The Matter of Voice

The Matter of Voice

Sensual Soundings

Karmen MacKendrick

Fordham University Press

New York 2016

Fordham University Press also publishes its books in a variety of electronic formats. Some content that appears in print may not be available in electronic books.
Visit us online at www.fordhampress.com.

Library of Congress Cataloging-in-Publication Data
available online at catalog.loc.gov.

Printed in the United States of America
18 17 16 5 4 3 2 1
First edition

To the memory of Helen Tartar

In the manner of those who, as Nelle Morton wrote, "hear each other to speech," Helen read me to writing. Her ear was poetically perfect—for content, context, style, and their ultimate inseparability. Her trust in my work finally gave me that bit of faith needed to get through the misery and fear and failure of it. I wrote for her. It is harder to write with her gone. But the memory of her reading still draws me out, and I hope this is a book that would have sounded good to her, and that there may still be more.

CONTENTS

Not for all the tea in China
Not if I could sing like a bird
Not for all North Carolina
Not for all my little words

—The Magnetic Fields, "All My Little Words"

Introduction: Hearing Voices

And everything that speaks is made of mortal flesh.

—LOUIS-RENÉ DES FORÊTS, cited by Maurice Blanchot, *A Voice from Elsewhere*

I came of intellectual age after authors were dead, which conveniently rendered their voices immaterial. This "death" had been given its official notice in Roland Barthes's famous essay, "The Death of the Author," which declared that authorial intent and biography were not central to literary criticism.[1] Such reading is too limiting, Barthes argued; context and history and the accumulation of readers added to a text layers of meaning that no author could have intended, so that the author's word on the text's meaning was not in fact final and absolute. Indeed—a more extreme claim—it was not to be considered. The authors' media—their poems, stories, essays, books—were no longer mediums, no longer channels for their very particular authorial voices. Barthes did not say that voices never matter, and in both *A Lover's Discourse* and *Image Music Text* he dwells lovingly on what he calls "the grain of the voice," "the *friction* between music and . . . language."[2] He considers voice in its very somatic texture, its feel in the throat and on the lips, its eroticism.[3] But that the matter of the author matters, that the materiality of the voice lives even in writing (as I shall argue in the first chapter here), did not seem to affect the authorial death announcement or its eager reception.

Without returning to authority, I do want to follow many others in returning to voice, thinking music in the text, in words. Specifically, I want to turn back to the materiality and carnality of voice, on which theorists and particularly philosophers had turned their collective backs long before Barthes. I shall focus especially on speaking and writing, where voice has been less attended to than in song. The melodic, timbral, and especially rhythmic character of the voice is essential to both song and speech, and music theorists began the return to vocal materiality rather earlier than the rest of us. Singing transfigures the voice. It is distinct from the speaking and writing voice in its range, in the parts of the body from which it is consciously sourced, and in the possibilities of its link to instrumentation. The musicality of the speaking voice is not that of song, but it is just close enough to be dismissed as merely ornamental. I want simply to ask what happens if we do not dismiss it, if we turn to it as that which does not quite transfigure words (as "real" music does), but does figure in them, necessarily, and without divorce from their meaning. That turning is all that I intend to do for the rest of this book, in considerations of writing, of pedagogy, of translation theory, of cosmology, and of something rather like semiotics. Like most minuscule undertakings, this one opens enormously. It will help, therefore, if I set forth some of the background of theories about voice, especially in philosophy and theology, but in literature too; about its materiality and its disembodiment both.

Authors' collective demise was helped along by a more general theoretical turn against subjectivity—without subjects, what did it matter who was writing? "What matter who's speaking, someone said what matter who's speaking."[4] The speaker—someone who is saying that someone said "what matter who's speaking"—adds, "There's going to be a departure, I'll be there, I won't miss it, it won't be me, I'll be here, I'll say I'm far from here, it won't be me, I won't say anything. There's going to be a story, someone's going to try and tell a story."[5] Someone—does it matter who? The passage seems well designed to muddle the who-ness so thoroughly that the reader on the roller coaster of the prose clings a little desperately to the hope that it doesn't.

This passage is quoted, a bit mischievously, by Michel Foucault when he echoes Barthes's "Death of the Author" by asking "What Is an Author?"[6] A citation, after all, takes someone's words and evidently repurposes them as one's own, as if to demonstrate that one person can speak them as well as another. But the sentence is just as mischievous in its earlier appearance, because in even the few lines just cited there resonates a particularly distinctive authorial voice, dry and sad and hilarious, curiously Franco-

Hibernian, and quite identifiable. "What matter who's speaking, someone said," and right away we can hear Samuel Beckett saying it.

His voice is at once singular and contagious. That's Beckett, all right, we think when we read this passage, but we are surprised then to see how often Foucault is cited as the author of that particular text. One voice takes up another, echoes it, and changes it—though we often recognize Foucault's voice, too, especially when the text, as in his many published interviews, reproduces his speech. Foucault, of course, is often playful with voice, as author and speaker alike. He begins his inaugural address at the Collège de France with the rueful wish that he mightn't have to begin at all, that he could "slip surreptitiously" into the stream of discourse as if he had been speaking already. Thus, "instead of being the one from whom discourse proceeded, [he] should be at the mercy of its chance of unfolding, a slender gap, the point of its possible disappearance."[7] It's as if the responsibility, the authority, of the voice's announcement is a little too much. (Stanley Cavell similarly remarks that during his stint as a musician, he came to love stage names: "Sometimes, and increasingly, it felt like a desire to know anonymity, as it were to have time to think, for a moment not to be on call."[8]) One of the puzzles of voice will have to be this question of a strange relation between the matter and the who. One phrase is reincarnated in multiple quotations; one bodily person voices many personae, sometimes under pseudonyms.

In the inaugural lecture, Foucault again takes refuge behind Beckett's already-speaking: "I should have liked there to be a voice behind me which had begun to speak a very long time before, doubling in advance everything I am going to say, a voice which would say: 'You must go on, I can't go on, you must go on, I'll go on, you must say words, as long as there are any, until they find me, until they say me, strange pain, strange sin, you must go on, perhaps it's done already, perhaps they have said me already, perhaps they have carried me to the threshold of my story, before the door that opens on my story, that would surprise me, if it opens.'"[9] Voices are hard to place: it's surprising if they open at all; they go on (they must) when they cannot; there is going to be a story, someone said; but does it matter?

One might argue that all this demonstrates just how dead authors are, that their distinctively voiced words can become or be mistaken for someone else's. But one might—and I would—consider instead that words are the agents as well as the objects of numerous remakings, not least in the makings of voices. Anne Carson, another author of distinctive voice, writes in her essay "Foam" about the sublimity of quotation. She acknowledges cheerfully that Longinus's essay on the sublime is unlikely to enlighten its readers about its purported subject, "But you will have been thrilled by its documentation," she assures us.

> Longinus skates from Homer to Demosthenes to Moses to Sappho on blades of pure bravado. What is a quote? A quote . . . is a cut, a section, a slice of someone else's orange. You suck the slice, toss the rind, skate away. Part of what you enjoy in a documentary technique is the sense of banditry. To loot someone else's life or sentences and to make off with a point of view, which is called "objective" because you can make anything into an object by treating it this way, is exciting and dangerous.[10]

Longinus exemplifies this excitement in his citations from the courtroom speeches of Demosthenes, citations that Carson traces from the judges hearing Demosthenes, to Longinus evaluating him, to her account, to our reading. (And my retelling, now, and your rereading, too.) "The passionate moment echoes from soul to soul," she says, without a trace of disembodiment; "Each controls it temporarily. Each enjoys it quote by quote."[11] Quotation is contagion, pleasure moving from body to body, soul to soul, by voice. But voice matters, every time. It is part of the thrill of contagion, of looting, of enjoying. It matters, but it eludes. It eludes because we are not *quite* sure whose it is anymore: we might not be surreptitious, but we always do slip (or leap, or stumble) into an extant discourse, even as it's one that we're helping to form. It eludes because, just as no language means in private, so, too, no voice speaks in solitude. We may perfectly well use meaningful words alone in our rooms, but the use and the meaning cannot have come from within the confines of our walls. The matter of speaking—speaking as matter, the materiality, the singularity in relation, the sound of the spoken and the subvocal vibration—all of this is a matter of voice. As Lawrence Kramer puts it, "voice, just insofar as it is human, is always bringing words and music together"[12]—and sustaining between them just that crucial bit of friction: "Both speaking melody and melodic speech," he writes, "are products of the uneasy, never completed fusion of speech with voice."[13]

That it might matter who is speaking, and even who is citing with intent ranging from reverent to sardonic, is hardly a novel notion. Even in the face of the declaration of authorial mortality, other theoretical voices were already sounding, offering alternative stories. For them, it mattered who was speaking, and it mattered in part because theirs were the voices that hadn't been allowed to speak very much, or, when speaking, had remained unheard. Voices shouted and whispered and murmured from the edges, and turned out to be not unintelligible after all: women's voices, queer voices, voices of the differently gendered and the otherwise abled, voices of color—coloratura voices, some of them, adding their unexpected timbres to the discursive chorus of the rather staid and amusical academy. In silencing their music, I want to say, theoretical language and thought have lost some measure of their own meaning.

It is probably already clear that the dichotomy, live voice or dead author, is at least a bit false. To listen to the voice is not to reestablish authorial authority, but it is to give added authorial weight, provided we don't go thinking of authors as speakers *ex nihilo*. So long as we avoid parodic extremes, these approaches are not as opposed as they seem: the uniqueness of each singularity speaking must play off of the choral multiplicity that keeps any voice from wholly owning the word or having the final say.

Authorial voice is generally understood to be a matter of writing style, and so as more merely metaphorical even than speaking—but style is material too.[14] "[T]here are approaches to literary voice," notes Birgitte Pedersen, "that not only have to do with the semantic positions of narration, with who speaks, etc., but that also approach the voice as a certain tone or intonation. . . . According to Horace Engdahl, style frames a textual soundboard that is not necessarily related to semantics, but rather to how the text is phrased."[15] Even Beckett's anxious narrator, awaiting a story, admits "there must be a body . . . I'll say I'm a body."[16] The writing voice may not be identical to the speaking, but it is the bodiliness of voice in both to which my thought, like my ear, is drawn: to vibration and audition, and to their alteration as they are *spoken*, and as they are subvocalized, too; as in them a trace of song somehow echoes.

I want to attend to the matter of the speaking voice, and to the question of the sense in which matter may be said to be *whose*, at all, and in which it may be said to matter, even, to meaning. Not all voices are so distinctive as Beckett's, of course, nor so easy to hear. Voices may mumble, or be inarticulate. They may be quiet, or talked over by more forceful tones. They may be deliberately bland, stripped of the signs of accent or authorship, "objective"—as if objects would all speak the same. Yet even the blandest voices set us apart. They are as distinctive as fingerprints—but unlike fingerprints, they also set us into relation, whether they invite us, command us, or fill us with the urge to be elsewhere.[17] Adriana Cavarero, in her marvelous book *For More than One Voice*, sets out both the distinctiveness and the connectivity:

> In the uniqueness that makes itself heard as voice, there is an embodied existent, or rather, a "being-there" [*esserci*] in its radical finitude, here and now. The sphere of the vocal implies the ontological plane and anchors it to the existence of singular beings who invoke one another contextually. . . . The ontological horizon that is disclosed by the voice—or what we want to call a *vocal ontology of uniqueness*—stands in contrast to the various ontologies of fictitious entities that the philosophical tradition, over the course of its historical development, designates with names like "man," "subject," "individual." For what these universal categories share is the neglect of the "uniqueness" of those human beings (or, to use the metaphysical lexicon, their "particularity" and their "finitude").[18]

Particularity and finitude, a uniqueness that is not pure individuation, are also characteristics of being in the flesh. The fleshiness of voice delights singers and intrigues poets, but, for a long time now, it has repelled philosophers.

To claim that in each voice others echo is not to posit an original speech that each subsequent voice would then reflect. The non-origin of voice is a matter not simply of imitative echo, but of a resonating that neither omits nor is reducible to the physiological. Resonance is not only in what comes back into voice, but also in the direction of its address—in call and response. I have argued elsewhere that all language carries an echo of prayer in that it addresses someone, not always knowing whom, and chapter five here will make more of that aspect.[19] Speaking and writing respond to a call by calling back, by the event of address that is redress, an address that becomes interestingly ambiguous as we acknowledge the trace of one in the voice of the other. In addressing another, seeking to be heard, I recall myself, though the moments of calling, or of my attention to the call, may not perfectly overlap. But there is no first call; voice is always response, the "first" silence already broken. In writing as in speaking, innumerable other voices echo; they must, simply for language to be. These other voices are both aural and written; in their writing, aurality echoes. Corporeality comes to writing and to speaking in rhythm, and in memory, and in the musicality of words—and it comes to us as both what makes words our own and what always keeps both our voices and our selves from being perfectly familiar.

As Mladen Dolar points out, the acousmatic voice—the voice without an apparent corporeal origin, always a little disturbing and uncanny—had its official start philosophically. "The Acousmatics were Pythagoras' disciples who, concealed by a curtain, followed his teaching for five years without being able to see him."[20] The Pythagorean intent seems to have been to make the voice not only grandly mysterious, but also more purely conceptual, by removing at least the visual element of embodiment. Now there are electronically generated voices, of course, but even hearing those, we look around for a source, for what is called, perhaps revealingly, a speaker.

Of course, myth often arrives at a point before philosophy does, and we find tales of disembodied voices speaking Greek before Pythagoras. Unlike the Pythagorean teacher, who moves from invisibility to a fuller flesh, these voices begin as those of bodies, albeit bodies then wasted by desire. The most famous is the tale of Echo, whose very name means *sound*, the chatty nymph whose stories distracted Hera while Zeus cavorted with other nymphs—until Hera caught on. Furious in the manner of the gods, Hera took away Echo's power of storytelling, leaving her with a voice only able to repeat the words of others. Among the words that Echo repeats are those of Narcissus, the striking young man whose beauty leads him to fall in love with his own reflection in the water. Alas, he desires his visual reflection only, and not his reflection aurally; he spurns Echo, who has fallen in love with him as she reflects back his words. Like many myths, this one has variations, but Ovid's is one of the most striking:

> Shamed and rejected in the woods she hides and has her dwelling in the lonely caves; yet still her love endures and grows on grief, and weeping vigils waste her frame away; her body shrivels, all its moisture dries; only her voice and bones are left; at last only her voice, her bones are turned to stone, so in the woods she hides and hills around, for all to hear, alive, but just a sound.[21]

Desire's duplicity in Echo's assistance to Zeus, its jealous possessiveness in Hera's response, its single-mindedness in Narcissus's rejection, and finally its own endurance in the voice leave Echo acousmatic, a mystery. Equally mysterious by a different means is the Sybil of Cumae, who issues prophecy from an extant cave said to have a hundred openings, each the home of a voice.[22] (A cave may hide still better than a curtain.) The Sybil beautifully embodies the voices, speaking them forth. In fact, she is so lovely that she arouses the desire of Apollo, who offers her anything she wants. She chooses a life of a thousand years—but neglects to specify lasting youth. Apollo, petulant at her refusal to become his lover even after he has given her such a nice present, takes advantage of this loophole. Even as she speaks and is spoken through, her body withers, and she begins to long for death.[23] What finally remains, as with Echo, is only voice. Yet like

Echo, too, the Sibyl speaks in a voice not her own, one of the voices of the cave, prophesying elliptically the meaning of the god. Without their own bodies, neither can embody her own voice.

Is voice, then, what is left before or after the body? Not quite. It is, rather, the body besides the visible, the body that hides and yet speaks—even from behind a curtain. Or it is the body that fades because its voice is no longer its own, but only the echo or the vessel of others' speech. Without speaking, we fade away; from speaking, we come forth. Echo and the Sibyl show us not the triumph of voice over flesh, but the loss of the voice that belongs to the body. When their desires are refused, their voices are taken from them and turned over to the use of others. But the very possibility of speaking through vexes the question of who "we" are. How much of the voice remains mine if the words are not? Philosophy will lead us to a long history of attempts to render language amusical, even soundless; myth and poetry will lead us into puzzles of personae—lines of thought that emerge and reemerge in the following chapters.

Dolar notes a surprising aspect of the bodily voice—though we seek its source (we seem to do so even from infancy), in fact the voice "stems from an undisclosed and structurally concealed interior" of the body.[24] As he indicates, we cannot simply *identify* voice with body, and not just in cases in which the two seem an odd fit for one another (I think exemplarily of Mike Tyson).[25] Voices are never wholly disembodied; no sound is, because sound is a physical phenomenon. But body is not the whole of voice any more than voice is the entirety of body. Voice is what resists the reduction of word to concept, what makes the *logos* in the beginning so much more complicated, and so much richer, than abstract principle. It is the meeting point of sense and sense: of meaningfulness and sensuousness. Voice's materiality resists the reduction not only of speaking to concept, but of matter to mechanics as well. It speaks to us of material vitality, of the singularity of living flesh.

Which may, of course, account for philosophers' tendency to disregard it. It is silly to speak of philosophy as if it were monolithic, but in general, ever since the paradigmatic Socratic question "What is . . . ?" refused answer by example, philosophers have asked after universals. This becomes increasingly true as subsequent generations begin to read Plato without the irony and poeticism that complicate his work.[26] The finite and particular have been pushed aside. I want to argue not just that voice matters, but that it matters to meaning; that this is another of those not quite right binaries that we have been dismantling for decades now.

"The Matter of Voice," the first chapter here, asks about the formation of what we think of as a singular writing voice, in the sense in which we speak of finding one's voice, or of distinctive voices. As I have already remarked, we do not, and cannot, become ourselves in isolation from anyone else; no more do we find our voices alone. The sense in which the written voice is distinctly auditory and bodily is important; to develop one's "own" voice is to find resonance among voices, to learn to hear in speaking. It is to discover one's own musicality, even if that happens to be atonal, or highly eccentric in rhythm, or surprisingly dissonant with itself.

This mutual implication of speaking and hearing, meaning and sound provides important resistance to the increasing and dangerous standardization of education, the assumption that voices and even bodies are irrelevant to any learning. Both allowing students to hear their own voices and enabling authorial voices to resonate in them resist the metrics of outcomes assessment. As will already be apparent in this discussion, uniqueness does not mean separateness: every voice takes up multiple voices, and more voices than we can count resonate within it. Thus the second chapter, by reaching back to the vocal and textual disciplines of monastic education, argues forward to a revocalization of our own classrooms.

Sound and meaning, the senses of sense, are entangled, yet we always feel the tension between them, the imperfection of each in grasping or expressing the other (each is insufficient to, and in excess of, the other). We are pulled by a dream of linguistic perfection. The third chapter, "Thou Art Translated!" considers this pull as the pull of body and word toward each other—echoing the myth of an original speaking, which is also a theological myth of a meaning perfectly embodied, in which sound and sense are so suited to each other as to be one.

The chapters in the second half of this volume are more directly theological. They begin at the beginning, with two considerations of creation. First, we move from the question of an original language to the tantalizing myths of language as origin, in the Christian gospel of John and the Hebrew book of Genesis. "The Voice in the Mirror" takes up the marvelous and original cosmology that Hildegard of Bingen develops in her poetic hymns and in her readings of the fourth gospel, especially its opening lines and their retelling of the Genesis story. Hildegard's is a synthesis, and a synesthesia, of resonance, of reflection, and ultimately of song. It demonstrates to us that the difficulties of determining address in a prayerful context actually reflect the complexity of the entangled and mutually vibrating cosmos.

The following chapter, "Original Breath," reflects more narrowly upon the opening books of Genesis, in which creation happens when "God said." This divine saying may be echoed when, in the same book, the first man names the animals. But the meaning of that resonance is subject to extraordinarily varied interpretation. At least one possibility, reading this tale in conjunction with the opening lines of the text, depends upon the ways in which the divine breath makes meaning in a surprising set of interactions with matter.

Finally, in "The Meaning in the Music," Augustine's complex semiotic theory encounters that of Friedrich Nietzsche (perhaps not the most readily anticipated pairing) to argue—with the help of several other figures, of course—against a strictly denotative theory of meaning. Augustine begins *De Musica* by comparing the rhythms of words to the beats of a drum, and his sense of language is always sensuous as well as intellectual. Ultimately, breath and matter vibrate with sense, and sense with materiality, at every level from the unique voice that can belong only to one, to the utterly choral song that is creation itself. I ask whether that vibration might not also be sense, be meaningful, even be part of the meaning of words. It matters how words sound, and in what voice. Matter means. The answer to Beckett's fretful query, "what matter?" may in fact be matter itself. Matter speaking. It may be voice.

I must note important limitations regarding my consideration of this material vocalizing. I have tried to explore, as I say, the materiality of voice. I am fascinated by sound, and by its synesthetic elements of touch and movement. But I have not attended to the intriguing possibilities of language that is unheard, not because it has been falsely stripped to pure concept, but because it belongs to those to whom sound does not. The kinesthetic action and shift and rhythm of sign language, it seems to me, must share a great deal with my account here, but also differ importantly from it, and I do not quite know how. I have always been cheerfully willing to wander into topics with precious little background, to speculate in areas that were not, disciplinarily, supposed to be my own at all. But this step seems to me a bit *too* presumptuous, and I will have to hope that someone else undertakes the additions and extensions and corrections of considering language without hearing—perhaps, if I am very lucky, in conversation with these thoughts on the matter of voice. I also hope to invite into conversation those at the other extreme, whose sensitivity to sound far exceeds my own, those who know in the flesh the pleasure of vocal music, even opera, and can perhaps play that knowing, whatever its kind, back into our mundane meaningfulness. For all of my love of music, I cannot sing, but only try to converse with those who can.[27]

Because these chapters arose in a wide range of contexts, they do not quite speak in the same tone. I considered attempting a little more to make them do so. I have decided, though, to leave that tiny bit of dissonance here, just because it better draws attention to voice itself—even allowing in a bit of the anxiety so easily provoked by trying to write about sound, especially about voice in writing. It is with such written voices that I begin.

CHAPTER 1

The Matter of Voice

> The prose itself is indestructible. It is all of a piece. It is a living person speaking. Mark Twain put his voice on paper with a fidelity and vitality that makes electronic recordings seem crude and quaint.
>
> —URSULA LEGUIN, "Reading Young, Reading Old"

We've started to hear them already—dead authors can speak in surprisingly lively voices. I have mentioned the distinctiveness of the spoken voice. But what of the writing voice? "[I]n the language of literary criticism," writes Cavarero, "*voice* is today a technical term that indicates the peculiarity of the style. . . . This use is interesting above all for the way in which it recalls a vocal uniqueness that is implicitly understood to be removed from the acoustic sphere."[1] This implicit understanding creates its own difficulties, and I have already noted that others imagine writing voice a bit differently. Yet even those who speak well may find writing infuriatingly awkward, and written voices often end up flattened or stilted. What might it mean for one to find an authorial voice, a voice proper to one's writing self? It is a question challenging enough to provoke encouraging advice columns in venues ranging from *The Chronicle of Higher Education*, to writers' blogs, all the way to full books on the subject, and plenty of them.[2]

The stereotypical academic voice has not been an especially pleasing one. Perhaps the emphasis on meaning over sound, the desire to strip the sensuousness from sense, forces us into a torturous style. Maybe, more kindly, that style is just an effect of the desire to put into recalcitrant language the complex knots of our thinking—which may well come to us in words, but seldom in full or connected sentences.[3] So how, then, does one develop an authorial voice, if it matters at all, whether by happenstance or by habit or by very deliberate effort? Where do those lively voices—and, for that matter, the pedestrian plodding—come from?

The most attractive authorial voices (those that are most intriguing, I mean, rather than pretty) have a persistent liveliness to them, a sense of life in the body. Work written with the *intent* of finding a personal voice often sounds stilted and artificial—precisely the opposite of the language in which one could feel at all like oneself. Of course, we are most often concerned with finding our voices when we are young and a little insufferable, so it may be no wonder that our voices would emerge so pompously—and that we then find ourselves stuck in them.

We often sound like those who speak around us, and so, too, we come to sound a little like those we read (for those of us who read a great deal, our speech may even begin to sound like what we've been reading). Let me dwell a bit on what it is to listen to text. It is true that we no longer move our lips when we read, and we can read much more this way, and in many more places—but we have to wonder, too, what we might have lost when we shifted our reading to silence.[4] (Beyond aural questions, too, what do we lose as we cease to heft volumes, turn pages, smell paper?) This loss seems especially important if we try to hear voices that are a little different, that come in from the edges, that aren't quite like the voices we have already heard. Can we do anything other than try to *understand* them—can we let them resonate in our chests and our throats and our ears? Would we gain anything, if we did? (It will be obvious that I suspect an answer.) Wayne Koestenbaum writes in *The Queen's Throat*, "The throat, not the ears, receives the diva: the throat, organ from which 'I' speak."[5] He adds, "Listening, your heart is in your throat."[6] When we hear voices by listening as deeply, as physically as possible, we will also receive the voice in the throat, and will understand another part of the sense.

There are dangers in voicing another too nearly, of course. A department chair once asked me casually, "So, what do you tell students who want to write like you?" "Don't!" I blurted, with an unintentional honesty that seemed to startle him a bit. But I do think that to write as if to set a model is probably a horrible idea. It is hard enough to attend to one's own voice, without intending to make it the voice of a generation of others. Nor is it much better to try to sound specifically like someone else. We have all read, and many of us have committed, writing that is too directly imitative.

Usually the effect is less like tribute and a little bit closer, uncomfortably close, to parody. I think I would be easy to parody, but the exercise doesn't strike me as especially useful (which could be a defensive response).

Except, perhaps, as an exercise in listening: we mimic in order to hear. As Kramer writes of his own (rather good) imitation of Henry James, "This voice is something we perceive in the way that we ourselves voice, or intone, the Jamesian language in our mind's ear. We have to imagine this voice, and to do that we have to imagine its tonality, its timbre, its pace, its flow, its quality."[7] Subvocalizing, we catch that image in our throats.

My dissertation advisor and I once mused on the strangeness of finding a voice, shortly before he had to deliver a lecture on the topic. All that I could add to his ideas was the suggestion that one must attend first to the subject matter, which has a way of telling one how it needs to be said (a slow, annoying, and roundabout way, to be sure). Or, as the poet Richard Wilbur puts it—more succinctly and more elegantly, as one would expect of a poet—"I have the feeling that the material chooses the form."[8]

This doesn't mean that one should write, for instance, frivolously of some matters, ungrammatically of others, or with as many semicolons as possible for others still. Instead, it means that one has to listen to the sort of thing one needs to say, to hear it before one writes it. This is a difficult concept to express; luckily, others have already done so, at least in the realm of fiction. Ursula LeGuin writes that she has a sense of inhabiting her characters bodily in order to tell their stories—or to let the characters tell them. Of the process, she says: "It is better to hold still and wait and listen to the silence. It's better to do some kind of work that keeps the body following a rhythm but doesn't fill up the mind with words. I have called this waiting 'listening for a voice.' It has been that, a voice. But it's more than voice. It's a bodily knowledge. Body is story; voice tells it."[9] *Voice tells body*. There is, for LeGuin, no separate sense of "meaning," but she does say that she finds stories far more satisfying than essays, which for her are more about concepts, and therefore harder to embody.

Virginia Woolf is only slightly more abstract, but helpfully so, in her description of style. She, too, begins with a very bodily sense—a sense of rhythm:

> Style is a very simple matter; it is all rhythm. Once you get that, you can't use the wrong words. But on the other hand here am I sitting after half the morning, crammed with ideas, and visions, and so on, and can't dislodge them, for lack of the right rhythm. Now this is very profound, what rhythm is, and goes far deeper than words. A sight, an emotion,

creates this wave in the mind, long before it makes words to fit it; and in writing (such is my present belief) one has to recapture this, and set this working (which has nothing apparently to do with words) and then, as it breaks and tumbles in the mind, it makes words to fit it.[10]

For LeGuin, the body makes a story that the (bodily) voice may tell; when we cannot find the (rhythm of) words, we should move rhythmically in the flesh and wait for the words to follow. For Woolf, the rhythm of the sight or emotion that wants to be described makes words to fit its waveform. Both writers are virtuosos with words, but for both, words follow not concepts, but something even more evidently physical than speaking. The classic philosophical idea that words outwardly express an inward meaning will not do.

My intent in fumbling toward the idea that one must listen to the subject matter is not altogether different from these formulations. One must listen in order to speak *or* to write. Jean-Luc Nancy gives us some hint as to the reasons that this might be particularly difficult in philosophy, in a way that might well extend to theorizing more broadly. In "Récit Recitation Recitative," he writes,

> In all the cases of philosophical and methodical path, the result is presupposed. This presupposition can remain relatively undetermined, like Cartesian intuition, Kantian freedom, or the Hegelian absolute; but it still remains a preliminary position, an already formed reservation and the provision for the journey. Despite the impressive travels philosophers can accomplish, despite the distances they cover, their paths harbor a secret immobility. This immobility stems from their gaze, fixed . . . on the idea of the result: of the fulfillment and the resorption of tension.[11]

The gaze may fix on immobility, but an immobile voice is no voice at all. The very condition of sound is vibration. Voices move. They move in time, according to rhythm and tempo. They move, rhythmically and speedily, in the body. They shift pitch and volume and timbre, and there is a rhythm to these shifts as well. We in the academy have tended to write as if writing could be voiceless, given only to the eyes as the quickest route to the intellect.

The sheer difficulty of finding the writerly voice in the sense of style makes more sense if we consider writing as the physical act that it is, even if that is not all that it is. Whenever we attend closely and consciously to complex physical activity, we tend to get in our own way—the same happens if we pay much attention to the act of speaking, in fact. "Get yourself out of the way" is often sensible advice, however difficult to follow, and we can get in our own way bodily as well as in our psyches. But there is a possibility that one could be in the way very differently. Perhaps, rather than putting oneself as a barrier between the sense and the sound, one could be that through which the voice resounds, as Nancy suggests:

> The word *person* might be considered as derived from *personare*, "to resound through," just as the voice of ancient actors reciting the drama had to speak through a mask. Not a person as interiority—unless we understand interiority as nothing but an infinite antecedence always more withdrawn into the very utterance of exteriority: the unsupposable, impossible to submit supposition of a subject of speech.
>
> The narrator is the necessary, improbable supposition of the narrative. He is the anteriority of the narrative to itself. The anteriority of the voice in itself.[12]

The voice is in the words, yet before them; its rhythms await the concepts as much as the converse. We become not in the words we generate as expressions or externalizations of our interior concepts, but in our emergence into an existing discourse (Foucault would be delighted). Thus, some writers find that they can best work using different *personae* for different voices—for the different manner of things that there are to be said. (The pleasure of the stage name is not dissimilar: "It was with names," says Cavell, "as I will find Rilke to say about the liberation of masks."[13]) The only way to think this matter well is to avoid reduction or a simplistic sense of primacy. We risk reduction in several ways.

Not So Simply

> I should be proud if I could convince a single teacher that the isolation of any mode of thought is misleading.
>
> MARY EVEREST BOOLE, *Logic taught by love: rhythm in nature and in education*

The first is to focus too narrowly on language as if it were somehow incorporeal. Many theorists have become skeptical about theory's focus on language; skeptical, that is, of the effects of the deeply influential and by now infamous "linguistic turn" across the humanities and social sciences. This skepticism arises particularly out of the concern that language became the focus of theorizing to the exclusion of all else, as the notion that "everything is a text" truly took hold of the intellectual imagination—in ways that thinkers like Derrida, who spoke that (in)famous line, are unlikely to have intended.[14]

The claim that all is text, which was meant to insist upon the central role of interpretation in knowledge, irritates philosophical realists, who want to argue for the more commonsensical notion that there is an extralinguistic reality not especially dependent on interpretation. It annoys historians, who like their texts to have context. It aggravates those whose influence by Marx disposes them toward history's material conditions. More recently, it has grated upon those who want to focus on body, particularly those interested in complicating old images of bodies as whole, self-contained, and singular material mechanisms—though it has irritated them, too, with its refusal to be An Object.

To be sure, voice in theorizing can take on a particular position not identical with language. Derrida, as Kramer notes, "takes voice as the privileged medium of a presence (of self, consciousness, truth, authority, divinity) that continually slips away from its invocation."[15] Pedersen points out the link to authorial demise: "The concept of literary voice is often linked to certain post-structuralist thinkers who position their work in opposition to the authenticity discourse of the physical voice which has been termed *phonocentrism* by Jacques Derrida. The critique of the phonocentric reading dominated the debate on voice in the literary criticism of the late 20th century, which was led by Derrida and continued in the post-structuralist tradition, for instance in the writings of Roland Barthes." Emphasizing bodily process, she continues, "The fantasy that the author is breathing behind his text is challenged in Derrida's and Barthes' theorization of the literary voice as something fundamentally different from the audible and speaking voice."[16] Pedersen and Kramer both note that the perception of voice is complicated further in the Lacanian work of Mladen Dolar and Slavoj Žižek, who do not find full presence in voice, but something more elusive, possibly dangerous, "felt most often as the punitive, unloving, and in a sense nonliving voice of law,"[17] as Kramer writes.

Against these deliberately discorporate abstractions, theory takes a turn to the somatic—and not to the phonetic. Language might not be entirely ignored in this turn to bodies, but it is subordinated to corporeality, and especially to neuroscience, instead of vice versa. In a sharply observed essay on "The Affective Turn," for instance, Patricia Clough notes,

> Affect and emotion . . . point just as well as poststructuralism and deconstruction do to the subject's discontinuity with itself, a discontinuity of the subject's conscious experience with the non-intentionality of emotion and affect. However, the turn to affect did propose a substantive shift in that it returned critical theory and cultural criti-

> cism to bodily matter. . . . The turn to affect points . . . to a dynamism immanent to bodily matter and matter generally—matter's capacity for self-organization in being informational.[18]

From such a theoretical perspective, the problem with the focus on language is not that it denies a reality beyond human construction, but that it abstracts the mechanisms by which we know *any* reality, taking them out of the flesh into pure structures of meaning, and taking the flesh out of the realm of matter, which is accessible to both scientific and political understanding, into heaven knows where—as if there could be a where without the material. Clough shows us that it is certainly possible to think about language without such reduction, and others, such as Anna Gibbs, make intriguing scientific arguments about language:

> [L]anguage . . . acts directly on the body. Metaphors not only derive from bodily processes (Lakoff and Johnson 1999) but they excite a "sympathetic" response in the form of embodied simulation in much the same way as mirror neurons do (see R. Gibbs 2006). . . . Because simulations are shaped by somatic memory, they have specific consequences for how metaphors (but also many types of nonmetaphorical language) can be understood. Language is in fact highly dependent on the body's physical capacities for its effectivity. It is also very selective, concentrating on evoking experience in one sensory channel at a time.[19]

But in this very interestingness the second risk appears, that of reduction to a narrow scientism. (It is not my intention to accuse Gibbs of something like this; the sample from her text is chosen simply because it is an interesting example of the use of the natural sciences.) The focus on matter, information, and neurobiology allows for a fascinating new approach to questions of embodied language, but we have to be careful not to think that approach exhaustive. Like, I think, most reasonably sane people, I am a great fan of science, deeply impatient with its pseudo versions and with attempts to replace it by myth. I would not for a moment deny the importance of bodily process, somatic memory, or sensory channels. But I am equally impatient with attempts to replace myth by science. In the shift in emphasis from language to matter, there has been a shift from a focus on the mad multiplicity of interpretation to the search for an "objective" basis even for the equally multiple movements of affective forces; from the sweeping Nietzschean declaration "gerade Tatsachen gibt es nicht, nur Interpretationen" (It is exactly facts that there are not, only interpretations)[20] to a presumably firm and factual ground. Matter seems more objectively solid than meaning, less prone to interpretive twists. I suspect that it is not in the least, and of course plenty of people suspect the same, but that is a matter for another time and text.

For now, let us just note that this second reductivism won't work either. The voice, when it stutters to a halt, when it rolls forward in joy, when it resonates with uncountable other voices, when it rasps with desire, deserves better than reduction. Again, I am in no way arguing against either conventional or novel scientific understanding, which is both useful and exciting; I *am* arguing against the notion that there are no other valuable modes of understanding, or that we do not benefit from multiple approaches. These are no more in competition (and no more to be identified with one another) than a chemical formula and a song.[21] An irreducible multiplicity resonates in the voice. Neither science nor myth can reduce the other, but we find between them as much intriguing echo—not identity nor identical claims—as active dissonance. And dissonance itself can be pretty intriguing.

In fact, several elements of thinking about matter dynamically will be familiar to anyone who has worked in twentieth- and twenty-first-century theory. "Affect," Melissa Gregg and Gregory Seigworth write,

> is found in those intensities that pass body to body (human, nonhuman, part-body, and otherwise), in those resonances that circle about, between, and sometimes stick to bodies and worlds, *and* in the very passages or variations between these intensities and resonances themselves. . . . Indeed, affect is persistent proof of a body's never less than ongoing immersion in and among the world's obstinacies and rhythms, its refusals as much as its invitations.[22]

The language here, often under a Deleuzean influence, moves us away from a resolute scientism, giving us a subtler sense of the ways in which bodies with bodies, words with words—but also, just maybe, bodies with words—might resonate, collide, or dance with the music of the voice. Thus, there are recognizable links to other modes and styles of theorizing in the emphases on movement and self-making, on intensity, relationality, and rhythm.

What the rush to science sometimes misses is that even the purest structuralism was never only about meaning; Saussure devotes no small part of the seminal *Course in General Linguistics* to sequences of sound and the physiology of phonetics.[23] Language has never been incorporeal, except as an abstraction for analysis: language as it is spoken, written, heard, and read; language as it shifts and stays, as it struggles, succeeds, or fails, is bodily.

We may think of voice not phonocentrically, but phonodispersively—or phonofugally, maybe.

Conversely, human bodies may be analyzed as nonlinguistic objects of matter and mechanics—but as they are lived and living, they are disentangleable from words. This does not identify the two: the body is linguistic, but not without resistance and remainder; it is likewise that language is bodily. Nor do the two simply share some part, some discrete and discernible portion, implying that the leftover body is mechanism, the leftover language abstraction. Rather, they exist in a paradox of mutual movement, of tension and attraction. At the heart of that paradox is voice.

A writing voice is not a speaking voice, but the elements of an audible style do resonate with those of writing. Language is utterly corporeal, even if it is not exhausted by corporeality, and it is odd to think that we would need to rescue bodies from it in order to theorize them; in turn, corporeality is far from exhausted by language, or reducible to it, but words are made flesh as much as flesh is made words. The notion that we must reduce or turn away from language in order to take body seriously, or that we can disregard corporeality in understanding words, misreads both. The two of them must make each other.[24]

The Subject as Responsorium

> The reader, as he or she begins to read, quickly enters the rhythmic pattern of a poem. It takes no more than two or three lines for a rhythm, and a feeling of pleasure in that rhythm, to be transferred from the poem to the reader.
>
> MARY OLIVER, *A Poetry Handbook*

Making words in the flesh, we are also made by them. Jacob Rogozinski, working out of psychoanalysis and phenomenology, argues that for each of us, "my voice" is not merely mine, but is constitutive of "me." I am called and recalled to myself not by abstraction, but by the resonance of voice, by language that is phonetic and auditory, tactile and kinesthetic. Language is given to me as an invocation: I am called into speaking; I recall myself by the voice in which I speak. I come to myself as I am called.[25]

This may seem to risk reintroducing a secure individuation of the *me* through the *mine*. But no word, even called in my voice, is ever entirely my own; likewise, no voice, however distinctive, is without its resonant echo, in which it not only returns to itself, but recalls innumerable other voices.

All coming to self is a coming back, a response to a self-call that is always recalling more and other than the self. As I shall remark in more detail below, that call to self, the voice that is *mine*, resonates with the voices to which I have listened, the voices from which I have, almost certainly without conscious intent, drawn my own voice. We dwell in our own memories. The call and the voice are quite fleshy things, pitch and rhythm and multiple resonance. Words are made mine by my body—by being in my voice, by being words enfleshed—but this is not to lay some sort of claim to language, as if by being mine it ceases to be anyone else's. The I is given to itself, calls and re-calls itself, knows its own voice. Yet at the heart of that voice persists an irreducible and carnal strangeness. It is, suggests Philippe Lacoue-Labarthe, already an echo: "The birth of speech: the starting-up of this echo by which a subject knows himself and feels himself—and here it is the same thing—preceded and followed by himself in an infinite, eternal alterity. Lost, consequently, further than any narrative, but reciting from this loss that he calls that of /his own/voice."[26]

Our voices are out of our possession even before we speak. Because, as Jean-Louis Chrétien reminds us, no voice is either first or alone (any more than the language in which it speaks), every call is already a response, and so too is every voice calling. As Kramer writes,

> [e]ach [voice] is at the same time identical with and non-identical with, continuous with and disjunctive from, any and every one of the others (including itself). The result is a kind of enveloping hum or resonance, a world of voice positioned indeterminately between word and tone, music and language. Between (any) voice and any other (voice) there is a relationship of calling in Heidegger's sense of a calling into presence. The resonant space of the voice as call, the call in voice, the invocative, is the space occupied by those beings who live in language.[27]

To hear our own voices from the outside—on a recording, for instance, or in the delay of a bad telephone connection—can unsettle and estrange us, set us for a moment beside ourselves. (To be sure, this may change with familiarity or with training. Those accustomed to recordings of their own voices may cease to be bothered by them, and singers, if not too self-critical, may even take pleasure in recordings of their performances. But this might suggest that we can even get used to being beside ourselves, for a little while, not that we cease so being.)

We echo, and in the echo, as we know if we have ever listened to one, even our own voices follow us as something other. Even when it is not thus dissociative, the ego's call to itself is always a call-back, and always altered and complicated by the echoes of further voices. There is something a little bit strange in these most familiar sounds, a strangeness that comes with the otherness of myself, an "essential plurality of voice."[28]

Each emergence, each response in the loop of invocation, makes evident the vulnerability of the speaking self. "The *I* appears in its dependency on the other," writes Michel de Certeau. "*I* speaks only if it is awaited (or loved), which is the riskiest thing in the world." Certeau remarks upon "the closing in of the *I* when it ceases believing itself to be awaited."[29] Indeed, the sense that no one listens, that one's voice has failed altogether to register, is sometimes credited with creating a more profound dissociation, the sense that I am not here with myself at all. But when I am awaited and given back, when I wait and give back too, then the voice that recalls me to me is at once strange to me and mine; always in question, always answering—and always resonating in the flesh. Speaking, I give me to others; heard, I am given myself. My speaking already doubles and redoubles my relation to myself, as Chrétien notes:

> In order to speak, I have to be able to hear myself, but in order to hear myself, someone must already have heard me and spoken to me, in a way that forestalls me—that is, comes before me, in both spatial and temporal terms. We have been listened to even before we speak. Between our ears and our voice, other voices and other kinds of listening are already active.[30]

This sense of resonance among voices is itself echoed in a more biological formulation (again, this is not to claim that the two approaches somehow say the same thing, but rather to look at the ways in which they too might play intriguingly off one another). "At the heart of mimesis is affect contagion, the bioneurological means by which particular affects are transmitted from body to body," writes Gibbs. "The discrete innate affects . . . are powerful purveyors of affect contagion, since they are communicated rapidly and automatically via the face, as well as the voice. This is because the distinct neurological profile of each affect is correlated with particular physical sensations, including muscular and glandular and skin responses."[31] This mimetic or contagious quality, extending between biology and this capacity and tendency of our voices to resonate one with another, to call from one to another without a first, echoes the sense of resonance that draws us into the deep, even apophatic elusiveness of the pull between flesh and word.[32]

Every resonance is already multiple. To claim that in each voice others echo is not to posit an original speech that each subsequent voice would then reflect. The non-origin of voice is a matter not simply of imitative echo, but of *response*, of a resonating that neither omits nor is reducible to the physiological. Resonance is not only in what comes back into voice, but also in the direction of its address—that is, in call as well as response. Speaking and writing respond to a call by calling back, by the event of address that is redress, an address that becomes interestingly ambiguous as we acknowledge the trace of one in the voice of the other. In addressing another (in seeking to be heard), I recall myself, though the moments of calling, or of my attention to the call, may not perfectly overlap.

Considering prayerful and prophetic voice, Chrétien ties voice's multiplicity to its directionality. Though it is a commonplace that Christianity marks a distinct inward turn from Judaism's more worldly and relational code of ethics, "No genuinely Christian thought," Chrétien writes,

> could ever privilege an inner voice over the chorus of God's witnesses: this would amount to substituting a private and solitary "revelation" for the Revelation that founds the Church. In order to announce Christ the voice is needed, "the voice of the one who cries in the desert" (Matt 3:3), the voice of John the Baptist. The call claims our voice in order to transmit it to others, and therefore to truly hear it in the process, but it is possible to think it and describe it without appealing to any inner voice.[33]

The call claims *our* voice. To be called, which is necessary for speaking, is also to have one's voice speak without its being perfectly in one's control. Pedersen notes that in the more purely aural terms of song, "You can feel overwhelmed by an experience of an opera voice as well as by a heavy metal voice. The voice at its limit tends to fascinate us, especially when it is powerful and close to the sound of a scream."[34] The voice taken over, the prophetic or oracular voice, may be particularly powerful, even as it speaks at the limit of sense; the voice at the limit of vocal sound is powerful too, as it, in its distinct fashion, stretches the limits of what we can do with words.

The language of calling has a religious resonance, as prophecy and prayer suggest, and it is perhaps in theology that we find the most complex history of that which draws us forth, not least into speaking. Maurice Blanchot makes this claim more strongly still:

> When the unknown beckons us, when speech borrows its voice from the oracle where nothing actual speaks, but which forces one who listens to tear himself from his present to come to himself as if to what does not yet exist, this speech is often intolerant, of a haughty violence

> that . . . takes us away from ourselves by ignoring us. Prophets and visionaries speak with a sovereignty that is all the more abrupt when what speaks in them ignores them.[35]

Blanchot's reading of visionary prophecy takes up an extreme form of being spoken through, but in all speaking, there is some touch of this *persona*, some absence of ownership and command—some sibylline echo. Any given language escapes a single "owner," a single speaker, but that there is speaking at all, that there is writing, that words are and meaning is—this, playing so intricate a part in making us, must likewise escape us all. Our speaking is drawn to limits: of ourselves, of knowledge, of the profane—perhaps sometimes, as in song, of the voice itself. Onomatopoetically, we may give up on reference to make meaning altogether by sound. Our words are enfleshed and our flesh is meaningful. Cavarero points out, with Nancy, that we may read voices as sharing in the divine: "For Nancy . . . the divine is that which is shared or distributed in the voices. It is the original, divine *sharing of voices* that is given in the singular voices of the poets and rhapsodes."[36]

Voices are lost, echoed, shared, dispersed. In Chrétien's analysis, control is lost when others claim and extend our voices. But it is already lost more fundamentally, as Certeau reminds us: "[T]o say is to want. . . . A beginning . . . of saying emerges at the point at which the enrootedness of speech in an in-finite volition (the 'inner yes') and its singular inscription within language (one little word to the exclusion of the rest; a 'no' to all things) coincide. At the threshold of mystic discourse, an elsewhere is engraved upon language."[37] What is remarkable about this elsewhere is that it is not somehow outside language, not even outside speaking, mystic or otherwise. Elsewhere and other are essential to my speech, right there "within" it—and they do not make it less mine, but are in fact the only ways in which it acquires its distinctive character.

Here, too, what is characteristic of the extreme ("mystic discourse") more subtly inhabits the everyday. Voices may be transmitted, amplified, and echoed in the voices of others. They may be appropriated, and this is not always a negative—consider, for instance, both theatrical performance and liturgical prayer, the voice that calls in ours as both echo and transformation. They may even meet their speakers with resistance (we often find ourselves reluctant to speak), or, for that matter, they may give away what we had intended them to keep quiet, such as strong emotion manifested in a break or a shudder or a squeak in the midst of our rational words. To invoke prayer and poetry, visions and prophecies, John the Baptist and mystic discourse, might seem to remove language from the body, though I hope that the sense of resonance and approach feels as deeply somatic to others as it always has to me. In case it does not, consider the quite corporeal, indeed animal, sense invoked by Derrida: "The narcissistic identification of one's fellow of the same species also works through the play of call and response between voices, of singing and sonic productions that are both coded and inventive. Whenever reproduction functions by means of sexual coupling . . . one has to register . . . some hetero-narcissistic 'self' as other."[38] It is not only in the mating rituals evoked by this passage that eros is outstretching and responsive, but more broadly, so much so that the play of reach and response might well be said to characterize it. *To say is to want.* Yet that reach and response are famously dispossessive, as if the self hyperextended and shifted beside itself even as it was transited by the desired.

This dispossession, this resonance into a void of origin, this call to an indefinite response, creates at the same time the very *mine*ness of my voice that it would seem to render impossible. Of course, this is not because voice is indifferent. Rather, each voice is a *particular* confluence of voices. That leads us to an unsettling notion: even though my voice is so very much mine; even though, in fact, my voice is that which (re)calls me to myself, there is always an incompleteness of presence and of ground in my speaking, of nowness in the moment of the invocation (every call is a calling back). Like other aspects of speech—address, desire, uncertainty—this incompletion is amplified in speech as it intersects the sacred, though it is not only there that we find it.

Our collective discomfort with this curious mine-yet-dispossessive aspect of speaking is of long standing. Blanchot notes that Socrates, in his condemnation of writing, must also condemn other modes of "impersonal speech," such as the oracular pronouncement and the hymn, in the urgency of his desire for the language of a fully present speaker.

> Socrates is undoubtedly right: what he wants is not a language . . . behind which nothing is hidden, but a sure speech, guaranteed by a presence: one that can be exchanged, one that is made for exchange. The speech in which he trusts is always the speech of some thing and the language of some one, both of them already revealed and present, never a beginning speech. And, hence, deliberately . . . he renounces any language that is oriented toward the origin, renounces the oracle as well as the work of art by which a voice is given to the beginning, by which a summons is addressed to an initial decision.[39]

Because it is never only my voice (even though it is uniquely my voice) in which I speak, this Socratic desire is ultimately as impossible as the unfiltered primal voice of a god: no voice can fully present all the voices resonant in it. No speech begins, and precisely because of this, no speech is that of a speaker fully present. So, oddly, even though the Socratic demand for a present speaker seems to be very much on the side of embodiment, it insists on what no body can give, or be. Blanchot notes that ancient gods, speaking through oracles, are never fully present in the speaking; moreover, those oracular pronouncements are unavailable for dialogue, the very criticism that Socrates makes of writing. It is the silence in them that is so awe-full: "What strikes him, then, what seems 'terrible' to him, in writing as well as in painting, is the silence, a majestic silence, a silence that is inhuman in itself, that makes the shudder of sacred energies pass into art, those forces that, through horror and terror, open man up to alien regions."[40] Those sacred energies have a long mythic history. Abrahamic cosmologies begin with divine saying, but this becomes a strange speech that addresses no one, echoes in no ear, once that cosmology turns to creation *ex nihilo*. Before this turn, the world must be, so that saying can resonate in it—not in a simple dialogue with the divine or the sacred, but shot through with its echoes. The mythic creation by voice allows for that voice to be spoken back by all of creation. (We shall revisit this notion in later chapters, with considerable elaboration.)

Like Socrates, we must renounce the idea that we can locate the origin of voice, but exactly because of this renunciation, we have to give up the notion that one can be the pure source of one's own speaking, that the speaker is ever purely or perfectly present. Nor is the echo of other voices the only non-presence. In our speaking are both resonance and silence, each allowing the other—sometimes rhythmic in their alterations, at other times awkward. The full presence of the speaker would enable the full presence of her speaking, not cut through by silence and lapses, not opening up the terrifying spaces in which she is absent to herself—but also not leaving the openings whereby entry is possible, where we can converse, or read, or be read, or respond. As the pause, silence is a structuring principle that makes speaking possible and is made possible by it. As a break and opening in speech, it can be a space of fear and absence. But it is also, in the same respect, a space of hospitality, where another may speak, whether to me or through me. Again, this is no abstraction, as Chrétien emphasizes. Silence

> is that which opens us, in the only way that anything can be opened: irreparably. Nor is it, even in the highest of its possibilities, a purely spiritual silence. Only what has a body can throw itself bodily into the fray. All

> attention takes place body and soul. . . . To suspend one's voice is not to suspend one's breath. The hospitality that breathing gives to the world, and the world gives to breathing, is broken only when life itself is broken.[41]

This is not a hospitality that offers full and true presence or even creational speaking. It is more akin to the hospitality of withdrawal, a divine contraction that allows the space for the world, resonating as we leave spaces in our speech, but also as we find our speaking broken: as we fail. In failure itself is renewal and possibility, as Blanchot suggests. We must always fail silence, any time we speak (of) it. "There is always yet to be born, birth in debt to itself, to the silence it failed by taking a vow of it, but through which, even failed, the gift of grace and the grace of the gift are maintained."[42] This realization that failure, silence, and absence may also be grace and be given, the realization that givenness can never be full possession or presence, has everything to do with finding a voice of one's own.

What Bodies Re-Call

> The "grain" is that: the materiality of the body speaking its mother tongue.
>
> ROLAND BARTHES, "The Grain of the Voice"

Resonance is not temporally straightforward. To resonate or to be caught in response, a voice must, however briefly, be remembered. But (outside perhaps of acting for stage or screen) it is rare for one to hold another voice in mind so as to call upon it imitatively. Rather, as Rogozinski writes, "The sounds, resembling fragments of remains, form an uncanny memory, prior to meaning. One would be hard put to say what it is the memory of: it recalls something that is not a past; it awakens what the body does not know about itself."[43] Neither in speaking nor in writing is the sound of my voice something I quite know about myself; it is of the body, but my senses cannot give it to me completely, and I sound a little bit different from inside my own head. Sound comes to me like my sense of myself, comes to me re-called, imperfectly present. It is never possessible; it is shot through with its own contradictions. (From where does it even come to me—outside or in?) It is all of this in breath and vibration. In this entanglement words are voiced, and voices speak their languages; sound strikes and vibrates the eardrum as we listen toward understanding. Nancy emphasizes the somatic character of resonance in speaking and listening both: "Timbre can be represented as the resonance of a stretched skin . . . , and as the expansion of this resonance in the hollowed column of a drum. Isn't the space of the listening body, in turn, just such a hollow column over which a skin is stretched, but also from which the opening of a mouth can resume and revive resonance?"[44]

This resonance, both an echo out of memory and the vibratory tuning-fork character of exciting conversation, traces the speaking voice; this voice, moving songlike in the throat, is traced out once more in writing—but writing, and reading, return again to resonate in speech. Blanchot cites and glosses Louis-Rene des Forêts's lines, "in which homage is made to *a voice come from elsewhere*," a voice that "has *in it something that lasts/Even after its meaning has been lost*. And why? Because *its timbre still quivers in the distance like a storm*." Blanchot asks, "Voice, timbre, music: Is it through these words that the answerless question of the *contretemps* [setback or difficulty; literally, a counter-time] opens up?"[45] Because words are voiced, there is more to them than definition. The music of voice is timbre and rhythm, altering the sound and sense of even the most similar verbal composition. Timbre resonates, and rhythm is structured not only by accents but by rests, by the stretch and silence in and around which our voices form, giving them style.[46]

Style as rhythm and timbre is famously resistant to reembodiment in a new set of words; the chance thus to play with sound is one of the almost illicit pleasures of quotation. Blanchot claims that the difficult transition from poetry, so focused on the sense of the sound, to prose is the gravest possible alteration of words. Poems "have their voice, which one must hear before thinking one understands them. *On a touché au vers* ['The line has been meddled with'—a phrase of Mallarmé's]. But Mallarmé still recognized in 'free verse' the old 'worn-out' alexandrine."[47] To echo a rhythm in a new voice, then, is not simply to reproduce it, alexandrine for alexandrine, iamb for iamb, but to be responsive to it, to let it resonate in what is nonetheless new.

Among those unexpected places is the forming of the singular voice: one might read one's own voice in places one would not expect. V. S. Naipaul offers an instance: "I found the material that was my own voice; it was inspired by two literary sources: the stories of my father and a Spanish picaresque novel, the very first published, in 1554, *Lazarillo Tormes*. It is a short book about a poor little boy growing up in imperial Spain, and I loved its tone of voice. I married these two things together and found that it fitted my personality: what became genuine and original and mine really was fed by these two, quite distinct sources."[48]

For Cavell, the found voice includes the ideas it will say: "The moment I felt that something about ordinary language philosophy was giving me a voice in philosophy, I knew that the something was the idea of a return of voice to philosophy, that asking myself what I say when, letting that matter, presented itself as a defiance of philosophy's interest in language, as if what philosophy meant by logic demanded, in the name of rationality, the repression of voice (hence of confession, hence of autobiography)."[49]

To come to voice may even be to respond by resistance, to push back against an overly influential voice with something very different. Beckett, Roger Boylan suggests, begins writing by trying to emulate his idols.

> But what he ended up with was a second-rate version of his master's voice instead of his own. The music is there, but it is played off-key. No wonder he gradually switched to writing in French; it wasn't only because French had so much less "style" than English, as Beckett claimed, but quite simply because when writing in English it was too hard to avoid Joyce's influence. Also, at around the same time Beckett started his career as a French writer, he came to the momentous realization that he was a taker-*out*, a minimalist, stripping words to their essence. By contrast, his idols Dante, Proust, and Joyce were all-inclusive putters-*in*, crowding their texts without limit. In an important sense, his artistic idols were his opposites.[50]

Beckett honors Joyce by writing otherwise, by finding his voice not simply in echo, but just as much in argumentative answer.

Whether we echo or answer or transpose to a foreign mode, we do not find voice by drowning out, but in an exchange of sounding with spaces. The rhythm of speech is sound and silence alongside assonance and stress. The rhythm of reading is structured by spaces, but that of writing, I find, is broken by something more like silence, where words cease in the stumbling song.[51] (When we read, space transforms into silence, telling us where to pause, when to draw breath between words.) Blanchot links our desires for a perfect music of language and a perfectly somatic silence:

> questions linger, words, silences, and also the glorious sun, the cries of birds, songs that escape the infernal necessity of language, jubilation of the creatures of the sky, music where, by anacrusis, the silence of what is still heard, or will be heard inside what is not heard, is sustained.
>
> *How many more times can one dream of a language*
> *Not subservient to words.*[52]

What is in language that resonates through words without being subordinate to them is its music: rhythm, tempo, tone, timbre; silence and sound. Nancy further attributes desire to this sensuality of language itself.

"[P]erhaps it is necessary that sense not be content to make sense (or to be *logos*), but that it want also to resound." Perhaps "to hear," he says, "is to understand the sense (either in the so-called figurative sense, or in the so-called proper sense: to hear a siren, a bird, or a drum is already each time to understand at least the rough outline of a situation, a context if not a text)."[53]

The rhythms, resonances, and failures in our writing are as corporeal as those of our speech, even if not quite so self-evidently. Silence gives meaning its space, and it gives voice to others, voices that will in turn echo within my own, will give me the voice in which I recall myself. Everything that speaks must also fall silent, must create and echo melodies and rhythms. To allow the possibility of speaking, we must leave silence, making space, which is a tacit acknowledgment both of the need for other voices and of what cannot be said.[54]

Voice, that is, does not simply belong to what we say. It is also in and of the unsayable of speech, the untranslatable rhythms and timbres and breaths of mortal flesh. Certeau links the haunting of text by voice to other traces of what cannot be said:

> Thus, in a thousand and one different ways, . . . the sayable continues to be wounded by the unsayable. A voice comes through the text, a loss transgresses the ascetic order of production, an intense joy or suffering cries out, the sign of a death is traced upon the display windows of our acquisitions. These noises, fragments of strangeness, may again be adjectives, scattered as memories always are, dislocated, but still relation to the substantive figure of the past that furnishes them with the reference point and name of what has disappeared.[55]

Language is meaning and order and interpretation, but it is noise and music and silence, too, which both make and disrupt order. And language, with the voices in which it is made, is necessarily choral. In order to speak, one must hear or otherwise encounter speaking. In order to write, one must read.

Writing Voices

> Ever since I was first read to, then started reading to myself, there has never been a line read that I didn't *hear*. . . . My own words, when I am at work on a story, I hear too as they go, in the same voice that I hear when I read in books.
>
> EUDORA WELTY, *One Writer's Beginnings*

Thinking back, finally, to the question of finding or giving voice, I realize that I have made at least one quite deliberate writing decision, at one of the points when one must think about writing in fairly direct terms. Not only did I choose to include in my dissertation figures who, at least much of the time, wrote well—Augustine, Freud, Nietzsche—but I also made sure to read other things that were well written, particularly poetry, to try to minimize atrociousness by contagion. This was an instinctive, untheorized move, but everyone to whom I spoke of it agreed that it was a sensible one (granted, those to whom I spoke were undoubtedly a preselected group of the agreeable). I make no argument for its success. In writing as in speaking, innumerable other voices echo; as I've noted, they must, simply for language to be. These other voices are both aural and written, and many of them, though certainly not all, are identifiable—though including poets around my dissertation reading is the closest I have come to being intentional about it. What strikes me about these voices now, however, is that the written voices echo in mine *as* aural and that this is a vital reminder of the corporeality of words. This corporeality comes to writing and to speaking in rhythm, as I have suggested, and in memory, and in the musicality of words—and it comes to us as both what makes words my own and what always keeps my voice and the self called by it a little bit strange to me.

Distinctive writerly voices bring out the somatic quality of words. Rhythm, when we take into account not just phrases and pauses but emphases and tone, can come through in writing as accent. Mladen Dolar notes, "We can have some inkling of the voice if we listen to someone with an accent. Accent—ad can-tum—is something which brings the voice into the vicinity of singing, and a heavy accent suddenly makes us aware of the material support of the voice which we tend immediately to discard."[56] It is possible to annotate intonations to some small extent, with italics, punctuation, or adverbs—or even diacritical marks, as Gerard Manley Hopkins sometimes did to help readers through his sprung rhythms. Even unmarked, though, accents may well come through in a text.

I was about fifteen when, for a high school English class, I read James Baldwin's story "Sonny's Blues." I had never read Baldwin, and can't recall that I brought any particular expectation to the story. Certainly I was not prepared, title notwithstanding, to hear the blues. (I should have heard jazz, too, but I didn't know enough jazz music at that point.) To the aching story of two brothers (one the narrator, the voice; the other a musician and a drug addict), the older blues rhythms, with their still older roots in call and response and songs meant for hard work, added a richness that could not have been imparted discursively, not by the definitions of the words or the order of events: it could only be in the music. I had loved words all my life, certainly within all of my memory, but I was astonished: I had no idea they could do *that*. The discovery was almost unbearably exciting.[57]

Better writers than I have shared this kind of astonishment. Jorge Luis Borges writes of hearing his father read Keats, when Borges was only a child:

> I hear his voice saying words that I understood not, but yet I felt. . . . I thought I knew all about words, and all about language (when one is a child, one feels one knows many things), but those words came as a revelation to me. Of course I did not understand them. . . . Those verses came to me through their music. I had thought of language as being a way of saying things, of uttering complaints, of saying that one was glad, or sad, and so on. Yet when I heard those lines (and I have been hearing them, in a sense, ever since), I knew that language could also be a music and a passion.[58]

In Will Stockton and D. Gilson's *Crush*, the narrator reads to a Mr. Williams, a lover of words who is slowly going blind.

> I pull a book off the shelf, little with an electric orange cover. Lunch Poems, by Frank O'Hara. I am five years old and it is the first book of poetry I encounter. The words in their queer combinations hold innumerable possibility, though I understand neither these combinations nor these possibilities yet. I am five years old and something sparks. . . . I am, unbeknownst, in love. I am, unbeknownst, learning from my forefathers an aesthetic of queerness, a lineage, a heritage, a bloodline.[59]

Only a little less vividly, Harold Bloom recalls, "I was preadolescent, ten or eleven years old. I still remember the extraordinary delight, the extraordinary force that Crane and Blake brought to me . . . though I had no notion what they were about."[60] Sometimes, music pulls us first; when we realize that words can make music and that music can make words mean before we can even conceptualize them, language may pull us very forcefully indeed. Marguerite Porete writes, "His Farness is the more Near," and Anne Carson responds, "I have no idea what this sentence means but it gives me a thrill. It fills me with wonder. In itself the sentence is a small complete act of worship, like a hymn or a prayer."[61]

The thrill I took from Baldwin's sentences extended to other distinctive authorial voices, a few examples of which will suffice to the point: I read James Joyce, drawn at first by the incorrigible punning; I read Flannery O'Connor, in love with her acerbic precision. And I realized—though, again, it took me decades to think about the implications—that one of the delights of reading either of them is that when one reads them aloud (or even subvocalizes clearly), one quite quickly acquires, for the duration of the reading, an accent—a Dublin lilt, the drawl and twang of rural Georgia. In fact, I have become slightly wary of citing long passages from O'Connor in talks.

This musicality and accentuation are part of what in language is irreducible to meaning and objective analysis—its sacred character, perhaps, but its bodily character, certainly. These writers' sense of rhythm is so precise that it brings the material support of the voice even to the printed text. For none of them is the voice inseparable from the meaning of what it tells. They let the material tell them how it needs to be said; the rhythms fill themselves with words and meaning. They know how words can move.

The movement of a text is not only in each word in relation to the next, but in the art of conceptual transition as well. Thought, too, has its rhythms and recurrences, its moves back to what is suddenly altogether new by its unexpected connections. John Ashbery remarks, "I think I am more interested in the movement among ideas than in the ideas themselves, the way one goes from one point to another rather than the destination or the origin."[62]

As a splendid instance, consider the movement of Anne Carson's texts. She begins with the perception of connection: "[it's] a basket of stuff that eventually looks like it has some informing idea. Then I grope around in it to see what that is, try different orderings and different concepts and then fix on one."[63] Her interviewer Emilia Brockes notes,

> Classicists are probably more sensitive than most to the suspicion that no original thoughts are left to be had in the world, but in any case, Carson believes that thoughts themselves matter less than the routes one takes between them. "I don't know that we really think any thoughts; we think connections between thoughts. That's where the mind moves, that's what's new, and the thoughts themselves have probably been there in my head or lots of other people's heads for a long time. But the jumps between them are entirely at that moment." She says, "It's magical."[64]

Those jumps make their way to her writing, in which we find ourselves moving in ways we did not expect—but which are wholly right as soon as we read them. The epigraph to her volume *Decreation* is taken from Florio's 1603 translation of Montaigne's "Essays on Some Verses of Virgil" (we enjoy it quote by quote): "I love a poetical kinde of a march, by friskes, skips and jumps." At times her text leaps by friskes and skips among its disparate ideas and figures; at others, it glides with deceptive ease. In these movements lies much of the joy of her writing. The transitions show us the connections, the conceptual common points. The ideas tell Carson how to write them; it is as if she wrote the musical score for the dance that emerges between them. But when she writes, we, too, move with the thinking that shapes the words and the words that shape the thought. Her awaiting of the movements, and Woolf's restless anticipation of rhythm, and LeGuin's inhabitation of her texts' speakers all sense movement, and they write in order to move along with it.

So, too, they move us. Whether we think in abrupt and discontinuous data points, linear slides, or Art Nouveau swirls, we find that our voices, which say these things, are also of these things themselves. While sensitivity to accents is unequally distributed, it is certainly true that many people acquire them quickly, coming to share the rhythms and intonations of those around them. Thoughts have accents too, the sensuousness in their senses.

For Dolar, accent is part of the materiality that resists meaning. Yet we could wonder whether this mightn't also be part of the paradox. In voice—in the fact that speaking is bodily, in its tactility, in its resonance—could be the very resistance to the telling that it makes possible, resistance whether in terms of constructed meaning or of neurobiological analysis. Even where the voice "tells"—gives away more than it denotes, in squeak or rasp or quiver—it resists. It cannot quite tell itself, but it must both re-call and receive itself from those who listen. Its resistance is in its very openness. The voice that tells and resists telling is created both in the silences that structure the rhythms of its speaking and in the voices that have made their unexpected way from hearing into sound. Every voice tells more than it can say, and it sounds even what it cannot tell, and in the end, it resists perfect knowing.

The rhythms of ideas that are given by thought, of stories that are given by character, of sentences that are given by accent are subject to contagion. One acquires voice by listening—and this includes reading materially and sensuously. Speaking and writing sound with the choral resonance of other voices. And, of course, one's own voice will not speak well unless it resonates as well with the said. As Carson puts it (in her own inimitable voice), "You write what you want to write in the way that it has to be."[65] To speak in my own voice, I have to fall silent and listen; to write in my own voice, I have to read others. In this brief absence, I begin to find my own rhythms, the unexpected sounds of speaking that sneak into text and form it beyond what it says. They come to me only as return—as rhythm does. The elusive bodiliness of all words, the speaking character of the movement between absence and presence in all relation and all generosity, mutually ground flesh and word. We say more than we can know how to tell, not because language is greater than body, not because body is more important than words, but because the two resonate in an infinite complexity of voices and voice. I speak only as a person, only as spoken through, only as other voices resonate in my own. And in this, my voice is unique.

CHAPTER 2

Speaking to Learn to Listen

> The teaching body dances its knowledge softly so that the audience will, like it, go into a trance and so that, through virtual mimicry of its gestures, a few ideas will enter their heads via the muscles and bones, which though seated and immobile are solicited, pulled toward the beginnings of movement, perhaps even by the written work's little jig.
>
> —MICHEL SERRES, "Variations on the Body"

Voices come to us in the way our bodies echo and alter: we read, we hear; we acquire an accent, however hard we might try for that perfect middle-of-the-Atlantic neutrality. The embodiment of voice demands that we attend to the sonorous sense even of a text given visually. Sometimes it makes sense to read aloud; other times, at least to subvocalize. But if we simply add reading aloud to our syllabi in the current academic climate, after centuries of the devocalizing of reason and the accompanying notion that we needn't hear in order to read, such addition becomes an oddly isolated move.

There is support for that move, though, and not just from wistful academics. In 2014 the American Academy of Pediatrics added to its recommendations for health care and feeding an urgent suggestion that all children be read to daily from birth.[1] Not only should we be surrounded by words as by touch, and spoken to by our parents or others who care for us, but someone, from the first, should enwrap us in the way that words on the page work in and on the voice. The Academy's recommendation is based upon concerns about vocabulary development and educational achievement, but we must suspect as well that in books we are also exposed to a range of rhythms, a set of mental movements, a range of voices, well beyond those of everyday speech. Our bodies' sense of words, our ability to embody meaning, is likewise expanded.

As a college professor, I teach those who have aged (however recently) beyond the range for which the pediatricians prescribe. They show, still, the effects of hearing an insufficiency of voices. Like many of my colleagues across a wide range of schools, I find that the students I teach have great difficulties with language at every point: speaking and hearing, writing and reading alike.[2] So far as I have been able to tell—this is something with which I am actively and constantly struggling—they hear words as a rush of sound with familiar blips that they can treat as keywords, and they write down text as if it were pictures. We cannot speak to each other of anything that requires focused textual work, though they are friendly and willing, and I am eager to engage them with the words and ideas that I find so exciting. Our college core curriculum, like the core and general education curricula of so many other schools, has been carefully modified to try to emphasize writing, with new instruments of measurement and new, cross-disciplinary requirements. It may be that these are helpful. It is not likely that they will help to the degree that our students appear to need. It may be that language itself is on the way out, in favor of a world of icons and quickfire images, of attention that cannot sustain itself for the length of a sentence (certainly not a compound sentence, or one with parentheses). But a lot of us in the humanities are too much in love with words and what words can do to easily let go of the hope that we can pass that love to others. It is in such hope that we continue to wonder how.

In my efforts to work out what might be going on in the classroom, I came across a study of a fifty-four-year-old woman (not a student) with a particularly vivid case of what is called dysgraphia, a certain kind of inability to write. This woman could speak and read, but could not write the letters of the alphabet. "The patient could accurately copy letters which she could not write," we are told. "The writing impairment . . . appeared to consist of a memory difficulty for the *motor movements* associated with letters."[3] Copying is different from writing. The woman treated letters as pictures. Dissociated from the movements that made them, she also could not make them *mean*. The research on this case indicates that the failure is not abstractly intellectual, but kinetic—"dysgraphia for letters may represent a specific type of motor memory deficit, dissociable from copying skills and the ability to draw letter-like forms."[4] A letter may be a visual sign, but it is not a picture in the illustrative sense. The problem is not that the dysgraphic woman has access to sound and sight but not to meaning, as might happen when we hear spoken and see written a language that is unfamiliar to us. It is (much more strangely) that one important part of corporeal meaningfulness no longer seems to be working for her, and so the complex but usually easy association between the sight of a word, the sound of a letter, the movement of a hand, and conceptual creation or interpretation has simply gone missing. The parallel with the students' problems is imperfect, of course. On one hand, this patient's rupture dealt only with writing, and not with language altogether. On the other, in writing, it was more severe even than that of the most devoted copier of PowerPoint slides. Nonetheless, the example remains telling—pathological cases often do tell us unexpected truths about the normal, differing primarily in degree. The association of language and flesh has broken, profoundly for her, more mildly for our students, and not imperceptibly for the rest of us. They, we, can neither dwell in the word nor stretch into the sentence—not, at any rate, without an effort that we are not always sure how to make. And that effort is not simply conceptual, but physical—a matter of the motor.

Time for Text

> What is the use of a violent kind of delightfulness if there is no pleasure in not getting tired of it.
>
> GERTRUDE STEIN, *Tender Buttons*

Difficulty with words is often, one way or another, a difficulty with *time*, and not only in the structures of rhythm. Students are certain that they are far more burdened by duties than anyone used to be (ever), and that this precludes, say, spending a lot of time reading Thomas Aquinas or worrying about the construction of sentences. (I have had students earnestly explain that Aristotle was able to write so much because people weren't so busy then, and that Teresa of Avila probably experienced visions as a way of relieving her profound monastic boredom.) Sociologists, for their part, are just as sure that those students suffer less from a lack of time than from a mismanagement of time: several studies show that students spend appreciably more time socializing, physically or virtually, than studying. This redistributive trend has been linked in at least one study to the rather alarming finding that most students learn pretty much nothing at all, or at least nothing that qualifies as intellectual, in their first two years of college.[5]

I would like to consider another possibility, in its way a more optimistic one: that the students' travails with time are really quite familiar, very like those of their professors, though perhaps more pronounced. Our schedules (mine and my colleagues' and our collective students') may well be overfull or badly organized, but we face a more fundamental issue—not of time management, but of time's structure, the very form of our lived temporality, and our bodies' ways of living it. This problem is one of tenses, not just in the linguistic sense of past, present, and future, perfect or not, but rather in the lived sense of tensions, of attention in its intensity and its extension. Time has become a great problem to us, though not, perhaps, a new one: Augustine complains in the early fifth century of being "scattered in times whose order I do not understand,"[6] while Teresa of Avila, in the sixteenth century, laments the difficulty of writing when other duties keep pulling her away (boredom notwithstanding).[7] We have lost—but we were always losing, we have always tended to lose—both density (the tight, intense focus of the attention in the moment) and extension (the stretch along a nonmomentary span), in favor of a scattered time—a dismembered, unremembered time, a time that is intriguing in a great many ways, but seems worrisomely to disallow learning, and especially learning through words. Learning demands attention (in fact, intense attention) and extension both; it requires focus and memory. There are, of course, a great many factors causing what feels like an increasingly fractured time, and a great many effects resulting from it. My focus in this chapter will be upon the relatively small subset of these causes and effects that are specifically pedagogical. Probably these cannot be altered in isolation from any of the rest of the sources of scatteredness and distraction, but it is possible, at least, that their alteration there can be a starting point rather than an isolated instance. That is, maybe if we learn in regathered time, we can learn a little bit about time's regathering. I should note that while I would not entirely discount our collective online time as a factor, I do not think that the internet alone can begin to account for time's fracturing (our records indicate that Augustine spent little time in online pursuits). Nor am I placated by the idea, which I have heard several times, that students have replaced textual with digital literacy. I find that those most capable in one medium (digital or print) actually tend to be the most capable in the other as well. Language is more than a skill set.

To revalue learning—especially to value reading and other practices of words—I want to look at a historical site at which reading has been very highly valued, to ask whether anything about that culture of reading might usefully be returned to our own. To turn ourselves to a more literate temporality, I would argue, must also be to turn ourselves to a time more attentive to body and flesh—a time that is both slower and more sensuous than ours often is. That this will seem counterintuitive to our tendency to understand body and language distinct from one another is itself, I think, symptomatic. As Catherine Conybeare writes in analyzing the language of Augustine's *Confessions*, "Too often it is pretended—held out, offered up—that words on a page are already somehow divorced from the body, involved in the realm of the metaphysical." The result of this pretense is "the disembodied subject (or 'transcendental ego')," the unfortunate "lovechild of linguistics and philosophy."[8] The time of our learning is doubly and destructively decoupled from body and from text as those two are unjoined from each other. We have lost our ability to *understand*, and not simply to *say*, that learning takes time—an understanding more primal than our ability to devote our time to it.

Marking Time

> A baby begins chewing on letters on wood blocks
> To get to the root of the problem at hand
> All your language is splinters it can't stick together
>
> SIMON JOYNER, "Born of Longing"

The timing of words: we suspect by now that this must mean, among other things, their musicality. The relation of philosophical to musical knowledge is no less intriguing pedagogically than it is theoretically. In a pleasingly strange passage of Plato's *Phaedo*, we hear indirectly from the poet Evenus. Like so much that is especially interesting in Plato, what we hear comes to us only as the rumor of a rumor; somebody said that Evenus said that . . . and so on. Evenus, it is rumored, said that Socrates, imprisoned for imparting impiety to the youth of Athens—ostensibly, then, for his pedagogy—has composed a hymn to Apollo.

The back story is slightly more complex. On his last day, Socrates muses to his friends that the relationship between pleasure and pain is very strange; one cannot have both at once, yet to pursue one is almost certainly to "catch" the other as well.[9] Aesop could have written about this, Socrates remarks: maybe the gods wanted to reconcile the opposition, but could not, so they made a two-headed beast such that one necessarily accompanies the other.

It is this speculation—about a story that someone else could have made (there is going to be a story, someone's going to try and tell a story)—that reminds Socrates's friend Cebes to ask about the hymn on behalf of Evenus.

Certainly if Socrates were to compose a hymn, it seems Apollo would be a suitable subject: Apollo is the god of reason and good measure in both learning and music, and it was his oracle who declared Socrates the wisest of men. Socrates assures Cebes that he has no aspiration to surpass the anxious Evenus. The rumor does touch on reality, though. Recurrent dreams have told Socrates to make and practice art—or to "make music and do it."[10] If philosophy is, as Socrates has always claimed, the highest art, then he is on the right track anyway. (Or is he? When he creates the persona of Diotima for the *Symposium*, Socrates goes beyond himself philosophically to declare the highest and most beautiful good something beyond reason or rational investigation.) But as long as his execution has been stayed—by the feast of that very Apollo—Socrates decides that maybe he should investigate whether music here means, in fact, music. It would be safer to try making some music, just to be sure. So he makes his hymn to honor Apollo, a fitting enough thanks for a few days' living.

A problem remains, because poets don't make arguments; they tell stories. Socrates himself is no storyteller, so he has taken some stories he already knows—the fables of Aesop—and put them into verse. After this admission, Socrates seems abruptly to change the subject to the good things that await good men after death. Not only is this in itself some fine storytelling, but Socrates may be doing one of his quick subject changes to avoid having anyone ask about the fable that he made up just a few lines earlier, regarding the two-headed beast—a fable Aesop should have made, but didn't. Who *is* speaking? It is the distinctiveness of the Socratic voice to leave us always unsure, even while we know that it must be he.

This near-deathbed scruple, this obedience at last to the repeated voice of his *daimon*, reminds us that the Socratic sense of philosophy is more complex and more musical than history has made it. Indeed, as most well know, Socrates does not work in silence at all; he does not write, but he speaks, and a great deal at that. (It is rather fascinating that in the *Phaedo*, Plato, who is home ill, does not hear, and must rely upon another's report of Socrates's words in order to report them to us.) Just as in *Phaedrus*, Socrates's *daimon* reminds him that he risks blasphemy in speaking ill of love, and that is safer to honor the god Eros with a long speech in his favor; so, too, it might be safer to honor the divinity of the dream by allowing music even into Socrates's speaking.[11] We must always be alert to Platonic polysemousness. The dream could mean that his philosophy has been musical all along, or it might mean that he has wasted his wisdom when he should have loved song.

But it seems most in keeping with the text that it would mean both: that he has attended all along to the most rational kinds of musicality, but also that music can never be wholly bound by reason. It is always a delicate matter to distinguish between Socrates, whose thought we have only second-hand, and the writer Plato, whose are the most important of the hands by which we have him, but we should not underestimate the subtle complexity of either. Plato, who seems so often dead set against the possible dishonesty of poets, is nonetheless too subtle not to undercut such a simplified stance. Socrates in the end demands that the philosopher hear the music of the daimonic voice, that she create poetic *mythos* and not simply logic. However directly he may defend the latter, Socrates gives voice to the former far too often for us to disavow it.

Plato gives us some clear arguments for the pedagogical value of, at the very least, Apollonian music. Laura Odello notes that, for Plato, "Music is put to the service of education because it allows 'rhythm and harmony [to] find their way to the inmost soul' (Plato, *Republic*, 401d). The politics of the *polis* are based above all on harmonic attunement, on being attuned to each other and to the law; music seems to be indispensable to the *polis* as the vital and sovereign unity of the political community."

Music is valuable both educationally, in the formation of the soul, and politically, in the formation of the state. Or rather, some music is: "We must not let music bewitch us, for music is also toxic; it is a *pharmakon*, one might say, a drug, a remedy, a cure, a medicine, but also a poison, a danger, a contamination. A certain sound regimen or diet is called for, under the control of a *logos* that gives the measure of which music is deprived."[12]

On this reading, which is true to the history of Platonism and certainly to at least one aspect of Plato, music seems to have value only insofar as it is reasoned, as it is the very science of measure and number (we shall later see a similar claim, with similar tensions, from Augustine). As sonorous measure, as what we hear and touch with our singing, this ratio remains deeply corporeal. Plato, and through him Socrates, runs the risk not of extending music into wisdom, but of loving wisdom *rather than* music. As Cavarero writes, "[t]he soul, as Plato ends up suggesting, can do without the bodily *phone* and contents itself with a metaphorical voice. And from this point on, the soul obstinately speaks with a voice that does not reverberate."[13] As this happens, that "inmost soul" becomes inner indeed: "The more serious side of this problem . . . does not lie in the metaphorical identification of thinking with speaking or in the interiorization of dialogue, but rather in the conviction that this interior discoursing is the condition of possibility for speaking to others."[14] Speaking then moves not between, but unidirectionally from inside to out—very nearly the wrong way round. It does not surround us and create us, but rather is created by us prior to its emergence; it emerges from our bodies, to be sure, but only as a byproduct of our souls, of our minds.

But this is too simple a seeming. Socratic intellectual and musical midwifery demands eros, which in its uncomfortableness is today duly excised from education.[15] Eros is far more ready than abstraction to burst into song. But we learn nothing if we cannot be drawn to it somehow, and abstraction has a hard time attracting us by itself. This is something that Socrates knew, and Plato knew that he knew it. "In contrast to Plato," Cavarero points out, "Socrates does not write; he speaks. Logos comes out of his mouth and effectively enters the ears of his interlocutors. The comparison with the flute [by Alcibiades in the *Symposium*] is therefore hardly coincidental. Just as Marsyas [the satyr whom Socrates resembles] puts the flute to his mouth and produces a sound that bewitches his listeners, so too Socrates makes his own mouth into a flute from which come bewitching discourses." These discourses, however bewildering, are, of course, meaningful too; there is no sense that Socrates is not setting forth concepts—only that this is not the *sole* thing he is doing, because concepts don't actually emerge all alone. It is not the well-known distinction between speech and writing that is at issue. "At stake, rather, is the seductive effect that Socratic speech shares with the acoustic—or, more precisely, the musical."[16] Socrates the teacher is a flute made of words, words played seductively in his voice. He attracts attention. His students, having hung upon his every word, remember: indeed, Plato sets more than one dialogue as a presentation entirely from the recollection of such a student. They can hum Socratic truth from memory.

Socrates may compose a hymn, but he also versifies—makes musical—stories that are all simile and metaphor and deceptive little animals. Claiming to be unable to make myth on his own, he opens with a fable that should have been, and goes on to tell multiple tales of the soul's journey beyond mortal living. It is not simply as the measure of reason that music sneaks in where logic fears to tread. And when Platonism meets with Christianity, with the latter's startling fleshy incarnation, a disciplined focus on the intersections of flesh and word also begins to develop: the *logos* itself takes on with flesh the power of *mythos* as well.

In fact, Christian monasticism will validate Socratic musicality. The daily office of monastic orders, the unchanging prayer practice that structures communal life, is centered upon the singing of psalms. As these contain history, prophecy, law, and emotional expression, they are particularly well suited to making each soul, to regulating and rectifying it—not by precept, but by the engagement of saying, and indeed of singing, the words. Gerald Gruber notes of medieval music, "What we find are psalms that were often uttered in a prosodic way. And the astonishing fact is that the text not only formed the voice but . . . the voice also carried the meaning of the text. As would happen centuries later in opera, the concentration of the listener is moved emphatically *by* the voice. The voice of psalmody *is* the message, the idea—there is no doubt about that."[17] In fact, says Athanasius in instructing monks in psalmody, it is important that the psalms are not just spoken: "it is fitting for the Divine Scripture to praise God not in compressed speech alone, but also in the voice that is richly broadened. . . . For thus it will be preserved that men love God with their whole strength and power."[18]

Setting forth what is proper to monks, Athanasius analogizes the soul musically; reason unites the powers of the soul "just as harmony that unites flutes effects a single sound," since "the reason intends man neither to be discordant in himself, nor to be at variance with himself."[19] Psalmody is the greatest harmonizing: "The harmonious reading of the Psalms is a figure and type of such undisturbed and calm equanimity of our thoughts. For just as we discover the ideas of the soul and communicate them through the words we put forth, so also the Lord, wishing the melody of the words to be a symbol of the spiritual harmony in a soul, has ordered that the odes be chanted tunefully, and the Psalms recited with song."[20] Indeed, the psalms make the singers into their proper measure: "For thus beautifully singing praises, he brings rhythm to his soul and leads it, so to speak, from disproportion to proportion."[21] While Athanasius does not remark upon it, singing builds community in deeply physical ways: choirs singing together begin, necessarily, to breathe synchronously, and even their heartbeats may align as a consequence.[22] Word and flesh entangle. Music and philosophy begin to seem a little more alike than we had thought, after all. Probably Socrates already knew.

Of course, not just any old singing will do. Athanasius does not favor song about anything one pleases, and reason gives the most beautiful measure. Desire, so readily aroused by music, is still a problem, and the instrument of the body must be properly tuned so the voice may sing God without risking the wrong sort of passion. This tuning, however, *is* of the body, and not of the spirit decorporealized; it is passion rightly directed but in no way diminished. At least one desire is necessarily good: the desire for God is not disordered; it cannot be so great as ever to be out of proportion to what it loves. By vocal impersonation, by taking on the words and the rhythms of the ancient hymns, the person of the monk is formed. He acquires the accents of devotion. Sometimes, devotion even sings back: "As studied by Bernard Lortat-Jacob at the Musée de l'Homme in Paris, the Quintina (literally 'fifth one') in Sardinian a capella vocal music . . . conveys an illusion: A fifth female voice emerges from the four male voices when the harmony and timbres are performed just right. (They believe the voice is that of the Virgin Mary coming to reward them if they are pious enough to sing it right.)"[23]

Even where the music is less overt, contemplation moves and resonates in bodies. Nearly every contemplative tradition recommends particular postures and the control of sensation. We usually think of seated postures and the careful withdrawal of the senses from the outside, but this is not the only variant. M. B. Pranger declares of the writings of the Jesuit founder Ignatius Loyola, famous for his widely practiced spiritual exercises:

> efforts to mitigate bodily concreteness by reinterpreting the famous five weeks of exercises as so many stimuli to arouse concomitant pious feelings in the soul should be rejected out of hand. . . . The combination of "concrete" places and images reintroduces the senses. Not unexpectedly, later theologians have tried to tone down this aspect and to turn the famous Ignatian "application of the senses" to scenes from Hell and the life of Christ into a merely spiritual affair.[24]

It is unlikely that words in a secular context, however well sung, could remake us quite so thoroughly as Athanasius held that the psalms might do to the monks, or Ignatius the various scriptural images and imagistic practices to his priests. We have less trust that any text could contain such perfection as they attributed to the psalms, and this mistrust might be for the best. But the sense that not only do words appeal to us by music, but that the music in them makes us understand them with a depth that goes beyond that of simple concepts, may matter still. If understanding both conceptually and bodily is not transformative, what in the world could be? The monks' transformation by music is of embodied soul; it is so complete that it accompanies a change of name. The monk who speaks in song is not the secular person left behind. Is it even possible, now, to make words as seductive as music? Can we desire learning in the rightly infinite proportion that monks held out for God?

Bodily Texts, Textual Flesh

> The richness of life reveals itself through a *richness of gestures*. One must *learn* to feel everything—the length and retarding of sentences, interpunctuations, the choice of words, the pausing, the sequence of arguments—like gestures.
>
> LOU-ANDREAS SALOME, *Nietzsche*

Even if not to the remarkable degree of monastic practice, learning means remaking the one who learns. First we become literate—not merely in plodding along deciphering, but in resonating with words. Already in the earliest monastic communities, as Harry Gamble points out, "monks were assisted toward literacy,"[25] and monasticism was associated with reading. Amusingly, Gamble notes a list of excuses that literate fourth-century Christians gave to John Chrysostom when he chastised them for not doing the private scriptural readings he encouraged as accompaniment to the public liturgy. Some cite a lack of leisure, of the books, or of interest, but Gamble also notes the response, "I am not a monk."[26] These excuses sound strikingly contemporary, though I suppose nonreaders would most likely argue instead of the last that they are not professors, our class having replaced monks in the popular mind as the sexless literati.

In fact, the preoccupations of monasticism may be exactly those of pedagogical time. Pranger points out that the deeply somatic temporalities of medieval monasticism respond to "the problem of compression and extension—that is, the problem of time."[27] Time is further problematized when we seem to *lose* both compression and extension in fracture and scattering, when we fail to gather time in the body. Brian Stock notes, "Medieval spirituality was concerned with the body in a more direct, practical manner than were the meditative practices of the ancient world, even though medieval thinkers were no less preoccupied than the ancients with emphasizing the superior status of the mind."[28] (We know better, of course, than simply to assume a modern mind-body dualism from this claim.) Can we, given the immense differences of culture and setting, adopt—or adapt—any of these corporeal concerns as our own?

Direct adoption will not be an option, of course, but perhaps adaptation will (with some necessary cautions and limitations thrown in). We might begin with the problem of speed. Pranger argues that monastic time is deliberately slowed and concentrated by multiple means—the training in classical genres, the slow timing of the sermon and scriptural meditation, and even the precisely constrained and ritualized time of daily living.[29] Moreover, this slow time is not directed at progress and conclusion. In monastic life, Pranger writes, "the progressive concept of time is bent, so to speak, and made curvilinear, so that it obeys the patterns and rituals of retardation and repetition."[30] To retard and repeat, to slow the "now" and return it to "then," is to curve attentive focus and temporal stretch into something quite other than the goal orientation that monopolizes so much of our educational focus.

Pranger elegantly details the ways in which monastic literacy is mutually structured with monastic time—reading itself is compressed and extended (in rereading, sermonizing, and meditating upon the text), slowed and repeated; and reading is what compresses, extends, slows, and returns time, too, in a life focused upon the Daily Office. In the dual movements of attention focused and stretched, the time of the body and the time of text return to one another and turn about in the slow curve of learning as living. Perhaps, though to an extent greatly limited by our spatial expansiveness and our lives' distractions, we can return to the power and the pleasure of such bodily time, such physical reading. For all of its artifice, this textual time is truer to the body than is learning in order to cease to learn, of teaching toward tests and outcomes assessments, so that the mind can eagerly abandon its knowledge once the calculations are finished—a practice that attempts to disembody learning and requires the assumption that the flesh does not form the habit of literacy, but rather begins and abandons forms rapidly and abruptly. Our overwhelming emphasis on quantifiable result, with the desired object of measure determined in advance, has been famously terrible for all sorts of learning, particularly in the humanities. One reason, I think, is precisely that it demands a model of learning that is so utterly at odds with the living, thinking bodies in which we learn, the voices in which we read. I certainly don't mean that bodies are somehow natural rather than artificial—but an art form that disregards its medium is going to turn out poorly, and the medium of teaching and learning is us.

Monastic Slowness

> What the reader wants from reading and what the lover wants from love are experiences of very similar design. It is a necessarily triangular design, and it embodies a reach for the unknown.
>
> ANNE CARSON, *Eros the Bittersweet*

We cannot create care by haste. Time's extension makes demands upon both memory and attention. Slowness (even "a retardation verging on . . . eternity," says Pranger[31]) combines the extension of attentiveness over time with the density of a contracture that plays out spatially as cloistering, temporally as the intensification of attention, a focus that can both tighten and stretch. To focus attentively on an extended time *is* a manner of slowing time, or more exactly of slowing our temporal sense into the peculiarity of absorption. I don't know that we need to learn more slowly in the sense of taking in fewer texts or less information over the same period of time, but perhaps we should relearn *slowness*, as the stretch of time. This, too, is part of hearing: that retardation to the edge of eternity is not least a *decelerando*, a slowing in the manner of music.

This deceleration and repetition are also in keeping with the way that bodies learn—and by which they may accelerate, if they want to. We know from explicit bodily instruction, such as that in dance or sport, and from the everyday learning of corporeal habit, that bodies learn slowly, a slowness linked to repetition. To create muscle memory demands repetition and temporal space, and it makes extension (the ability to sustain) and focus (the ability to dwell in); that is, there is a feedback loop of what we need to do and what we are able to do.

We recognize here a parallel to the dual time of reading. The process of creating bodily memory is sometimes described as that of repeating an act until it becomes unconscious, but of course we are seldom actually unconscious when we dance, or run, or even, for that matter, when we tie our shoes. Probably one reason for the notion that the act is unconscious is that in it we are usually not *reflective*: we are in the movement, not outside it analyzing or taking its picture for Facebook. We may be distracted—tying our shoes does not, most mornings, take up very much of our attention. Or we may be utterly absorbed—it is sometimes a bit surprising to find oneself having finished a performance or a book, after one's attention in and to its moments seemed almost to keep time from passing, to slow it to the point of a-temporality (a slowness verging on eternity). But we have not ceased thinking, we have simply been thinking with an unusual focus; we have learned with the clarity of slowness. The sense of body slipping readily into a long-familiar discipline and the delight of a movement newly becoming "natural" are echoed in the delight of new revelation in a well-studied text and the simple pleasure of knowing the words already (I cannot be the only person who sneakily enjoys reciting the various formulations of the categorical imperative, for instance), or of finding an astonishing new text and trying to follow it through. Thus, too, when we read with a sense of the sounds, we repeat in order to know; we take the luxuriant pleasure of slow simplicity and indulge in the virtuosity of complexity and speed. The mind moves its muscles, and they are not other than those of the flesh.

While we don't learn text by the same pure drilled-in repetition by which we learn movement, we do better in both to start by slowing the movement down, giving ourselves time to consider each part of it. Reading and remembering, whether as brief as the extent of a sentence or as long as the labor of a life, take time; speaking and listening remind us of this time's fleshy character. And flesh's character as song and music gives meaning its rhythmic sense, but it also gives the very *feeling* of understanding, of saying, of words. Instead of learning in order to reproduce for an exam—as I have suggested above, learning in order to forget—we may instead learn by heart.

Taking time is importantly not the sort of laziness that creates the scattering of attention here and there with longer inattentive stretches between, such as the brief moments of focus on an assignment between long stretches exploring internet cats.[32] It is, rather, a matter of attending precisely instead of rushing past. Working toward an analysis of the glacial tempo of monastic sermonizing, Pranger pauses to remark on "the Romanian conductor Sergiu Clibidache," who "was famous for his extremely slow tempi. . . . Listening . . . , however, one did not notice this slowness. What came to the fore was a high degree of clarity, conveying to the ear the majestic structure of the piece so as to cause movement and rest almost to coalesce."[33] Pranger's is not, to be sure, an opinion universally shared; it is possible that music may move so slowly that one quite loses the thread of it—and the same holds for both speaking words and bodies dancing. With very difficult movement, both of flesh and of thought, we may do well to learn with great slowness—but we might find, too, that there are truths revealed anew when we are able to approach the now-familiar thoughts and movements more quickly.[34] The wrong tempo may even lose a voice—keep the Virgin Mary from singing back, for instance. But we can know the right tempo only by finding it, and we can find it only by knowing the steps. In my efforts to teach, I will often move very slowly through the material, then end a class session with the "two-minute version." This version may be comic in its hurriedness, but it makes clear to me, and I hope to the rest of the class, the connections and movements between the pieces that we could only clarify with slowness.

Clarity comes of remaining in the moments and attending to their series, rather than awaiting only completion—in the near-coalescence of movement and rest, we *dwell* on passages, on ideas, on words; on them, and in them, too. But we do not dwell in stasis; rather, we attend as we move and we attend to our movement. We cannot attend, though, to moments or to movements when we are too focused on what comes after, on prespecified goals that have nothing to do with the pleasure and difficulty inherent in the moment and the movement. When we become exclusively focused on results, we also become reluctant to linger, or to repeat—to reach clarity and not just finality. The results suffer too, and the more narrowly we focus upon them, the worse they become. Of course we cannot teach, much less grade, without desiring some accomplishment—but we can return the focus to the accomplishment of process itself, a communal process of remaking ourselves more than of acquiring skills as if they were possessions, or even tools. The requirement of some evaluation is real enough (however much the idealist in each of us might wish for pure teaching for the joy of it). But evaluation of any kind should be subsequent to and consequent upon what we actually do pedagogically, rather than driving and directing our teaching and learning from the outset. To pay attention slowly means to pay attention *now*—for as long as now may take.

Paying attention, or focusing—concentrating and extending the moment—is not necessarily a matter of remaining on a single track. Time slows, attention stretches, and we wander. It is actually our reluctance to pay slow attention (our desire to reach the end) that leads us to fear digression as if it were hostile to learning. Pranger notes the contrary argument of Gregory the Great, who declares that commentary should be like the flow of a river: "For, when a river flows through its bed, hitting on both sides open valleys, it immediately changes its course. And when it has filled those open spaces sufficiently, it all of a sudden returns to its bed."[35] Learning, too, should be able to flow into possibilities, without fear that the line of thought will be unavailable for return. Attention, though certainly not identical with joy (little focuses the mind so obsessively as a toothache), is assisted by joy, by delight—and delight may equally well obsess over a single thought or leap, by friskes and skips, to a quite surprising tangent. Returning from the tangential, we find our earlier understanding enriched by both knowledge and pleasure, and we repeat the earlier ideas, readings, or topics with renewed attention. More still: a willingness to digress respects the openness of time and of text, the fact that we do not know in advance what we might learn, however often the text might be repeated.

It must seem, speaking of digression, that we have wandered well away from the corporeal and sonorous here. But I would argue that we are undertaking precisely a corporeal way of thought, which may not be restricted to voice but must include it. Repeating the "same" material from a new perspective, or enriched by our tangential thinking, we slowly form the habits of thought, so that we do not have to think so much about thinking, and we can begin, as we acquire and embody the techniques of thought, to move in it with some measure of skill and perhaps even grace—not to be done with moving, but to be able to move, to be skilled in flesh and word, even more. We may begin to use words as we may play music, not with an eye to ending, but with pleasure (a pleasure that in no way denies attendant frustrations) in the widening of our range of abilities and possibilities. Our minds might begin to sing.

We need to be able to focus extensively, but we also need to be able to shift our focus, which is not the same as losing it. While, as I've noted, slow attention is importantly different from inattentiveness, sometimes inattention will be required. Even tangents are always connected, and we must sometimes disconnect. Taking time means leaving time enough—not only time to digress, but time between. Learning can interfere with learning if the temporal space is too crowded. For instance, studies show that learning finger patterns back-to-back tends to lead to forgetting them all, while learning such patterns with a temporal gap between allows us to retain multiple sets.[36] Not dissimilarly, Seneca remarks, in Brian Stock's paraphrase, that "reading is like physical exercise, which achieves its best results if spurts of activity are followed by periods of relaxation."[37] This must sound a bit counter to the arguments I have been making: what is broken time if not activity in spurts, the incapacity for attention conveniently creating the necessary breaks? The difference between Seneca's exercise of reading and the loss of language, however, is at least twofold. One aspect is simply quantitative; his bursts, one suspects, were not merely a minute or two in length, and the quantitative difference in reading time becomes a qualitative difference in the nature of attentive absorption. Thus, relatedly, the second difference holds between "active" time, the clarity of slow precise focus, and an uninvested, half-focused attention with an eye always on afterward. Taking a break after or between is different from being disengaged during. We must engage in the flesh, letting words make and remake us.

Learning takes time: wandering time, open time, and repetition (inclusive of rhythm), waiting for the moment when the body-mind *gets it* and the focus, though no less, can stop standing outside to reflect upon itself. Eager for efficiency, we do not allow thought its time, but test and forget and hurry on. We do not allow words their flesh: the "speed reading" techniques first developed in the 1950s and encouraged still today (for purposes of more efficient test-taking, for example[38]) mostly work by eliminating even *sub*vocalizing, the inward representation of the voice that is accompanied by the movements of some of the speaking muscles, such as those in the throat or jaw. Newer versions offer to train readers online, with quickly moving text to force one to learn to keep up.[39]

Thus stripped of its music and of its right to wander with curious pleasure, learning in the moment is rendered joyless, and understanding fades with discouraging speed. Neatly lined up, eager to get our reading over with, we find that it is over too quickly, forgotten as we move urgently on. Certainly it has had no time to restructure our selves and our passions, to awaken our desires for the infinite possibilities of learning itself.

Movement slowed by intent is different from movement slowed by disruption; it does not remove the dense intensity of attention from time. In fact, it enables that attention, to allow us to dwell in moments, in movements, in texts rather than having always to anticipate what comes up next (of course, there can be pleasure and value to such anticipation—but not if it is a constant, or our only option). And just as we can build strength and endurance in the muscles, so, too, we develop them in our ability to dwell and think in words. We do that by keeping words in our ears, on our tongues, and in our throats, by keeping language in time; by keeping time, in language.

In attending to the sound of sense, more than one sense is engaged, and with them the possibility of more modes of learning. Musician and music researcher Deniz Peters argues that sound-making is always synesthetic, tactile as well as auditory. And sound-sensing, when it moves from hearing to listening, when it is active, adds this synesthesia to perception: we see the weight of a body, feel the rise of pressure and resistance in pitch. Peters argues that as observers, we contribute adverbially—we do not *infer* weight or stress, but experience them corporeally. The emotion of sound, too, is directly encountered in the body, not derived by inference from it.[40] We really do, or can, feel poetry, and the poetic qualities of prose.[41] People learn in different ways, but the value of engaging multiple senses, and multiple kinds of knowing, may well be that of opening the greatest possibilities for learning at all.

Urgent Memory and Constrained Spaces

> So, when I see a word I'm interested in, what that means to me is that the word's the surface of an extended volume. It's as if the word has density.
>
> RICHARD FORD, IN NANCY COMPTON, *Writers on Writing*

Pranger writes that the curiously intense, concentrated lives of early medieval monks exemplify a sense of slowness (reiteration, amplification, minute attention), but also of urgency.[42] Both urgency and lingering are aspects of attention, with its echoes of awaiting built into its sense of immediate focus. Without the memory that the extension of time might grant, we lose intensity, too.

Ideally, learning would add a synesthetically tactile-kinesthetic-sonorous element to the vision of words, taking its time and following the course of collective curiosity and returns to key points. Even a daydream, however, has to be a little bit realistic; in this case, we have to acknowledge that such focus is far harder in the contemporary academy than it was in the medieval monastery, and that communal memories will be difficult at best to construct. The enclosure of the monastery is not only temporal but spatial; "the enclosed garden of the monastic site," Pranger notes, is particularly adapted to bearing the "violent love" of an insatiable divinity.[43] It is, as well, a space of memory, not least as successive generations of monks inhabit it, and even a space of mnemonics. It's unlikely that such a place would be created in contemporary campus architecture. If it were, we might feel claustrophobic in it. Yet we should take a hint from Pranger's observation that a monastic enclosure is also an enclosure within language: "The dense structure of [the monk's] existence is reminiscent of the compactness of a book. . . . That which, for the extramural reader, is bound to remain a matter of imagination has become reality for the monk. In the compact, 'curved' world of the monastery he becomes identical with the rhythm and density of his linguistic corpus."[44] Dense, intense attention to text is also attention to the rhythms that we read with and in our muscles, our heartbeats, our breaths—and the voicing of words. We have to attend to the body of the text with, or even as, our own embodiedness. Thus attentive, we enter into a history of thought, a tradition of thinking. We can use it, if we like, to think about quite nontraditional things.

We remain extramural readers, but in our small and temporary ways perhaps we *can* recreate this attention within our more temporary enclosures, even if to a lesser extent than was true for those who lived entirely in learning. We do it already in studio spaces, as any visitor to a school of music, dance, visual arts, or theater can attest: often there is a focused creative seriousness to such a space that is distinctly absent from many academic classrooms. Undoubtedly there are relevant architectural differences, but there are temporal and corporeal differences, too. And again, part of the distinction is a focus in the present, in its difficulty and its delight. This is the delight that lets us digress or move slowly not because we are tired of the text, but precisely because we are not; not because we are measuring our learning, but because we are dwelling in it, eager to think more and think more readily. This is particularly difficult when we must treat syllabi as contracts for required outcomes and not as scores for collaborative performance with space for improvisation.

In practices clearly devoted to performance, delight is not contrary to discipline, but entirely caught up with it. It matters to us, as teachers and as students, that texts are affective, and that there can be a pleasure in the disciplined development of the body ensouled. The texts with which the monks spend so much of their days don't *illustrate* discipline, development, the ascent of the soul, even the infiltration of joy into daily despair—they *induce* them. This induction requires a great absorption in the text. With a few exceptions, such as the handbooks of monastic Rules, the texts aren't how-to manuals; rather, they implicate the reader, such that reading becomes a doing—also a creation, as Rebecca Krawiec notes, of social memory,[45] of an us within which the self is transformed, expanded by its very spatial and temporal constraints, by its presence in the monastery and its location in the body, into the community and into history.

The best academic classes manifest a communal pleasure precisely in and through the concentration and extension of the attentive attendants. When we lose these tensions in the "everyday" character of our time and space—time and space to which we do not pay exquisite and living attention—we lose some of both community and the sacred in our worlds. Pranger dates the emergence of our strong sense of the individual subject a little later than most, to the twelfth century, precisely when we begin to lose the monastic enclosure and the density that it allows.[46] Contemporary concerns intensify this movement of disenclosure; as we extend ourselves virtually, we forget to contract our attention, to enclose it in a thought, a text, a motion of the muscles, a collective breath. And forgetting to attend, we simply forget. We become only ourselves, and the chorus of our voices thins.

The question of enclosure is vexed. The monastery en-closes, but it also closes out, demanding a *contemptus mundi* that we actively want *not* to instill today. We want, quite the contrary, to link the love of learning and of text to the love of the world; the perception of that disconnection, the negative heritage of monasticism, may even be a factor in turning off the desire to work and dwell in words. This makes the argument for the reembodiment of learning and the resensualization of language all the more urgent. We must attend to language not only as a sign-system, though this is terribly important in helping us to understand how our views of the world are constructed, but also as a bodily resonance that vibrates with what Merleau-Ponty calls the flesh of the world.[47] To include so much (in) time, to concentrate the moment to the intensity of the eternal, to stretch the attention span out beyond closure, we must be a bit ascetic, too. Pranger quotes Robert Musil's strange and lovely *The Man Without Qualities*: "So I offer you my conclusion that beauty and excitement come into the world as a result of things having been left out."[48] As Nietzsche points out, asceticism may derive from rejection, but it may also be a consequence of absorbed delight.[49] It is true that absorption in anything will mean cutting out something else, however briefly; it is not true, though, that absorption in text must mean cutting off the lived, corporeal, relational world. In the occasional asceticism of textual work, we enrich and extend our modes of attention and recollection. We can close out by focusing in, rather than by foreclosing or rejecting out of hand.

We cannot, of course, make our classrooms into tiny monasteries, nor do we usually want to—though the temptation must occasionally strike, most often in early spring. But we can embody the movement of attention that is not distraction, attention to textual flesh and sensual text, attention to the wanderings of the subject itself, with its subsidiaries and tributaries. We can attend to the rhythms and returns of an argument, the flow of sound in a poem, the outward stretch of an ancient hymn. We can, for a few hours, pay attention. We can read together, and aloud; we can take pleasure in voice and breath and vibration, and make reading, too, not something to have done with.

All of this abstraction needs some fleshing out, and some bringing back into voice. Texts from just about as early as we have texts—from the Sumerian epic of *Gilgamesh*—tell us to attend not just to what they say, but to the reading of them: "Climb the stone staircase," we are instructed in the preface to the poem. The palace at Uruk is described in sumptuous detail, the place set, before we are instructed to retrieve the tablets on which the tale itself is inscribed:

> Climb the stone staircase, more ancient than the mind can imagine,
> approach the Eanna Temple, sacred to Ishtar,
> a temple that no king has equaled in size or beauty,
> walk on the wall of Uruk, follow its course
> around the city, inspect its mighty foundations,
> examine its brickwork, how masterfully it is built,
> observe the land it encloses: the palm trees, the gardens,
> the orchards, the glorious palaces and temples, the shops

and marketplaces, the houses, the public squares.
Find the cornerstone and under it the copper box
that is marked with his name. Unlock it. Open the lid.
Take out the tablet of lapis lazuli. Read
how Gilgamesh suffered all and accomplished all.[50]

The text itself, in Stephen Mitchell's gorgeous rendition, slows us down, makes us wander with it—and then draws our attention to what we and the text are doing together. Or consider the equally lovely, more contemporary setup of Italo Calvino's *If on a Winter's Night a Traveler*, which takes us through the process of finding and buying the book, and urges us, with examples, into a comfortable, pleasurable reading position—including hanging upside down, should we wish.[51] Here, too, is an enclosure, not in the walls of the city, but within the space of the book:

> Let the world around you fade. Best to close the door; the TV is always on in the next room. Tell the others right away, "No, I don't want to watch TV!" Raise your voice—they won't hear you otherwise—"I'm reading! I don't want to be disturbed!" . . . Or if you prefer, don't say anything, just hope that they'll leave you alone.[52]

Pay attention to how you read, these texts urge us. Attend, and give the words space. Attention makes the spacing. This also the urging of Irenaeus, who writes to those who must decipher continuous script—words without spaces, text without gap or punctuation—and who must, in the reading, work out when to breathe and pause.[53] At times, as he notes, the very meaning of the text depends upon where we draw breath. He writes of an ambiguous Pauline text,[54] "If then anyone does not pay attention to the reading and neglects to indicate by pauses the person of whom Paul wants to speak, he will read not only incoherence but blasphemy, as if the coming of the Lord would take place by the working of Satan."[55] As Jennifer Glancy reminds us, "The reader's pause is nothing other than a breath, the corporal movement of an orthodox spiritus."[56]

Irenaeus's worry is based on a text where the absence of spatial divisions means that a reader might divide words in the wrong place. Our texts, of course, come not only with word breaks, but with useful punctuation. However, I have found that the inability to read aloud and the inability to punctuate tend to occur rather widely and in the same persons: losing the aurality of text, the sensual side of the sense of the sentence, we lose its sense as meaning, too. That is, when students cannot use or understand punctuation, we encounter very Irenaean problems: breaks in the wrong places, or the wrong breaks, and these mean also a loss of continuity and connection, a time out of joint, out of flesh.

To read thus physically is to read slowly and, as Gamble reminds us, repeatedly. This, too, was more vivid in text without breaks, but again the point holds: "The initial reading of any text was inevitably experimental because it had to be decided, partly in retrospect, which of the possible construals of scriptio continua best rendered the sense."[57] To read such script is to reread, to move the eyes back over as well as forward, to *sound* out, to carve into muscle memory the contraction of the throat and the intake of breath. This we may continue to do, even with breaks already given.

Reading is an ascetic practice, a shutting out of the world outside the walls, of the television in the next room; but it is not ascetic out of loathing. It may even retain its focus through the shifting ranges of speedier technologies—from the laboriously pressed tablets of Gilgamesh, through bulky rolls of papyrus, into heavy illuminated codices, all the way to the Kindle, even the iPhone, easily pulled out of the pocket to make a book available anywhere. Intensity of focus, of attention, breathes with the words and lets a great deal drop away—but we need not demand a monastic contempt for all of that. We only need space enough to hear ourselves sounding out other voices. One attends, and one lets drop away, and one concentrates, and for that time, time is mended.

It will shatter and scatter again. But for those moments the discipline, the constraint, the persistent imposition of artifice is, rather like the monastic text, precisely the source of freedom, and of the sheer *life* of mind as of movement, of the voice in the words remaking everything. Not a rejection of the extramural world, but a practice of dwelling by which our lives in that world may be enriched.

Sense and Senses

> It is this displacement that I want to outline, not with regard to the whole of music but simply to a part of vocal music . . . : the very precise space (genre) of *the encounter between a language and a voice*.
>
> ROLAND BARTHES, *The Grain of the Voice*

We actually lose memory as we make readings simply things to remember and reproduce, make reading itself a product and not a process, an object and not an event—and a painfully unconcrete object, at that. Reading for the sense of sound, we learn how to close ourselves into a text. The process of voice or the event of speaking keeps us from being too sure that ideas are eternal things. Monastic reading reminds us that the contractions and extensions of time and of space are not simply abstractions, but a quite corporeal process and experience. Monastic asceticism does not deny the flesh, but rereads and rewrites it. Pranger insists that even, indeed especially, in monastic life, "The basic facts of Christianity, even though they must be learned from a book, are so preeminently a matter of sense that, upon hearing the biblical narrative, we feel that we could have seen, heard, felt, touched, and smelled what was going on at the time of its creation and foundation."[58] The monk *attends*, not least to sense, with a density that has now become profoundly elusive, and this density is at once an attention to and a discipline of the sensitive and affective flesh, the enticeable ear through which entering sound remakes the very self. (There is even a variant story of the conception of Christ, by the breath of the announcing angel entering through Mary's ear. "God spoke through the angel and impregnated the virgin through her ear," Augustine declares.[59] It is not only ideas that we conceive.)

We seem to think now that if we take care of the sense, the sounds will take care of themselves—or at least they needn't demand our attention as well. Lewis Carroll, who made this punning suggestion, knew better—as the very fact of the pun already indicates.[60] When we read for sense, as Augustine long ago noticed, we read in anticipation and recollection; we hear the syllables pass as we strain, waiting, for the end of the sentence; we remember them as we gather the sentence together and see what the meaning was. And this is good: in it is the work of memory and the kind of anticipation that does not let go of the present. But when instead we try to *remove* the present from time, as he also realized, we are left with no time at all. The problem of sense and sound is itself a problem of time. We can only really attend to the sense if we do not disregard the sensuous. If our reading, however nonscriptural our text, is not quite *lectio divina*, in all its contentious interestingness, it is nonetheless not altogether distinct from the latter's attention to sound, its metaphors of mirroring,[61] speaking-with, even digestion.[62]

We try to turn learning into a "merely spiritual" or purely mental affair, but neither reading nor writing, neither listening nor speaking, is a properly spiritual exercise when it is not also an exercise of the flesh and the senses. It's not that we don't train bodies; in a process beginning no later than kindergarten, we render them docile, but a little hostile to learning, too. I say this not because my students are physically fidgety—they are not, to an almost disturbing degree. Nor is it simply the inverse, that their passivity disturbs me—although it does, a bit. But what disturbs me more, though its physicality is less obvious, is that with which I opened: the increasing inability to process language, which seems an extension of a broader passive disengagement. (One element of attending properly to reading might even be getting rid of particularly horrible classroom furniture, of the sort that absolutely requires one to distract oneself from bodily discomfort and so from the body altogether.)

Body and language do not become identical in voice, but they do engage and intersect. We can attend to their mutual shaping: by reading aloud, returning sociality and text to one another; by reading slowly, returning sensuousness to sense; by thinking digressively, returning wandering pleasure to sharp focus; by returning, to text and so also to us. By giving voice, training each voice as a part of the communal chorus of bodies that think.

We need to focus on the text, to breathe in its rhythms and to read it in time with our breaths, to stretch ourselves into its sense, to let it form us again, to allow the time its density. My best student readers—especially in terms of reading aloud, but in terms of their ability to understand as well—are often theater majors. Their training in attending to the rhythms and the affect of language also forces them to attend to meaning (again, the strict separation is a false one). After all, if you don't know what a text means, you're unlikely to get the affect right—to give the right reading of the lines.

Julia Kristeva cites Nietzsche as having declared, "To be mistaken about the rhythm of a sentence is to be mistaken about the very meaning of that sentence."[63] This is so even in ways that Nietzsche could not have known—musical and linguistic syntax share "neural resources involved in structural integration in working memory."[64] In fact, as Aniruddh Patel notes in *Music, Language, and the Brain*, "Humans are unparalleled in their ability to make sense out of sound." In our reception of both music and language, we "convert complex acoustical sequences into perceptually discrete elements . . . organized into hierarchical structures that convey rich meaning."[65] That there is a kind of training that allows attention to the meaning of rhythm provides, at least for me, a glimmer of hope. We must read more, and read aloud, and enact.

We have trouble remembering, collectively, that the discipline of the flesh is not always its mortification, nor that of the spirit its disembodiment. Divorcing text from its somatic quality, we have taken the possibility of textuality from the flesh. Because we no longer read in the time of the body, we can no longer embody the time of the text. The early monk is trained as a reader. This in itself is fascinating, as contemporary scholars have shown and are showing us. But he is trained, he trains himself, also as a text: not only by being available to the superior's interpretive skills, but also by embodying textual time, a time of movement and pauses, of urgency and slowness taken together, of the need to dwell and the urge to know more. Most of us are not training monks; many of us, myself included, are not training scholars. The students who come seeking only a certification that will allow them more profitable employment—not an unreasonable quest, particularly now—may not see much ground for this slow dwelling; thus it is increasingly important that we model both the practice and the pleasure. The skills with words and texts, habits of focus and sustaining, can only do well by those who form them, and to widen rather than constrain people's possibilities has always seemed to me fundamentally ethical. While there is a need to be gentle and honest in facing the students' economic concerns, there is an equally urgent need to broaden their concerns to the aspects and pleasures of living not quite so attentive to profit—nor, bureaucratic demands notwithstanding, to measurement.

In attending again to the bodiliness of text, we also textualize the time and the affect of the flesh. And this is not a distortion, but an art, of the body—like all arts, a potential source of deep delight emergent from a difficult discipline, a remaking of the self for the expansion of possibility. Certainly up to the point at which we attempt to teach them, most undergraduate students have had little reason to associate discipline with pleasure. We cannot impose the pleasure, but we can, in modeling the slow discipline of it, perhaps impart it—or rather share it—just a little nonetheless. Perhaps, like Socrates's students, ours will be able to hum along a tune or two that they have learned by heart.

CHAPTER 3

Thou Art Translated!

[T]ranslation rests for Jerome on the painful and frustrating acquisition of an utterly foreign tongue, and it is not the transcendent mind but rather a resistant throat that "channels" the Hebrew word.

—NAOMI SEIDMAN, *Faithful Renderings: Jewish-Christian Difference and the Poetics of Translation*, cited in Virginia Burrus, "Augustine's Bible"

Languages have distinctive sounds. We can sometimes even recognize that a particular language is being spoken without understanding the words. They have their own music, and to shift across them must mean to sing the words a bit differently too. We may even have to translate within a tongue. Cavarero cites an instance:

> For the poetry of the English tradition . . . pentameter is the most apt meter. But "the hurricane does not roar in pentameter," laments [Kamau] Brathwaite. In addition to making the English language bend to the sonorous universe of the Caribbean, the Caribbean poet must also force it to vibrate in a meter that it—for environmental, cultural, and historic reasons—does not foresee. The language, no matter how modified or hybridized, remains English—but its music becomes something else.[1]

Music resists translation—this is certainly one reason that poetry is still more difficult to translate than prose; not because music is other to words, but because it isn't. Cognitive neuroscientist Steven Brown offers the possibility that language and music evolve from "musilanguage," a common ancestral sense of phrasing and rhythm as meaningful modes, a concept to which we shall later return.[2] But there is much, as it happens, that translation finds resistant. In this chapter, I want to think about the question of translation by beginning with some thoughts about unusual translational modes, more dramatic shifts that highlight the shiftiness of all translating. These will eventually lead us backward to the notion of a term through which all translations shift.

In *A Midsummer Night's Dream*, William Shakespeare offers us a particularly comic instance of translation. In the first scene of the third act, the mischievous fairy Puck has set into motion all manner of havoc, including the substitution of a donkey's head for the ordinary head of poor Nick Bottom, a weaver who had been innocently engaged in rehearsing a play that he and other "rustics" intended to perform for visiting royalty. Bottom is, understandably, a little cranky and confused about this buffoonish substitution—he had offered to play the far nobler part of a lion[3]—and he does not react happily to the responses that it generates among other members of his company. The first to see him is the tinker Tom Snout, who declares, "O Bottom, thou art changed! what do I see on thee?"[4] Snout is followed by Peter Quince, a carpenter and the author of the ill-fated play that had been in rehearsal, who will give us our relevant line as he exclaims in surprise, "Bless thee, Bottom! bless thee! thou art translated."[5]

Indeed he is. Bottom, when he later declares the events a dream, proposes that Quince shall write a ballad of this transformation.[6] This ballad might be seen as a further translation, of the kind Umberto Eco calls "intersemiotic"—a translation across forms, rather like that of interpretive dance, which is sort of famous for translating badly. What is not quite clear, though, is how layered this translation may *already* be just in Nick Bottom's appearance. The use of "ass" for buttocks (i.e., for the bottom) is first definitively attested only in 1860, more than two and a half centuries after *A Midsummer Night's Dream* was written, sometime in the 1590s. But there is some speculation that the pun may already have been current, if cutting edge, when Shakespeare translated Bottom to ass, and certainly such a pun would not have been out of character for the author—after all, we also find a Snout among the would-be actors, and Shakespeare's brilliance is hardly incompatible with crude punning. The translation of the flesh is in this instance also a translation of the word, not just in parallel but somehow of one another, and the visible head of the indignant ass betrays the indignity of the rustic weaver sporting the name of Bottom.

John Parker points out that this translation may be more complex still:

> In addition to its more common uses, ["translation"] had once denoted a particular form of labor: a weaver might be said to "translate" a garment by making adjustments to it (OED, 2nd ed., 4). Quince probably glances at that meaning in his outcry at Bottom's ass-head—as though the weaver had on accident made an adjustment to himself sewing, as it were, an inhuman costume out of human flesh. But the term here of course strongly implies a verbal as well as a mechanical transformation and on the Elizabethan stage, it was both: translation of received narratives (Apuleius, for example) into novel scripts had become for the first time a highly profitable form of labor.[7]

The body through work translates material. The body is translated—not just by narrative becoming performance becoming labor, and by the weaver making his own costume, but by that costume making over his body (or, at any rate, his head) in accord with the text—quite differently from the manner in which the psalms might do the same to a house of monks. Translation and transformation are not very far apart; the former implies some greater preservation—but it is more difficult than one might expect to work out what must be preserved.

Let me offer one further instance of bodily translation. The translation of relics (that is, of pieces or close possessions of saints) is their movement from one location—specifically, from one church congregation—to another. This sounds markedly unexciting, I grant, but that's only if you don't know that throughout the Middle Ages the relics were sometimes said to have translated *themselves*, moved of their own volition. This was held to demonstrate the desire of the relevant saints for the newly privileged location—which means their desire to patronize and to bless the new church or congregation. This happened especially often when those with less devotion would more likely say that the relics had been stolen by members of their new communities.

In the translation of relics, an original—a whole, intact body—is the very source of meaning. To translate is not merely to cross from one to another, but to claim an origin. The relic matters because it belonged to the body of a saint, and each fragment is held to contain, miraculously, the wholeness of saintly power and sanctity.[8] But as a rule, that original is impossible to find; the meaningful pieces are only ever fragments. (In fact, studies of older relics often show that they are not even fragments of humans. Pigs are popular.) *Now* the relic means what it is translated to mean: the saint's blessing upon *this* congregation. Sometimes, devotees claim, the translation even demonstrates that the previous meaning, patronage of the other congregation, was false.

Both the ass-headed Bottom and the wandering saint piece remind us of the remarkably mobile character of translation, and of its corporeality—which may mutually alter and be altered by the verbal meaning, too. The pull of meaning and flesh on one another also shows up in translation as we more commonly conceive it; specifically, it shows up in the recurrent lure of a perfect third term, an originary speech, such as is presupposed most famously, though not only, by Walter Benjamin. This third term is mythic, the source language echoed in both terms of a translation, by which they may be translated: it is what allows us to register whether there is a proper equivalence. An insistence on corporeality alters the reading of this mythical origin, but there are elements that remain intriguing on any interpretation. The rest of this chapter is my effort to think about what that third term might be, or what we might mean by invoking it, and to argue for a reading of it that demands the sound and the flesh of speech. Cavell writes of "a fantasy of a voice that precedes language, that as it were gives itself language."[9] The third term is that of a first language, in a first voice.

What Are We Trying to Keep?

> Hold fast the form of sound words . . .
>
> 2 TIMOTHY 1:13, KING JAMES TRANSLATION

We should ask the fairly obvious question of what in the world translation is trying to do, what it is that it holds fast. The naïve presumption is that in translating, we replace words in one language with words that mean the same things in another language, choosing as exactly as we can, adjusting as needed for word order and other grammatical considerations. But theorists have long left that naïvete behind. Benjamin suggests that a translation that communicates only "meaning" is as bad as a translation that misses it altogether.[10] There is more at work in a good translation than a set of dictionaries and the help of Babelfish or Google Translate can quite capture. Indeed, Benjamin argues even more strongly that "literalness" is not a matter of "meaning" conserved, but of fit:

> Thus no case for literalness can be based on a desire to retain the meaning. Meaning is served far better—and literature and language far worse—by the unrestrained license of bad translators. . . . Fragments of a vessel which are to be glued together must match one another in

> the smallest details, although they need not be like one another. In the same way a translation instead of resembling the meaning of the original, must lovingly and in detail incorporate the original's mode of signification, thus making both the original and the translation recognizable as fragments of a greater language, just as fragments are part of a vessel.[11]

This image of the fragmented vessel echoes a Kabbalistic cosmology, in which the power of divine light is too much for the vessels carrying it out into the created darkness, so that they shatter, and the light is scattered throughout the world in sparks. Not only do we have a metaphor that nicely illustrates part and whole, we also have an image of a scattered divinity, and this, too, will make its way into Benjamin's thoughts about language, though in a manner different from Nancy's divine that is scattered in voices. It is not just that we can fit a translation together and hold something close to the original; if we fit our words together rightly, within them we can lightly hold a bit of the divine.

So what else is there to "fit," if it is not simply a matter of reproducing denotation? What more could meaning mean? Benjamin uses the language of *effect*: "The task of the translator consists in finding that intended effect upon the language into which he is translating which produces in it the echo of the original."[12] Jacques Derrida argues still more strongly: "the effects or structures of a text are not reducible to its 'truth,' to the intended meaning of its presumed author, or even its supposedly unique and identifiable signatory."[13] So, too, Umberto Eco: "the aim of a translation, more than producing any literal 'equivalence,' is to create the same effect in the mind of the reader . . . as the original text wanted to create."[14] Pedersen even suggests that, rather than "cling to the personal, to the imagination of the authentic self," it might be preferable "to describe the voice, not as a prolongation of the self, but as the production of an effect." She is particularly interested in the "transmedial" perspective—that of Eco's intersemiotic—as it renders audible "the silent literary voice."[15]

Such an effect may carry over even into the extreme—the translation of a poem to a musical score to a ballet,[16] or a novel to a film, or the suffering of an actor to a ballad, or the comedy of the name Bottom to an ass in the place of a head.[17] We might not wish to call such adaptations translation, properly speaking—and it would be awfully hard to reconstruct the original from them—but they do share something, a nebulous, mobile, attractive *something*, of the translational pairing of movement and retention, or preservation, something that fits.

Unexpectedly, intersemiotic translation might even intensify or clarify the effect of the original. Consider, for instance, the interplay of poetry with music. Settings of Paul Celan, whose poetry is at once deeply musical and seriously elusive, include Horace Birtwistle's intriguing *Pulse Shadows*. Interleaved with instrumental passages, the movements of this composition set Celan's words to music for soprano and chamber ensemble, sometimes with linguistic translation (in *Todtnauberg*, for instance, the poem is sung in German, with each line then spoken in English). But there is also a wordless musical translation of Celan's famous *Todesfuge*, itself named for a musical form. Like the original, Birtwistle's version evokes traditional forms without reproducing them, and layers coherence with dissonance.

The right fitting "something" seems to be behind, and maybe even before, the languages that it crosses. It is perhaps what Thomas Wall calls "communicativity *as such* . . . [which] gives nothing to be thought; it gives no message to which we might listen but, in effect, says: there is (*il y a*). Communicativity *as such*—where *what* is communicated is not outside it but instead buries language in itself—is poetry, the original and absolute singularity of what does not cease to take place."[18] Joseph Brodsky suggests that "the works of the better poets" take on this as-such of language; in them, the poet is "simply talking back to the language itself—as beauty, sensuality, wisdom, irony—those aspects of language of which the poet is a clear mirror."[19] But what original speaking as-such speaks through all the rest?

Poetic Feet

When I cannot look at your face
I look at your feet.
Your feet of arched bone,
your hard little feet

PABLO NERUDA, "Your Feet"

Poetry, in the difficulties it poses for translators, forces us to think carefully about this effective and affective aspect of translation. Eco argues that "*every translation proper has an aesthetic or poetic aspect*. If to interpret always means to respect the spirit (allow me this metaphor) of a text, to translate means to respect also its body."[20] It is not simply by metaphor, I think, that we speak of the body of a text, or of a body of work. The disciplines of writing and dancing are not so dissimilar as we might suspect (even given the shortcomings of interpretive dance), nor translating from a text altogether different from reinterpreting movement in a different body.[21] Hélène Cixous offers us an unusually carnal sense of poetic feet when she writes:

> Mandelstam asks very seriously in his "Conversation about Dante": how many pairs of shoes Dante must have worn out in order to write *The Divine Comedy*, because, he tells us, that could only have been written on foot, walking without stopping, which is also how Mandelstam wrote. Mandelstam's whole body was in action, taking part, searching. Walking, dancing pleasure: these accompany the poetic act.[22]

The whole body takes part in word-making. Benjamin writes, "In the realm of translation, too, the words 'in the beginning was the word' apply."[23] In the realm of translation, we may also add, the word has to be made flesh, and dwell among us. It is the pull of flesh and meaning that at once eludes all language and gives to each word its multiple senses of "sense."

The effect of language is not something isolated in the psyche, as if anything really could be, but rather something quite physical—though not merely mechanistic or otherwise physiological. Words *move* us—and, like wandering relics in translation, words *move*, whether from one language to another, one body to another, or sound to sonorous sense. Cixous writes of Thomas Bernhard's short story "Montaigne," "The text is a real lesson in writing, paragraph by paragraph, step by step. . . . The text flees paragraph by paragraph. 'Montaigne' comes to an end in twenty-two steps or paragraphs—twenty-two bounds. Since you read with your body, your body paragraphs."[24] The body paragraphs much as the body follows music when we dance, in a relation that may be direct and simple or terrifically complicated (including the possibility that the body leads, and paragraph and musical phrasing follow). There is, as we have noted, considerable overlap in the ways in which our brains process "meaningful" words in sentences and the ways in which they process the abstract yet somatic organization of musical sounds. Thinking, reading, we dance and we pace among words. Language layers here: these meditations upon motion, with their worn shoes and bodies paragraphing step by step, are those of a writer upon writers about writers: Cixous on Mandelstam writing of Dante and on Bernhard writing of Montaigne. We enjoy them quote by quote.

Your body paragraphs. Words move us. And words just plain move. Theorists intrigued by that Benjaminian third term have often focused upon the motility of words and even letters themselves. This is particularly evident in the Kabbalistic tradition that letters combining into words *are* the force of creation—a more graphic, rather than phonic, version of Genesis's "and God said," a more explicit and developed version of the Johannine word-in-the-beginning, which also tends to unfold into a more aural tradition. The Kabbalistic *Sefer Yezirah* asks of the creator, "How did He combine, weigh, and interchange [the primordial letters]? Aleph with all and all with Aleph; Beth with all and all with Beth; and so each in turn. There are 231 gates. And all creation and all language come from one name."[25] For Kabbalist Abraham Abulafia, "Since, in the letters of a Name, each letter is already a Name itself, know that Yod is a name, and YH is a name." As Eco glosses this, "each letter . . . already had a meaning of its own, independent of the meaning of the syntagms in which it occurred. Each letter was already a divine name."[26]

From its utterly literary or literate tales of creation, Kabbalah moves on to equally alphabetic meditative practices of movement and combination. Again, Eco cites a representative instance:

> And begin by combining this name, namely, YHWH, at the beginning alone, and examining all its combinations and move it, turn it about like a wheel, returning around, front and back, like a scroll, and do not let it rest, but when you see its matter strengthened because of the great motion . . . and rolling about of your thoughts, and when you let it rest, return to it and as [it] until there shall come to your hand a word of wisdom from it. . . . Afterwards go on to the second one from it, *Adonay*.[27]

Words are in motion as soon as there is a *there is*: the prime mover is the sound of speaking, or the inscription of the letter: the physicality of the word. In the beginning is, if not the word, the fragments of words' composition, moving choreographically into word-ness. And in every motion is a transition, like the leaps that unexpectedly connect ideas; in every translation a reception (one meaning of the multivalent term *Kabbalah*).[28]

Among the dozens of theorists influenced by Kabbalistic notions of language, the optimistic fourteenth-century Franciscan Raymond Lull stands out, both for his efforts to create a perfect and universal language as an instrument for conversion and for the intricacy of his effort. His thinking presumes a possible transparency between words and thoughts: clearly, he reasoned, the infidels retained their infelicitous fidelities only because they did not properly understand the Truth, and they did not understand because their languages did not properly communicate it to them.[29] Lull's linguistic system entails several complex figures, some of them mobile concentric circles likely influenced by the "wheel or spinning disc" that represents the combinatorics of the *Sefer Yizirah*. If we choreograph language just right, Lull thinks, it will translate as purely and divinely as a relic moving itself to its desired congregation: it will go straight to those who need it.

Here, the perfect third-term language is imagined not as a static and lost origin, but as something mobile and creative, something that lives and changes and seeks out, finding just the right fit with those who hear. The created world signed in or made by language in motion may itself signify mobilely, and indefinitely: its meaning may keep on moving. Perhaps its meaning is even life and change itself, though one suspects that Lull would balk at this particular move. Signs and meanings and sounds and senses slide in and among one another. Early semiotic theory, such as Augustine's, reads the world as a sign of its creator. As Eco points out, such is the hermetic tradition broadly speaking, for which "every object exists not only in itself, but as a possible sign, deferral, image, emblem, hieroglyph of something else. This worked also by contrast: an image can lead us back to the unity of the infinite even through its opposite."[30] Every sign moves, into and out of an infinite everywhere-center, for which "there was but a single divine breath, one principle of motion pervading the whole of the infinite universe, determining it in its infinite variety of forms."[31] Divine breath drawn in pulls the word back to the flesh, the sign to the senses again; breathed out it forms the word by the body: the word and the flesh move toward one another, scatter apart, reach across in a pull of desire sustained by difference. Sometimes they fit. The breath moves into the ear, and meaningful sense is conceived.

This sense that language, even perfect language, is live and mobile is both relevant and frustrating for the attempt to translate; moving from one to another is difficult enough without the added issue that neither end holds still. Of particular importance—if we are to keep with the notion of translating an effect, if a relic is to translate to a place where it is happy and signifies truly, if the head of the ass is to translate poor Bottom—is the motion of moving-with that is also a moving between or across, a resonance. Cixous writes of the resonance between languages: "I speak to you today . . . through two languages. From one day to another, from one page to the other, writing changes languages. . . . This is what writing is: I one language, I another language, and between the two, the line that makes them vibrate; writing forms a passageway between two shores."[32] The transition between reader and text is not a replacement, nor a shift of both into the place of one, but resonance: "The sentence that has just been uttered . . . is it in the book or in you? It is delocalized."[33] Along the paths between, vibrations transit.

Perfect Language

> In the absence of his graspable and audible body, only the elusive text remains.
>
> VIRGINIA BURRUS, "Augustine's Bible"

As the reader with text, the body (more literally) resonates with speech, and in speaking and writing, meaning and movement mutually echo—and echo, perhaps, some deeper mutuality, the mutuality of the perfect third term toward which we have been roundaboutly wandering. Eco has developed this notion in a long discussion of the search for the perfect language—a perfection that can lead us to created languages (such as Lull's or, most famously, Esperanto), but more often leads us backward toward a universal, mythical original. Intriguingly, many cultures have stories of a primal language that splits—from the story of Babel in the Hebrew bible, to the ancient Greek tale of Hermes, who divided human languages to spite his father, Zeus,[34] to the story told by the East African Wa-Sania people, which holds that a famine reduced humanity to a mad jabbering that persisted as linguistic multiplicity, to the Haudenosaunee tale of a more intentional divinely directed dispersal of people and tongues—and there are many more.[35] The Babel story and its variants are often read together with the Eden story and its variants: both are losses of some primal perfection expressed by a perfect unity. In the case of Eden, on the very influential Augustinian reading, the loss is of the unity or perfect harmony of human and divine will. (There are many other, and some better, ways to read that story, but few that have been as central to the history of Christian thought.) In the case of Babel, we lose the unity of all language, and of all meaning.

Particularly intriguing for my purposes here is a variant on the Babel story as it is retold by the Andalusian Muslim philosopher Ibn Hazm, in the eleventh century. As Eco summarizes it, there is first "a single language given by God . . . thanks to which Adam was able to understand the quiddity of things. It was a language that provided a name for everything, be it substance or accident." So the language is perfect in its completeness and its exactitude, and thus it must be "so rich in synonyms that it *include[s] every possible language*."[36] Babel, then, is a fragmentation of this original: every language as it now exists is partial, some portion of a primal whole. Here the relation of translation to origin is clearly one of fragmentation and mending, of matching part to part, like Benjamin's reassembly of vessels—but the fit is between both terms of the translated and a third original, rather than between a simple original and a copy.

Maurice Blanchot develops this sense of translation as the effort to mend an always-prior breakage in his essay "Translation," more specifically in his discussion of the poet Friedrich Hölderlin. In his renditions of Sophocles, writes Blanchot (moving again from writer to writer, step by step, quotation by translated quotation), Hölderlin

> was no longer a poet, nor a translator, but . . . was recklessly advancing toward the center in which he believed he would find collected the pure power of unifying, a center such that it would be able to give meaning, beyond all determined and limited meaning. . . . For with the unifying power that is at work in every practical relation, as in any language, and that, at the same time, exposes him to the pure scission that is always prior, the man who is ready to translate is in a constant, dangerous, and admirable intimacy . . . with the conviction that, in the end, translating is madness.[37]

The very effort to mend or to unify shows us the breaks, the seams that both separate and join even the most perfectly fitted fragments. Things fall apart—but as beautifully, sometimes, as a shower of sacred sparks.

Pleasingly, it turns out these myths of primal language may have some empirical counterpart. Eco scrupulously notes, "Even faced with the results of comparative linguistics . . . monogenetic theories refuse to give up the ghost. The bibliography of belated monogeneticism is immense. In it, there is to be found the lunatic, the crank, the misfit, the bizarre mystic, as well as a number of students of unimpeachable rigour."[38] Among this last group, Quentin Atkinson, an anthropological researcher at the University of Auckland, has used computer analysis of the geography of phonemic diversity to argue for a single original, phonemically rich language out of sub-Saharan Africa. The claim is controversial, of course, but not unsupported, either by evidence or by other scholars.[39] As languages split, they tend to lose some of the diverse phonemes of the source language. That is, the source does not have all the words, but it has the set of *sounds*—an echo at the phonetic, very bodily level of Ibn Hazm's claims for an all-inclusive original speech that splits and scatters its words. We do not find primal perfection, but it is not impossible that we find an original set of sounds that we make to make meaning. Here is gathered the potential for *all the voices*. Whether or not this monogenetic theory turns out to be probable, that languages lose sounds as they dissipate does argue for some sense of a gathering that becomes a dispersal at the bodily as well as at the intellectual level of language. We know, too, that we are born with a fullness of vocal possibilities; it is only after coming into one language that we lose the easy ability to make the sounds characteristic of others.[40] Daniel Levitin notes, "Similarly, it seems that we all have an innate capacity to learn any of the world's musics, although they, too, differ in substantive ways from one another."[41]

The pull of these origin stories of perfect unity is profound. Most monotheistic creation stories move from the absolute singularity of God to the multiplicity of the created world. Benjamin provides both the tightest and the clearest connection between this pull and that of the perfect translation: as "in the original, language and revelation are one without any tension"—that is, in an origin in which language is purely transparent to meaning, identical with that which we know in it and through it—"so the translation must be one with the original in the form of the interlinear version, in which literalness and freedom are united. For to some degree all great texts contain their potential translation between the lines; this is true to the highest degree of sacred writings. The interlinear version of the Scriptures is the prototype or ideal of all translation."[42] Perfect translation thus would preserve the very original that it alters. Blanchot makes explicit the messianic character of this vision: "To each translator thus his own messianism, if he works toward making languages grow in the direction of this ultimate language, attested to in every present language by what each language contains of the future. . . . "[43] In messianic timing, the origin pulls us toward the future. The messiah rewrites and teaches us to reread.[44] The translation to come envisions a future, like many messianic futures, that is at the same time a return—a return not to, but before, the origin in fragmentation.

Though we know that there are more or less secular messianisms too, the religious resonance of the term reminds us that these pulls toward origin and unity are, unsurprisingly, likely to be linked to the sacred. For Dante, whose theory of linguistic origin we shall explore more fully in chapter five, speaking is first a response, to the (possibly unspoken) word of God, a protolinguistic response that is deeply corporeal. Eco writes:

> While the first sound that humans let forth is the wail of pain at their birth, Dante thought that the first sound emitted by Adam could only

> have been an exclamation of joy which, at the same time, was an act of homage toward his creator.
>
> . . .
>
> When Adam spoke to God, it was in response. Consequently, God must have spoken first.[45]

Jacques Derrida, himself engaged in thinking about the messianic, remarks, "Even the desire for translation is unthinkable without the *correspondence* with the thought of God."[46] Adam's is a co-responding of joy. The desire for a perfect translation pulls toward the desire for a perfect language, so transparent that it is without fault or failure, so inclusive that it is divine as well as human—like a perfect Platonic Eros, daimonically pulling these realms together.[47]

The notion of sacred text plays a crucial role not only in translation, but in interpretation, itself a kind of translation at the level of meaning that may occur within a language; translation across languages is of course a delicately interpretive act as well. In fact, just as the intralinear Scripture is the paradigmatic item of translation, so, too, sacred texts are the paradigmatic objects of exegesis. Eco notes, "As soon as a text becomes 'sacred' for a certain culture, it becomes subject to the process of suspicious reading and therefore to what is undoubtedly an excess of interpretation. It had happened, with classical allegory, in the case of the Homeric texts, and it could not but have happened in the patristic and scholastic periods with the Scriptures, as in Jewish culture with the interpretation of the Torah."[48] But this excess of interpretation need not, as Benjamin reminds us, provide any definitive result, any final version in a desired language.[49] At once perfectly, purely translatable (the intralinear ideal of translation) and wholly untranslatable (incapable of coming to rest in a definitive or even a finite meaning), the sacred text can only be overinterpreted and incompletely interpreted, can only demand further interpretation.[50] And the suspicion of the really hermetic readings, as well as of most late ancient and early medieval semiotics, is that every text is sacred.

This process of suspicious reading opens onto an infinitizing sense of mystery. In the late ancient and medieval idea of the world as text, or in hermeticism,

> interpretation is indefinite. The attempt to look for a final, unattainable meaning leads to the acceptance of a never-ending drift or sliding of meaning. . . . Every object, be it earthly or heavenly, hides a secret. Every time a secret has been discovered, it will refer to another secret in a progressive movement toward a final secret. Nevertheless, there

> can be no final secret. The ultimate secret of Hermetic initiation is that everything is secret. Hence the Hermetic secret must be an empty one, because anyone who pretends to reveal any sort of secret is not himself initiated and has stopped at a superficial level of the knowledge of cosmic mystery. Hermetic thought transforms the whole world theatre into a linguistic phenomenon and at the same time denies language any power of communication.[51]

Fond though I am of many of Eco's readings, I find the notion of emptiness here an odd one, and am inclined to something more optimistic: the secret is never ful-filled, but that is only because of its infinite capacity. Emptiness is not quite the right metaphor. The kind of desire that drives infinite interpretation is never only lack; it is the desire for and the possibility of knowledge reaching into the always-more. (Thus, we hope to learn to learn, toward this always open possibility of learning more.)

Derrida metaphorizes this ungraspability differently. He argues that the sacred in the text is both original and untouchable: "The kernel of the original text is untouchable by the translation, and this untouchable something is the sacred, which says: don't touch me."[52] That sounds unpromising, even if intriguingly Johannine, playing on the book as body with its echo of the *noli me tangere* of the fourth gospel's story of resurrection. But Derrida too is drawn to the power of drawing; he adds, "The desire for the intact kernel is desire itself, which is to say that it is irreducible."[53] Translation and interpretation, then, pull on desire, pull with the teasing promise of wholeness, the intact kernel—intact, prefragmentary, desirable, but untouchable—and unsayable by the flesh that has to touch words so that they may be made at all.

The desire for this intact speaking is sustained by its infinite possibility and its impossibility, by the multiplying of incomplete and imperfect translations, each of which nonetheless gives us so very much more than nothing. It draws upon some strange sense of another unsayable beneath, within, or before the said. This precedent substratum of language, the murmur of the neuter, is again linked to poetry. Thomas Wall writes of Blanchot:

> A mute communication precedes any *dit* (said). This communication is unspoken but irreducible . . . that precedes any message. Language that precedes itself, or that "begins" in repetition, is poetry, and this preemptive "speaking" belongs to no subjective intention to say anything. Older than the subject, it is a language spoken by no one, or by an anonymous "someone" (Blanchot's *il*, "he," the Neuter) who cannot

> speak in the first person. Unable not to communicate, this anonymity cannot cease "his" saying just as it is unable to manifest "himself" in any statement, for "he" *is* only insofar as, and for as long as, "he" speaks.[54]

A word is not simply the elusive thought, idea, concept, or thing beyond itself that it attempts to capture, something that we cannot quite say, because we have to use words for the saying. It is also the making of the something, never quite complete. We have a pretty good sense of the ways in which what we want to say can elude our saying it—and this despite the fact, or intertwined with the fact, that our saying is all we have of it, besides that sense of elusion. Translation, even more than everyday speaking, tells us that the word is never self-identical or wholly reducible to meaning or sound. Even its speaker, its writer, is unsettled. Cixous remarks, "We write, we paint, throughout our entire lives as if we were going to a foreign country, as if we were foreigners inside our own families."[55] And, even more strongly,

> I kept thinking: what I have just written didn't come from me. *I* could write a thesis, but the texts I wrote were never mine. For a long time I lived in a state of serious uncertainty—sometimes I even told myself I shouldn't sign my name. Or else I felt great uneasiness when people talked to me about the texts "I" had written. They think it is me, but I only copy the other, it is dictated; and I don't know who the other is.[56]

For Derrida, too, others play a vital role in my own signing: "[I]t is the ear of the other that signs. The ear of the other says me to me and constitutes the *autos* of my autobiography. When, much later, the other will have perceived with a keen-enough ear what I will have addressed or destined to him or her, then my signature will have taken place."[57] Benjamin is both broader in scope and more concise in declaration: "[A]ll translation," he writes, "is only a somewhat provisional way of coming to terms with the foreignness of languages."[58] All language is a little bit strange, a translation reminds us, unsettlingly strange, in a way with which we can come to terms at best provisionally. Language is never quite *mine*, even when I speak or write in my first or only language. Even our "own" languages dispossess us a bit. I own neither meaning nor lettering nor sound; the accents of my voice come to the me that they make.

Not only meaning, neither is a word only matter; we know this, but translation makes it more evident still. In fact, we can have before us the matter of words and yet not have them as language. It is hard to make up a language—the efforts tend to turn into code—but there are certain ancient alphabets, such as Meroitic, for which we know *only* the correspondence of sight to sound. That is, we can look at a Meroitic text and, if properly trained, pronounce it aloud. We can translate the words across senses, from vision to hearing, sight to sound. Yet we do not know what many of those sounds and images *mean*; they seem distant from the languages we know, and the best efforts of archaeologists and linguists have not yet yielded their sense.[59] This reminds us that words, like other bodies, can be dead matter too (though perhaps more revivable than most). The dream of a perfect language, a language that would enable every translation with the originary perfection of interlinearity, may also be the dream of a perfect union between the flesh and the meaning of a word, the animation of the body of the text. This allows us the dream that there may finally be no dead languages, that all can be eventually reanimated.[60]

The perfect original tongue of so many myths, the tongue that splits and scatters languages all over the world, is perhaps this dream of a perfect union, not of all the world's dialects, but of sensuousness and sense, of meaning and sound (with all its synesthetic counterparts). From this pairing comes the transmission of an effect, a sense that resonates at perfect pitch, yet never makes the one and the other identical. At the heart of both translatability and untranslatabilty, the infinitude and the impossibility of translations and interpretations, is the pull of the mythic origin, with its ties to the sacred—the pull of an infinite desire for perfect sense. The pull is that of the "original" which is also the perfectly unified, the "original" text as the myth of a Word not foreign either to its flesh or to its meaning. This is also, for many monotheisms, the pull of the sacred (word made flesh, word made world): the pull between *logos* and flesh. The crossing point of this mythic chiasmic origin-language, the point where perfect translations meet, is pure meaning *and* pure sensuousness, grapheme or phoneme, signed in sight or sound. At the origin, there is no original. There is desire, desire for the origin that isn't, for the perfect union of the word, meaning and scription and sound all together. At the beginning of translation is the sounding word, at least for those engaged by Benjamin's thinking. But at the beginning of the word is translation. This primal translation is not a successful transposition but an urgent translative desire, a desire for a transition (or, perhaps more precisely, a resonance, a desire to take up) from meaning to enfleshment and back, the pull of flesh and word toward the impossible perfection of the doubleness of sense.

CHAPTER 4

The Voice in the Mirror

> [S]mall mirrors or silvered paper can be used with architectural drawings (or small scale models) in a darkened room to reflect light from a point source. The patterns of reflected light demonstrate, during the design process, the effect of room shape on the distribution of sound.
>
> —DAVID EGAN, *Architectural Acoustics*

The myth of the original, perfect language draws us into myths of an ultimate origin, and origin myths draw us into cosmologies—by this route, especially into cosmic creation by voice. The next chapter considers the stories of Genesis more directly; this one draws out some creational as well as prayerful implications of creative vocal resonance in the work of medieval polymath Hildegard of Bingen.

It matters who is speaking, we have seen—not in the sense that there is a who, and then there is speaking, but that speaking, like "who," is singular and unique and relational all at once. The voice and the who are not identical, but they are made together. In trying to think through what voice might be, we thus find ourselves also thinking about the one who is speaking. This one is not so much imprecise as it is shifting and multiple, even when it is unique; it becomes particularly interesting when the one who speaks and the one who hears cannot be altogether told from each other. Such is the case in an exemplary hymn from Hildegard, a hymn that allows our exploration to open onto her wonderfully musical cosmology—and allows us to reflect more particularly upon the explicitly musical singing voice. Thus, she will lead us both through further puzzles of the singular voice and into a consideration of the broadest imaginable chorus. And she will begin with very literal voices, sung forth by the nuns of her house. "Voice, which must be listened to as well as heard if it is to concern us, must be observed to be understood," writes Kramer. "Understanding voice does not *begin* with the observation of voices; it *is* the observation of voices."[1] Hildegard observes and creates for voices, and when she extends this understanding, she avoids ever reducing it.

In Hildegard's texts, we find ideas and language turning about on themselves in the unexpected ways that reveal mystery—as her melodies, too, turn and twist about in her famous melismatic lines. She performs these turns not by stripping the mysterious of its concealment, but precisely by showing us that not all is showable. I focus here on an antiphon to the Father from Hildegard's *Symphonia armonie celestium revelationum* (the Symphony of the Harmony of Celestial Revelation). The *Symphonia* is not a symphony in the modern sense, but is Hildegard's assemblage of her musical works into a song cycle for the liturgy and daily office of her nuns. Like the psalms in the Athanasian view, the hymn (which would itself open onto a psalm) is sung in a formal, cyclical, repeated setting, as much for transformation as for worship. As Bruce Holsinger notes, this transformation is once more of a body and soul non-separated: "the body itself was invested with the miraculous potential to burst forth in sonorous melody at any moment. It may not be an exaggeration to say that, to many medieval Christians, the most fundamental attribute of music was its inextricability from bodily experience."[2] Hildegard brings forward the Athanasian sense of self-transformation, but she takes the music further. My interest here, though it must necessarily intersect with the sound of Hildegard's hymns as sung, is still more with the marvelous interplay between her conception of music and the music of her concepts. That is, I am especially drawn by this instance of something I mentioned earlier: the sense that ideas tell us how we should write them, how they should sound, and that there is a movement between them that is no less motile than a musical movement must be.

In this particular hymn, the strangeness of address and indication that emerge within it open up onto the mutual address, the responsorium, that is creation itself. Hildegard's sense of divine address, of the way that "we" use "you" in relation to God, is unusual even among mystics, and in it her musicality extends even more deeply and surprisingly than we might have thought. Address, typical of the voice in prayer, multiplies and becomes resonance; word becomes song. And, as we shall see, the God who says *I am* speaks in the voice of the chorus.

The greater proportion of Hildegard's songs are antiphons like this one, meant both to hail and to respond, often to psalms. A third of them are responsoria—hymns in call-and-response form. Though her works are not written as polyphony, relationality is already highlighted in their very form.[3] In the responsorial pieces, the sung tones might have overlapped more polyphonically as the nuns sang call and response across the aisles; today, Hildegard's pieces are sometimes performed with a drone to create a subtle polyphonic effect. The greater polyphony always echoes; the world mirrors creational song.

This particular antiphon is the first piece in the incomplete Dendermonde version of the *Symphonia*, the sixth in the larger Riesenkodex version. It is short enough to present here entirely: "O magne Pater, / in magna necessitate sumus. / Nunc igitur obsecramus, / obsecramus te / per Verbum tuum, / per quod nos constituisti plenos / quibus indigemus. / Nunc placeat tibi, Pater, / quia te decet, / ut aspicias in nos / per adiutorium tuum, / ut non deficiamus, / et ne nomen tuum in nobis obscuretur, / et per ipsum nomen tuum / dignare nos adiuvare."[4]

Barbara Newman offers us both poetic and literal translations of the song. Her sense of poetry is elegant, but to work as closely as we can with Hildegard, we might best turn to the more literal version: "Great Father, / we are in great need! / Now then we beseech / we beseech you by your Word, / through which you created us full / of the things we lack. / Now, Father, may it please you, / for it befits you, / to look upon us / and help us, / that we may not perish, / that your name be not darkened within us: / and by your own name, / graciously help us."[5]

If Hildegard were not an unusually famous mystic, one might be tempted to read this straightforwardly: we, a group of humans, ask another fairly anthropomorphic being (who can look, be pleased, assist, be addressed in parental terms, and so on) for assistance. But the more we think about this song, the stranger its request for assistance becomes, and the less tidy its divisions, a melding amplified by Hildegard's famously close fit of the words to the music. Address and petition become curiously blurred; the name fails to *be* named, and addressee and petitioner seem to turn about in a manner that renders the usual directionality of the *you* (and, accordingly, of the *we*) impossible to identify—without instead identifying the two terms with each other.

The vocative element of all language is evident in hymns even more than in other prayers,[6] and this in itself is enough to make the language a little strange. The strangeness of address here, however, runs more deeply and a little differently.

The Multiple Music of Mirrors

> Such music-making lends the surface of language the complexity and interest of the surface that's being observed.
>
> MARK DOTY, *The Art of Description: World into Words*

Resonance, which is essential in Hildegard's thought, takes the time of the echo, and the sung text necessarily unfolds at a much slower pace than the spoken, itself slower than the text read silently. There is time for language to do more, to be more complicated by the voice.[7] Most of the lines of *Magne Pater* begin and end on an A or an E, perhaps resonating slightly over one another as overtones.[8] The sound fills out what the denotation lacks.

The lines of Hildegard's hymn echo its musical phrases. The song opens on two modes of greatness that mirror each other as both image and opposite—the greatness of the father, the great need of the petitioner. And musically, *magne* (great) in the first line most nearly mirrors not *magna* but *necessitate*, as it is not our greatness, but our need, reaching toward the first line's father. In addition to these musical echoes, Hildegard is fond of both the act of poetic mirroring (that is, the use of these sorts of structures in which one phrase or image reflects another), and the metaphor of the mirror (as a description of the way in which we are the image of the divine). "All celestial harmony," she declares in her *Causes and Cures*, "is a mirror of divinity."[9]

The transformative character of Hildegard's music is expansive; for her, the whole world is made and remade by song. Her own songs, known for their unusual range, expand as if to stretch their tones over the world.[10] The symphonies of celestial harmony are symphonies of the mirror of divinity. The chorus of song is not itself celestial harmony, but it comes as near as we can to giving that harmony a human voice. Each song sings in a voice of the mirror.

As this suggests, the reflection of the Father's greatness in the petitioners' need is neither singular nor simple; Hildegard's language evokes less a figure gazing at its reflection than the dizzying recursion of an image in facing mirrors. The poetic structure itself repeats and redoubles in the words that open lines: *magne* and *magna*, then repetitions of *obsecramus*, *per*, *ut*, and *et*, with musical mirrors and repetitions complicating the story.

This multiple, recursive gaze-that-sounds peers out from the very moment of creation, as Hildegard shows in her exegesis of the prologue to the fourth gospel in her visionary *Book of Divine Works*. She writes of the opening phrase "In the beginning was the Word": "I am the One by whom every reasonable being [i.e., every being that has reason] draws breath."[11] As the close affiliation of reason and breath makes clear, Hildegard is typically medieval in her sense of the union of spirit and flesh—hardly irrelevant to her use of language in song. The musical notation for those songs is not that of modern notes and measures, but of pneumes: indications of rhythmic mode and relative pitch, of the shapes and movements of phrases, whose very name bears the *pneuma*: literal and physical breath, but also the spirit or soul. "The body is the garment of the soul," Hildegard writes, "and it is the soul which gives life to the voice." The two together breathe music; they sing praise.[12] They make hymns.

Hildegard is too original to repeat anyone else, but others echo in her work—notably Augustine, whom she read with some pleasure. In his sermon on the birthday of John the Baptist, Augustine equates John himself with voice, and Christ with the Word that the voice speaks.[13] For us the voice comes ahead of the word, as hearing ahead of understanding. Never one for too much simplicity, though, Augustine muses that all things are made through the Word, so "Why be surprised if the Word made himself a voice?"[14] The timing, he decides, is doubled: "So if John is a voice, Christ a word, Christ comes before John, but with God; Christ comes after John, but with us. It's a great mystery. . . . "[15] The wonderful thing about hearing a voice, he suggests in this sermon, is that the listener gains by it what the speaker does not lose.[16] So this multiplicity and entanglement of voice and word is a great mystery, but also a grand recursion, a reflection in sound in the image of God. The image in sound is the word, and Hildegard's antiphon soars as it approaches *Verbum tuum*, finally hitting the hymn's high A. This high point recurs a few lines later, with *tibi Pater*—it is not the opening's "great father," but "*you*, father," echoing "your Word," the father spoken and addressed, that hit the high points: the image of God, the image of the Word, in the rise of the voice, reflecting back what the speaker, or the singer, does not lose.

So, too, says Hildegard, writing in God's voice: "And so to gaze at my countenance I have created mirrors in which I consider all the wonders of my originality, which will never cease. I have prepared for myself these mirror forms so that they may resonate in a song of praise."[17] The mirrors in which God delights in gazing, the mirrors that are creation itself, also, in a curious synesthesia, delight resonantly in songs of praise—and the divine gaze upon a creation made in order to reflect strangely mirrors the delighted song of creation reflecting upon the maker who gazes. As the maker gazes toward those voicing the hymn (*Ut aspicias in nos*), the musical line descends, drawing the ear-gaze downward. Even recursion is not complex enough for a mirror so deeply synesthetic and so causally complicated.

In this divine gaze at the wonder of mirrors that sing, as in the antiphon, delight is not neatly distinguished from desire. We are reminded in Hildegard's exegesis—"I have prepared for myself these mirror forms so that they may resonate in a song of praise"—of the famous opening of Augustine's *Confessions*, in which he declares to a god for whom he is still searching that "to praise you is the desire of man, a little piece of your creation. You stir man to take pleasure in praising you, because you have made us for yourself."[18] This opening is full of desire, too, and of bafflement, as Augustine prays to find God without being sure how to look—and so, necessarily, without quite knowing where to address his prayer and his stirring.[19] For neither Augustine nor Hildegard, however, is this praising function somehow a matter of reassuring an insecure god or stroking a divinely inflated ego. It is, rather, a resonant mirroring of a desire and a delight that amplify in complex ways: the desire and the delight of humanity amplify those of God, and vice versa; desire amplifies delight, and vice versa again.[20]

As an invitation, resonance also demands silence: if I invite what resonates, I must give it the aural space in which to do so. The words of the song are those of desire requesting—*we beseech you*—but Word itself is given by and as the aim of the desire, by and as the god sought (the exegeted prologue continues, "And the Word was with God, and the Word was God"). There is a gradual ascent as the hymn beseeches (*Nunc igitur obsecramus*), rising up to reach out, to call toward: our word, too, reaches to be with God, to be with the Word.

All words are called through the Word. Hildegard's Father has made humanity through words, as words are humanity's means of beseeching God: "I spoke within myself my small deed, which is humanity," God declares in this same exegetical passage.[21] And God has made humanity so that they may make words: "Human beings were to announce all God's wondrous works by means of their tongues that were endowed with reason."[22] The Latin is even more revealing: God has made humans "per tubam uocis racionalis omnia miracula eius pronunciaret," to pronounce all his miracles by means of a rational voice.[23] "Rational voice" appears with all the calmness of the self-evidently noncontradictory; song and reason belong to, rather than exclude, one another. This is not because song is pure reason, number alone, but because body and its joy interweave in the pronunciation of the miraculousness of being—a pronunciation that surely must be sung. Hildegard's Word is made Flesh even more truly than Augustine's. And for Hildegard, there is an important qualification both to the divine creative voice and to the praising human one—they do not simply speak, but sing, and that will matter.

What Matter Who Is Singing

> It is nothing new to say that all utterance is erotic in some sense, that all language shows the structure of desire at some level. . . . Already in earliest metaphor, it is "wings" or "breath" that move words from speaker to listener as they move eros from lover to the beloved.
>
> ANNE CARSON, *Eros the Bittersweet*

Making occurs through desire and desire's expression—not its satiation. Matters become stranger still as the song continues. Through the Word, we are *created . . . full of the things we lack*—in the only exception to the rule that the hymn's lines end on A or E, as if the lack left our sound, too, out of place, without fulfillment. And through words, we, in Hildegard's company, create anew the fullness in this lack, create the expression of the desire and beseeching, an expression that is the creation of beseeching and the sustaining of desire. Language desires, and desire languages, is pulled into words (not always, to be sure: it may sometimes stop our speaking, creating both the rushing flow of words and the stuttering gap).[24] Full of the things we lack, we are not only full of lacking, or empty of fullness, but we also possess that fullness of which, and by which, we are dispossessed, the fullness of delighted desire. The words by which we beseech are our words, too. We give back not simply *what* we *were* given (words in desirous song), but that *by which* we *are* given—words, through Word itself. We give our own givenness, because we are given in desire (the divine desire to delight in the song of its own countenance), full of the things that we lack, given by the fullness of the words by which that lack takes on a fullness of its own. Here, too, Augustine echoes in Hildegard's thought. For him we may be given over, in memory or in the commitment of desire, to a god we nonetheless cannot fully find or grasp. It is a great mystery.

Even without its synesthetic element, this is an entanglement too deep for simple reciprocity. That is, we cannot simply say, "God makes us by verbal means, and we sing God a song back." We do not reciprocate in the sense of an economic exchange, but rather, like those singing mirrors, we resonate, reverberate. There is a great deal of mutual implication already in these opening lines, especially when they are set in the greater context of Hildegard's work: delight and desire, word and Word, song and gaze, praise and petition, mirror and song, sight and audition.

Other puzzles remain in this strange little song. What, for instance, are we asking (for)? Aside from repeated but interestingly open requests for help, two things are specified, though it is not clear how distinct they may be from each other: that we may continue to be, and that we may read internally the divine name: *that we may not perish, that your name be not darkened within us.* The name we call out to in prayerful song is the name within us—and as the metaphor of darkness (or obscurity) suggests, it is a name both sounded and written: read aloud, perhaps, since we need light (not-darkness) to call it, in a sinuous line that rises back to the hymn's high pitch on *nomen tuum* (*et ne nomen tuum in nobis obscuretur*).

In being read aloud, the name eludes the vexed divisions between writing and speaking. In its sounding and its inscription, we are both made and sustained, created and kept from perishing. We call as if to draw ourselves to it, even as we draw and desire what we do not have. Synesthetically, the name is visible to the ear, is read aloud (and read musically: this is not just a poem, but a song) in the resonating chamber of our empty fullness. It is by that name that we are helped—helped, in part, to call it. We participate in our own sustaining.[25]

We should avoid reading these resonances and intersections as if they were identifications, even of a complex sort. A voice echoed and multiplied is not exactly the same voice. It is here that Hildegard's distinction from at least some lines of mystical thought becomes evident. Hildegard is no pantheist, not even an emanationist.[26] For her, emphatically, God is not every thing, not even in the curious panentheistic manner of someone like Meister Eckhart (for whom God is distinct from all things by being alone indistinct from all things), but is unique and singular—and forgetfulness of that fact is grounds for the strongest condemnation. In the same passage of analysis in which the creator God delights in the mirrors' song of praise, Hildegard writes in the voice of this unique God: "By my Word, which was and is without beginning in myself, I caused a mighty light to emerge." Here again, we see the synesthesis of the aural and the visual. "And in this light are countless sparks, which are the angels. But when the angels came to awareness within their light, they forgot me and wanted to be as I am. Therefore, the vengeance of my punitive zeal rejected in thunderclaps those beings who had presumed to contradict me. For there is only one God, and no other can be God."[27] The angels' rejection of divine uniqueness, their desire not for God but to be (as) God, stands as a warning to human arrogance (but also to a common mystical desire for theosis): no other can be God. Our relation with God, nonetheless, is both more complex and more intimate than is commonly conceived.

Correspondingly, Hildegard's firmness about the distinction is not quite so discouraging to the possibility of ubiquitous divinity as it might seem. To be unique and singular is not to be isolated or disconnected, and Hildegard's is a cosmology not only of image and repetition, but of dense interconnection. Image and repetition are often for her the language of that connection, as they would have been for many of her contemporaries. "God, who created everything, has formed humanity according to the divine image and likeness, and marked in human beings both the higher and the lower creatures."[28] These "marks" are signatures and similarities: body parts are paralleled with the creation account, the humors (black and yellow bile, phlegm, and blood) with the elements (earth, air, water, and fire), the planetary bodies with the health of the human body, the forms of plants with their medicinal uses, and so on. Humans are no more disconnectable from other organisms than from God, from other heavenly bodies, or from the earth.[29] To pluck one string of the cosmos—the human body, the natural world, the art of music, the planets, the elements, the humors, the angels—is to set all of it vibrating.

Vibrating, it sings—and in this antiphon, the human soul sight-reads the helping name. Not obscured, the name is nonetheless a mystery. The addressee goes unnamed in the song, unless we count such terms as *Word* and *Father* as naming. The name read is unnamed; the demand of the call is only to keep reading (aloud)—that is, to keep calling out. The *name* at the highest tone, resonating with *you*, vibrates finally at the end of the hymn with *us*, in Hildegard's own harmonic version of union, as if the "us" had found the right reading, to resonate on the same pitch at which *you* has sounded throughout—to join in the graciousness presented in the gracefulness of the final line.

As a mystery, the obscured undarkened name is a paradox. At its root, a mystery demands closed eyes (it is not to be seen by the uninitiated) or closed lips (it is not to be told to them, either)[30]—but for Hildegard the mysterious name is undarkened and sung out. This it can be, perhaps, only because it is and is not a mystery (it is both concealed and revealed), is and is not a name. It is *you*, addressed by *we*. So who are *you*?

Deixis and Deities

"YOU!" said the Caterpillar contemptuously. "Who are YOU?"

LEWIS CARROLL, *Through the Looking-Glass and What Alice Found There*

The directionality here is downright odd, and that oddness is in some measure a deictic one, a matter of where the words point. Among the many strange things that can happen to deixis in mysticism, including a dissolutional fusion of the *you* and *I*, Hildegard's is perhaps one of the most intriguing, grounded as it is in the connective point of language to music, and of both to the origin, sustaining, and celebration of creation. If every image is a recursion, every utterance a resonance, where does any word point? The deixis of *you* and *I/we* is also one of voice: here is the matter of who is speaking. Yet it matters, too, that the terms be relocatable; as Nancy writes, "it is not evident that the simplest act of speech does not imply that 'I' who speaks (an 'I,' subject of my speech, and at the same time putting myself forward as speaker) should not withdraw into the interchangeability of all 'I's,' an interchangeability which is nothing but a general condition of language as speech."[31] The very possibility of speech makes possible this multiple dislocation.

Deictic terms, such as *I* and *that*, are those given some measure of their meaning by context; they point, but in order to know at what, we must know something of the context of the pointing. Because it functions in a particular setting, deixis is not quite ostension. A deictic term such *she* or *this* will pick out different objects when voiced by different users or within different contexts. Ostension will, at least presumably, always find the same object or set of objects; it means only to define by pointing to, often by pointing to an exemplar standing in for an entire set. Ostension is a common intuitive theory of language; to know what a word means, we find examples of those things named by that word, and we point to them, or at least to one of them—perhaps quite literally—and, having formed the proper association, we may be said to *know* what the word means. No doubt one reason this seems at first pass so reasonable a linguistic theory is that it is in fact the way many of us first acquire some important nouns, with the aid of parental pointing and terms such as "doggie!" uttered in tones meant to encourage mimicry—and as this is one of the most deliberate ways in which we teach language, we tend to focus upon it as the way that words work.

Of course, such pointing is pretty limited, which is why this intuitive view nonetheless is not a widely held theory of the way that languages work. It runs into particular drawbacks in theology. In *The Teacher*, Augustine's son Adeodatus, as he tries to work out how words mean, suggests an ostensive theory of language, which Augustine gently but thoroughly dismantles. The first problem comes in relation to verbs—how does one point at "running" without making the viewer think that "running" is the word for feet, or perhaps indicates the motion of striking the ground? The deeper concern is more abstract. The poles of being itself—that is, nothing and the fullness of being that is God—cannot be pointed to (and this despite the fact that, engagingly enough, a little-used sense of "ostension" is the display of the sacramental host for adoration).[32] While it is alarmingly easy to have conversations with minimal meaning, it is hard to talk about nothing—our desire to reify is strong. Perhaps the primary effect of this fact is the amusement of logicians ("I'm sure nobody walks much faster than I do," says the insulted messenger in Lewis Carroll's *Through the Looking-Glass*, to which the king replies, "He can't do that, or else he'd have been here first"[33]). Clearly, however, we cannot point at nothing and point at all. Rather more detrimental effects come from our desire to point to God—particularly the effects of theological certainty and unyielding dogmatism, the sense that we *know* just what we mean by the term and just what the term means for us.

Ostension, where the consecrated host is not involved, is not very theologically useful. And though, as we've duly noted, ostension is not deixis, such pointing-in-order-to-mean doesn't seem to perform much better, theologically speaking, when it depends upon its context. There is, at least for Augustine or Hildegard, no place from which we can legitimately say of God, "that's him," "that's me," or "here it is, this one." That is, we cannot establish the very context on which our meaning would depend. Our pointing can be neither exemplary, the way it is ostensively, nor, it seems, contextual. How, then, can we say of a mystic's god, or more properly *to* such a god, "you"?

To see properly the strangeness of Hildegard's *you*, let us spend a moment upon the divine *I*. Asked for its name, the God in the Hebrew tradition, taken up by Augustine and Hildegard's Christianity, declares instead, "*'ehyeh 'ašer 'ehyeh*," generally rendered "I am that I am," though more literally "I will be what I will be" (Exod. 3:14). The "I am" as it begins could almost be a straightforward statement of presence, but then it explicitly turns back upon itself. In thus circling, it renders strange, as if it were so purely pointing (its name is nothing but its self) that we who are not it have no idea where *we* would point if we wanted to speak of it. The way that the "I" here names itself seems to negate the very possibility of properly naming at all. It reflects, refracts, resonates with its very self, neither singular nor not.

As Nicola Masciandaro points out, a curious (if lesser) negation is actually inherent to deixis: "What makes deixis work . . . is that it says by not saying, and more precisely, that it negates its own inability to signify by speaking language, that is, by referring to the actual event of our being in language, in the same manner that 'I' means 'the one who is saying 'I.'"[34] This negation is not Aristotelian; it does not resolve into the elimination of one contrary—rather, it circles back. "The negativity of deixis," Masciandaro writes, "thus resolves to a deeper auto-deixis, its pointing to itself."[35] This appears as the only way out of Nancy's dislocation.

The name "I am" says only I, pointing to itself as if purely indicating. By circling back in this way, the *I* says a mystery, names a mystery by offering only this circle instead of a name. Yet offering only the "I," it offers, if we listen to Nancy, language itself. The loop cannot be closed, shutting divinity off from its creation. The indicative requires a certain immediacy, even a presence, but we see now that it is odd enough that even simple repetition can trouble the sense of the present: it is all very well for "I" to point at itself, but where do the rest of us point? Obviously, if each of us simply says, "I am," while pointing to him- or herself, we have altered rather than resolved the puzzle, shifting it from the mystery of a god without name to the staggering multiplicity of all of us as godlings. Nor are matters much simplified if we turn to the future "I will be," which mystifies us not only as to the whereabouts of the I, but even as to the when.[36] (We can make this even more puzzling with a turn to the Christian gospels; Jesus declares to a skeptical crowd, "before Abraham was born, I am."[37]) There is nowhere to point, but we do not point at nothing. Hildegard's *we* calls out to a divine *you*, not to nothing, and it calls out urgently: we are in great need. We ask help through the name that says only in a looping *I*, while we call to the *you* presumably named by it.

Like pointing (to oneself or not), calling is sometimes fairly clear, but this hymn is not one of those times. "You" has a particular effect upon the reader or listener. Unlike the "I" or the "he" or the "this," the "you" makes it hard to pull back, to feel oneself to be wholly outside the deictic context. Perhaps this is why its use in writing is relatively restricted; beyond prayer or the deliberately addressed epistle, the second person appears infrequently in essay or literature, but often in poetry, which may well seek to connect with its readers rather more directly than narrative or drama might, and not infrequently in pornography, which in its own rather different mode certainly seeks such a connection. The basic, doubly deictic question, "Is that you?" is so common that we tend not to hear its strangeness—the strangeness, in this instance, of the fact that an honest negative answer is impossible. "You" is simply the second person, the one (or, in English, more than one) beyond the first person, the condition of the possibility of conversation. If *I* ask, *you* can only answer in the affirmative.[38]

The effect of a *you* that somehow *fails* to call is thus both odd and poignant. Perhaps it will be useful to consider it, for comparison with a you that calls by resonance and reflection instead. A few examples may illuminate not only concept, but affect too. In David Markson's 1988 novel *Wittgenstein's Mistress*, the narrator, who is either the last animal on earth or quite mad (or both), hears a voice calling—"*You?* Can that be you? . . . And here, of all places!"[39]—but she finds no caller, only, in a moment that at once echoes and alters Hildegard, her own reflection in a window, or in a highly glossed canvas.[40] In a sense, of course, the *you* is present here, as the narrator herself, but she cannot occupy the second-person position after all—there is only one person, and the addressor is absent, or merely imagined. The "I am" becomes a circling "you are," but no one is there to say it. Hildegard's divine reflection is far from this unexpected solitude; the mirror that shows back the face is capable itself of calling.

Rainer Maria Rilke offers us a different, more directly religious, failure in his poetic account of the Christic passion in "The Olive Garden": "And why is it your will that I must say / You are, when I myself no longer find You . . . I am alone with all of human grief, which through You I undertook to lighten, / You who are not."[41] Rilke comes close, in this *you*, to drawing together Augustine's impossible ostensive poles, nothing (no one) and God—but only by addressing each in its failure, by speaking with bitter awareness that his words fail to point themselves at an addressee. The addressor is narratively present here, but alone, or at least without one addressed: the poetic voice addresses a void, addresses the realization that address is impossible now. It is not that the I circles upon itself in resonance, but that it cannot reach out to, cannot vibrate in, anything or anyone at all.

Finally, in a more complex and even incomplete failure, T. S. Eliot's grim rejoicing in "Little Gidding" includes the description of a self split in order to address: "I met one walking, loitering and hurried . . . Both intimate and unidentifiable. / So I assumed a double part, and cried / And heard another's voice cry: 'What! are *you* here?' / Although we were not. I was still the same, / Knowing myself yet being someone other / And he a face still forming."[42] One doubles to address what is nonetheless not oneself, calling out to the reflected face, but hearing it call out, too: *Could that be you?* This *you* does not address falsely (from or to one who is not), as in both Markson and Rilke; nor does it perfectly point back on itself, though it comes closer to this latter. Rather, in the double part assumed by the *I* is the double cry of a mutual *you*, a cry that forms those addressing and addressed by it, neither quite the same nor fully formed yet in their distinction. It is this lingering indistinction that keeps this final *you* from being quite successful. This will come closer to Hildegard's strange address, in which the voice is redoubled, but she will insist nonetheless upon a clear priority and distinction between creator and creation—a priority and a distinction that do not preclude mutuality. And the wistful echo of loneliness—"Although we were not"—is overcome in her celestial chorus.

Resonance: Singing the World

I took my lyre and said:
Come now, my heavenly
tortoise shell: become
a speaking instrument

SAPPHO, translated by Mary Barnard

For all its reflections, Hildegard's antiphon is not simply reflexive; it does have a second person. There are a choral many *we* who address; there is an addressee in the *you*, a Father in whose existence the singer seems confident. But her—or, given the *we*, our—spoken or sung words give back to the Father what the Father through the Word gave to us: the fullness of lacking; that is, desire. That curious creative combination of fullness of lack (desire is never only lacking) flows multidirectionally through the Word/word—and not least through the strange high-reaching word *you*. The address lacks a name, but it does not lack the full force of desire: it is entirely beseeching, asking only to address, to call upon. The name preserves its legibility. But the address is also directed through the Word by which the one calling was created—called into being as desiring, and by the divine desire to see and to hear. The antiphon vibrates, *resonates*, at the frequency of *you*. It echoes a divine eagerness to resonate, for which creation is made, and a human eagerness to resonate, as that for which we are made: it draws up to you and your word; down to us in your gaze; together in resonant song.

Resonance is particularly appropriate to Hildegard's cosmology. Nancy, struggling to make sense of sense itself, writes, "Perhaps it is necessary that sense not be content to make sense . . . but that it want also to resound."[43] As re-sounding or sounding again, resonance emphasizes the sense—the sensuality, even—of sound. Nancy writes of the act of listening to music, in which we attend to resonance explicitly (and to language, if at all, with as much attention to sensuousness as to meaning):

> It returns to itself, it reminds itself of itself, and it feels itself as resonance itself: a relationship to self deprived, stripped of all egoism and all ipseity. Not "itself," or the other, or identity, or difference, but alteration and variation, the modulation of the present that changes it in expectation of its own eternity, always imminent and always deferred, since it is not in any time. Music is the art of making the outside of time return to every time, making return to every moment the beginning that listens to itself beginning and beginning again. In resonance the inexhaustible return of eternity is played—and listened to.[44]

We can begin to see how central her musicianship is to all of Hildegard's work. Hildegard claimed that her songs were received in her visions, though it is not clear if by this she included their melodies or only their lyrics.[45] What is a little clearer is that this distinction is imperfect. Marianne Richert Pfau notes, as we have, that "the words and music in Hildegard's compositions are mutually influential. The text determines many musical choices; the music may clarify textual syntax and large-scale form that in turn contribute to the meaning."[46] For Hildegard, the world brought into being by divine voice is interconnected by resemblances that musically vibrate—as bodies do, breathing and pulsing in unison. Such connections and vibrations characterize the universe entirely, and like much of Hildegard's thought, this characterization is presented in the microcosm of her music. To say that for Hildegard humanity is the image of God is accurate enough, but it oversimplifies the complex of images that she sees at every level of the cosmos.[47]

The human voice is the image of the creative divine voice—but it is not a weakened copy. If anything, it is a weaker version of its *own* original perfection; Hildegard both takes up and nuances the Augustinian reading of original sin, as the loss of harmonious voice. For Augustine, the original disobedience is one that resonates or multiplies in images of itself: Adam's disobedience of God echoes in the continued dissonance not only of human and divine will, but of human will with itself and with human flesh.[48]

Hildegard, however, makes explicit, and makes more than metaphorical, the musicality of this image. In a letter to the prelates of Mainz, she uses her reading to make a subtle argument in favor of song—and against the injunction that forbade her house from musical celebration (her argument was evidently effective, as the injunction was subsequently lifted). "Adam lost [the voice of the living Spirit] through his disobedience," she writes. "Because he lost his innocence, his voice in no way harmonized with the voices of the angels who sing God's praise . . . a harmony he had possessed in Paradise."[49] The loss of Paradise is the loss of song. This may be behind an oddity in Hildegard's musical morality play *Ordo Virtutum*, in which all of the virtues sing, and only one role is non-singing: that of the Devil, to whom and perhaps even through whom Paradise is lost.

Music is not completely lost to humans together with Paradise, however. Music as it still remains reminds us of Heaven to come: when the prophets composed songs and accompanied them on musical instruments, they acted "[s]o that human beings would not live from the memory of exile, but with thoughts of heavenly bliss . . . and furthermore so that human beings would be enticed to praise God."[50] (To sing on the basis of pneumes, which are much less prescriptive than modern musical notes, must be also to remember the music, to bring forward this memory of hope.) Music is the best form of praise because it acts as its own enticement, thereby enhancing itself, and because it echoes the perfect praise of the voice that harmonizes with the very angels. Indeed, Hildegard insists, "before the Fall [Adam's] voice carried in itself, in full, harmonious sound the loveliness of every musical art."[51] Our music is imperfect, but it is as close to perfection as the praising voice can come; when we only speak, or when we are inharmonious, our praise is lessened. The Devil, Hildegard argues, so hates songs of praise that he sows discord—from that between humans and God in Eden all the way to that between Hildegard and the prelates—in order to silence them.[52] If creation is song, then this silencing (so different from the silence essential to rhythm and exchange) unmakes it: it is the musical counterpart to the nothingness that is Augustinian evil, opposed to the goodness of being and being's source.

In this antiphon, address and deixis become musical forms. The *you* does not point, but neither does it fail: it resonates. I am who am; you are who are. We find neither identity nor difference, but "alteration and variation . . . modulation." *You* resonates with the *we* as the plural of "a self deprived . . . of all egoism and all ipseity," a self full of the things that it lacks, made a resonating chamber for the divine "I am" that does more than simply reflect.

That singing, praying self resonates with its addressee; God reverberates with the creation that the resonant divine voice has called into being, and eternity returns to the measured time of the song. Reason breathes from the diaphragm, and the body gives voice to the soul.[53]

It is creation that allows God to see God, creation that acts as a mirror—a mirror that shows (wonder) by singing (praise)—but in singing it does not simply show, it necessarily shares. Creation mirrors God in this synesthetic image, an outpouring of divine joyful desire echoed back, as such desire so often is, in song.

The knowledge or seeing thus given back to the creator is not an epistemological necessity (it does not seem that Hildegard's God requires creation for self-knowing), but rather a gift that returns joy by holding that mirror up to it. Resonance is responsive, but it is not simply response, nor even a circle of response and call; in it, the singing vibration is shared and thereby multiplied: the speaker or singer gives, and loses nothing. God says, and the world is—both because God's speaking is creative power and, less evidently, because all speaking does implicitly address: to speak, God speaks to, and the face (thus) formed in the mirror (thus formed) sings back in praise. Hildegard's *we* calls out from creation to the resonant joy and desire found only in the great need and the *you*—a you read within and sung out, illuminated by its very self.

Musical cosmology is not unique to Hildegard, of course, but hers is an unusually melodic version, with an unusual measure of joy. Plato, an influence on every Western mystic after him, has a more austere version that throws into relief Hildegard's exuberance. His features a Siren singing from each celestial sphere (his own symphony of celestial harmonies), but each Siren voices only a single unchanging note in wordless song.[54] Here there is no room for response or uplifting in joy, and no play among melody and lyric, though there is still a resonance among voices that sustains the world in its beauty, and this is no small thing. Walter Benjamin repeats a Jewish tale that both echoes and temporalizes Plato, as Gershom Scholem summarizes: "the creation of angels [is one] of existences meant to sing one note of praise to God and then vanish. It may well be taken as an emblem of the ephemerality and eternality of voice. . . ."[55] Augustine gives some bodiliness to Plato and to the angels; Hildegard gives them both a little more, by making the cosmos a chorus.

Hildegard's *you* does not simply point; neither does the pair *we-you* simply collapse, as if conflated—not only would this be for her a sin worthy of severe condemnation, but it would silence the music, the rapid back and forth of vibration. Despite Hildegard's frequent use of mirror imagery in descriptions of creation, the song is no simple mirror either; the singing *we* are not a poor imitation of the divine voice that sang creation into being, but the closest that postlapsarian creation can approach to the perfect harmonies of Paradise, where perfect humans sang. The antiphon does not quite serve as a responsory, even in the complexly looped manner of much prayerful call and response, in which an originary voice is hard to pinpoint, and every call seems already to be and to have been an answer. Nor does it, quite loop in the manner of autodeixis, in which the context refracts the pointing back to the source of the term. Rather, altogether musically, deixis, of both self and addressee, becomes reverberation, in which one vibration—the call of created desire, the creative divine desiring voice—sets up another on the same frequency, so that we have the "same" sound, but more so, louder but just slightly altered by addition, enriched by another voice, closer to paradisaical perfection. Address is resonance. Humanity's very need, put into song, perfects divine delight. Hildegard's musicality informs her cosmology both intellectually and sensuously. Taking seriously the notion of a world called into being by voice, she likewise takes seriously the fullness of desire that calls back, the soul as a resonating chamber for the voice that reads aloud the unnamed name of the *you*, in an address and a reply that can only call to both gratifying completeness and endless need—and all of it only made in the calling. In the beginning, the Word is sung.

CHAPTER 5

Original Breath

The paths to God are as numerous as the breaths of the creatures.

—IBN AL'ARABI, QUOTING A SUFI SAYING, IN WILLIAM CHITTICK, *The Sufi Path of Knowledge: Ibn al'Arabi's Metaphysics of Imagination*

Articulation before the letter, apparition of something where there was nothing or something else.

—MAURICE MERLEAU-PONTY, *The Visible and the Invisible*

In the beginning, God speaks.

For all of Hildegard's exuberance about primal song, it's not clear that this beginning marks a very promising start for a fully corporeal sense of the voice. If we could somehow take a text by itself, out of its context and history, it might: that a divinity speaks, and so the world becomes, seems material enough. A voice that forms the world must surely give matter to meaning. But, of course, this story of Genesis enters into the long history of the Abrahamic faiths. There it encounters in subsequent millennia a slow but increasing abstraction, until it reaches an insistence on a God who is beyond and outside all time and place. This already makes speaking very strange, since words follow one another temporally, as we can hear even in reading them. And the speaking becomes stranger still with the insistence, beginning early in the Christian tradition, that creation must be *ex nihilo*, that before this speaking creator there is *nothing*, not even the matter out of which a world can be formed—and that the speaker is likewise immaterial. Without a material body to form the words or air to carry the vibrations, "speaking" here is something odd indeed.

If creation is the work of a creator whose eternity is utterly separate from time, and if creation comes out of nothing, then the creational speaking can at best be a rather stretched allegory or metaphor; the "voice" is disembodied, speaking at no time from nowhere to no one. Genesis, however, does not give us much ground for these disincarnating claims. "In the beginning, when God created the heavens and the earth" (Gen 1:1),[1] we cannot, admittedly, have the heavens and the earth already in place and formed: that leaves no room at all for creative activity or beginning, and so the story goes nowhere. But that does not mean that we cannot have the heavens and the earth at all. Rather, "the earth was a formless wasteland, and darkness covered the abyss, while a mighty wind swept over the waters" (1:1–2).[2]

God speaks, and *There is*: thereness, in the possibility of place; isness, filling *there*. The world becomes, though in a way that, as formless, cannot quite be specified except by negations—of shape, of fertility, of light. That *there is* gives us a new possibility for reading the voice, as something still strange and wonderful, but closer to and more resonant with voice as we know it, voice by which we speak, voice as vibration given meaning in flesh.

The first things spoken in the story are well known: "Let there be light" (1:3), God says; "Let there be a dome in the middle of the waters, to separate one body of water from the other" (1:6); "Let the water under the sky be gathered into a single basin" (1:9), and so on. God seems to speak in a kingly, even imperious, fashion, commanding; and if we were to understand creation as *ex nihilo*, then we would see those commands as sufficient to bring about results even if there were no one (indeed, before the light, no thing) to follow them. But if there is *not* no thing, then it is the earth and the water and the wind, and the darkness and the light, that follow God's commands—or, more promisingly, that *respond* to God's speaking, and even, in their very movements and formations, *answer*. If they respond, then that speaking is something different from the disembodied voice of the ultimate ruler, something much more promising for material speech.

Such a possibility arises not only in the presence of the water, earth, abyss, and dark, but from the ambiguity of that which blows over the waters. I have used the New American Bible translation here, and it declares that "a mighty wind swept over the waters" (1:2). Most often, however, English versions render the phrase *ruach elohim* not as "mighty wind," but as "Spirit of God." Sometimes this spirit "moves" upon the waters, or "sweeps" over them. Often it more vaguely "hovers."[3] Both words in the translated phrase are ambiguous—breath, which here as in many languages bears the implication of spirit, or wind; god, or divine, or mighty.[4] Cavarero writes, "As is well known, the thesis of creation through speech—a pervasive commonplace in western culture—suffers from the Christian rereading of the Old Testament. For ancient Israel, neither creation nor self-revelation comes from the speech of God but rather from his breath and from his voice."[5] As is usual with translations, this one presents a problem of choice. If, however, we choose not to choose—if we choose the ambiguity of divine breath *as* a mighty wind blowing over the abyssal and unformed—then we hear an intriguing voice beginning to sound, not just in the sweep of the wind, but in the creation of the world. Nor will we have to fall into clumsy literalism thus to read it.

Not, at least, once we begin to listen. The resoundings of the creative voice echo in bodily speech. All of our speaking is modulations of breath, raw material shaped and stretched and cut by our body's movements, from our diaphragms to our lips, made into sound, breathed out on our own small wind. (One hopes it is small, anyway: for a human to be called windy is not complimentary.) The divine breath in Genesis's first beginning moves upon the abyssal waters and the dark sky and the formless earth; they move responsively. Again, we might read them as responding to command, and although the God in this story is not the omnipotent divinity of later theologies, gods do tend to be in charge. But imagine this as something more intimate, a breath given form by matter and matter its meaning by breath: a voice, a speaking (or a Hilegardian singing) in which chaos moves into the shape and the song of a continuously emerging world. My reading of Genesis is not quite Hildegard's reading of John; I am less wed to an absolutely separate creator. It would not be quite wrong, though, to suggest that the two readings resonate.

God says, and light moves, and water, and earth, and it is good. Even this first word is breathed, there on the waters when God began creating: a wind moves upon the waters, and it is as if in conversation with that breath that the formless is made into world. World is at once divine word given voice by the earth and the earth's form shaped by divine breath, bearing that trace of its own brush with divinity.

The idea that God writes twice, once in creation and once in scripture, allows the possibility of reading divinity in the world and the enticing complexities of reading the world within scripture. If we take creation as breath moving matter—that is, as voice, in fact as voice speaking—then this inscribing is also a voicing; the world becomes a strange sort of book that is its own co-author, a song (with room for improvisation) that makes itself in the singing. Breath without body does not speak.[6]

Promising though it might already be, this forming is not the end of the Genesis stories of making. Once formed, the world is filled. First, there are plants, about which there must be a great deal to say, but this is not the discussion in which that belongs. If, however, we listen ahead for the animals, we find that they are addressed more directly. The first set of animals—"the great sea monsters and all kinds of swimming creatures . . . , and all kinds of winged birds" (1:21)—are urged to "Be fertile, multiply, and fill the waters of the seas; and let the birds multiply on the earth" (1:22). One presumes that they go forth obligingly to do so.[7]

The animals do not speak back to their creator, but, like primally chaotic matter, they respond, giving the speaking its meaning within the world, embodying it in their very movements. They are brought forth from the created earth (1:24–25), and they, too, have "the breath of life" (1:30, NRSV).[8] Walter Benjamin writes, "God breathes his breath into man: this is at once life and mind and language."[9] Is this shared breath uniquely human, though? Our own breath is not: all animals that are born out of their mothers draw breath when they are first separated, as if one separation leads only to a new rejoining, all of us sharing the life-giving air.[10] A newborn human gasps and cries out. In some way, it begins to seem, the very world speaks. The animals' actions, their ways of being, speak in turn, harmonizing with the request given to them, further harmonizing with the matter of the world in which they tend to find themselves rather more at home than humans do.[11]

It is only then that humans come about. God, having spoken amongst Godself—"Let us make humankind in our image, after our likeness" (1:26)—creates human beings to whom it likewise speaks. God gives them, in fact, just the same commandment as the other animals, and they, too, head out toward fertility. Here human beings are not the first animals, and they share fertility in common with the others. Like the other animals, they do not appear to have words to answer the divine commandment. They are, however, given a special place: like other animals, they are commanded to multiply and are given plants for food (1:29), but uniquely, they are given dominion over the earth and its living species (1:26, 1:28)—an infamous moment that has been used to justify human disregard for the rest of the planet as something simply placed at our disposal. After this, God rests.

All this would be complicated enough. But famously, it is here that Genesis takes a deep breath and begins again, as an older story is imperfectly tacked on to the first. In the second beginning, we do not learn of the response between matter and breath/wind, nor hear of divine creative voice. All of that is condensed into a preliminary statement: "At the time when the Lord God made the earth and the heavens—while as yet there was no field shrub on earth and no grass of the field had sprouted" (2:4–5). But we do read of a first human shaped out of the matter of that earth, as the animals were in the previous version: "the Lord God formed man out of the clay of the ground" (2:7). Here too, now more explicitly, breath moves: having molded a man from earth, God "blew into his nostrils the breath of life, and so man became a living being" (2:7). With that divine breath, the man lives. In his breathing, then, is divinity. But because he appears so early in this creation story, there is nowhere to put him.

So, once again, we read that God makes plants, as a paradisiacal garden is quickly put together for this created human. The garden supplies all the man's physical needs, including the aesthetic (the trees are pleasant to see as well as supplying fruit [2:8–9)]). Once again the man (this time minus the co-created woman of the first story) is in charge of the land, but here is he is told "to cultivate and care for it" (2:15), rather than to dominate it. In a move the first story is missing, he is also warned against eating from the tree of knowledge of good and bad (2:17), a warning that will become significant in the story's next chapter.

Speaking, With and Over

> A word, so long as it's not absorbed without remainder to a sense, remains essentially extended between other words, stretching to touch them, though not merging with them: and that's language as body.
>
> JEAN-LUC NANCY, *Corpus*

No longer homeless, the first man is nonetheless lonely, or at least alone, and God feels that this is not good for him (2:18). Even God has an "us" with whom to speak, both in the first story (1:26) and in this second (3:22). So from the same earth, God makes the animals, which he then sends before the human.

The interaction here is intriguing: "So the Lord God formed out of the ground various wild animals and various birds of the air, and he brought them to the man to see what he would call them; whatever the man called each of them would be its name. The man gave names to all the cattle, all the birds of the air, and all the wild animals" (2:19–20). Just as God's speaking enters into some relation with the matter of the world, so, too, does the man's speaking enter into some relation with the animals (which is not to imply sameness in those relations, only the importance of entanglement for the possibility of speech). The breath needs something to move, or it cannot be voice; the voice needs something to name, or it will not be words.

So what sort of relation *is* language making here, when the man calls the animals by their names? Patricia Cox Miller, in "Adam, Eve, and the Elephants," warns us of an often overlooked conflation in a widespread answer to that query. The scene of

> Adam naming the animals in Gen. 2:19–20 is understood, by an intertextual sleight of hand, in concert with Gen. 1:26, the passage in which God gives humankind dominion over the fish, the birds, and the domestic and wild animals. . . . Such a view of the dominical Adam separates the human from the animal rather than placing the human in a continuum with the flesh-and-bones materiality of the natural world.[12]

With this conflation, we can ignore the breath that moves over and forms the unformed world, and moves into and animates the living animals, and declare that only breathed into human nostrils is divine breath anything special: divinity speaks to, and through, us alone.

This interpretation is of very long standing, Miller notes, and it justifies a further claim:

> The intertextual reading that understands naming as a being-over rather than a being-with is indebted to a certain strain of Patristic commentary on Adam and the beasts. Especially in the Hexaemeron tradition as exemplified by Basil of Caesarea, Ambrose, and John Chrysostom, Adam's dominion over the animals as namer is attributed to his creation in the image of God; only humans have reason and hence are superior to the irrational beasts.[13]

That sense of superiority grounded in these texts remains strong long after late antiquity, and across a range of traditions beyond Christianity. I would like to offer a small sampling of exegeses of the passages and of philosophical thinking about the first words to illustrate the point and the connections that Miller has summarized: humans are rightly dominant because they are superior; they are superior because they are rational; rationality is demonstrated in speech. And in several of these stories, rational speech is demonstrated in naming the animals.

The Genesis story is homiletically elaborated in the "legends," synthesized from a number of late ancient and medieval sources, in Louis Ginzberg's *The Legends of the Jews*. Here the God who creates the first man confers (as does the God of the Qur'an) with the angels, who are not at all sure that making humans is a good idea. Human wisdom is linked to convincing the angels that humanity is a good thing after all; the human ability to name is connected in turn to human wisdom. We are told,

> The wisdom of Adam displayed itself to the greatest advantage when he gave names to the animals. Then it appeared that God, in combating the arguments of the angels that opposed the creation of man, had spoken well, when He insisted that man would possess more wisdom than they themselves. When Adam was barely an hour old, God assembled the whole world of animals before him and the angels. The latter were called upon to name the different kinds, but they were not equal to the task. Adam, however, spoke without hesitation: "Oh Lord of the world! The proper name for this animal is ox, for this one horse, for this one lion, for this one camel." And so he called all in turn by name, suiting the name to the particularity of the animal.[14]

The animals are named first, properly so that their names accord with their particularities, and then Adam goes on to self-name (a privilege reserved in many philosophical traditions for God alone, given the creative power of naming). He calls himself "Adam, because he had been created out of Adamah, dust of the earth." What is more, Adam knows God's own name, though he does not create it: "Again, God asked him His own name, and he said, 'Adonai, Lord, because Thou art Lord over all creatures'—the very name God had given unto Himself, the name by which the angels call Him, the name that will remain immutable evermore." The tale stresses that such naming is human, but beyond ordinary human capacities: "without the gift of the holy spirit, Adam could not have found names for all; he was in very truth a prophet, and his wisdom a prophetic quality."[15] Adam creates the names, but in perfect accordance with what he is naming (in the perfect prelapsarian accord that we may recall from considering translation).

The God of the Qur'an (seventh century) chooses similar means to convince the angels that humankind is worthwhile. Unlike Genesis, the Qur'an explicitly attributes omniscience to the creator God, who "knows all things" (2.29). Here God does not await Adam's naming to see what the animals will be called; rather, "God taught Adam"—and *not* the angels—"all the names" (2.30), and had Adam "present them to the angels" (ibid.). This makes the man so impressive that even the angels—with one exception—bow down before him (2.33–34), and, of course, that one exception gets into trouble.[16] Though there is no explicit granting of domination here, human superiority is well established in this act of speaking and naming; Adam is superior even to the angels. However, Adam's speaking is not a creative act. He has memorized what God has told him; he has learned his lessons flawlessly.

This shows, some Islamic philosophers argue, human participation in the divine intellect, as God shares knowledge with Adam.[17] On some readings, these names are even more than they seem, and so the knowledge even more clearly divine. As William Chittick summarizes, "the Qur'an tells us that God taught Adam all the names, and one of the interpretations of this verse is that these were the names of God, that is, the names that designate *wujûd*, the Real. This special knowledge that God taught to Adam explains his superiority over all other creatures."[18] (We encounter again the perfection of that first speaking.) The philosophers vary as to where in the cosmic hierarchy they place the participation of human in divine intellect: "Al-Fārābī, Avicenna and Averroes identify the active intellect with the lowest of the cosmological intelligences, and argue that the human intellect is able to conjoin with the active intellect. Several scholastic authors identify the active intellect with God on the authority of Avicenna and Augustine."[19] But in either instance, the human ability to name proves not only superiority over other species, but a special and even unique connection to divinity—a share not of creativity, but of intellect. The injunction to dominance and the story of naming, then, need not be overtly conflated for the sense of the first to influence the second.

Jewish philosopher Moses Maimonides, whose work became central across a number of theological traditions (particularly in negative theology), took Islamic thought seriously—unsurprisingly, given his residence in Spain, Morocco, and Egypt in an Islamicate context. In his *Guide for the Perplexed* (1190), Maimonides replies to a smug-seeming interlocutor who raises the challenging question as to whether Adam did not gain his greatest perfection (the ability to know good from evil) in his worst act (disobeying God). Maimonides declares,

> [T]he intellect which was granted to man as the highest endowment, was bestowed on him before his disobedience. With reference to this gift the Bible states that "man was created in the form and likeness of God." On account of this gift of intellect man was addressed by God, and received His commandments, as it is said: "And the Lord God

> commanded Adam" (Gen. 2:16)—for no commandments are given to the brute creation or to those who are devoid of understanding. Through the intellect man distinguishes between the true and the false. This faculty Adam possessed perfectly and completely.[20]

Maimonides clarifies that the only reason Adam does not already know right from wrong is that such knowledge is not actually a matter of intellect. Intellect judges the true and false rather than the good and bad.[21] Maimonides declares human superiority, by virtue of human intellect, over the "brutes." (He also, conveniently, omits the command given to animals in the first creation story.)

Much influenced by "Rabbi Moses," whom he often cites, and by Islamic thought broadly, Dominican friar Thomas Aquinas rejects the idea that the human intellect *participates in* God's.[22] Like Maimonides, however, he does believe that Adam's knowledge is perfect before the Fall. In his *Summa Theologiae* (1265–1274), Thomas reads the naming of the animals as a sign of that perfection in knowledge which is lost to postlapsarian humanity: "Man named the animals. But names should be adapted to the nature of things. Therefore Adam knew the animals' natures; and in like manner he was possessed of the knowledge of all other things."[23] (Adam knew the names of all things.) The peculiarities of the animals, like the universals designating their names, must be known to this superior being; they do not know him back.

Finally, we may return to the linguistic theory that Dante Alighieri puts forth in *De vulgari eloquentia* (ca. 1302–1305). Dante actually rewrites Genesis in order to maintain not only human, but male, superiority. Strictly interpreting the difference between direct and indirect discourse, Dante will declare that the Bible lists the woman as the first speaker. Hers are indeed the first human words *quoted* in the second story, though God has been quoted already (2:16–18). We read *that* the man gives names, but we do not hear his voice. In the third chapter of Genesis, the woman speaks in conversation with a serpent (who actually speaks first). The serpent asks about the rules governing the fruits that may be eaten, and the woman confirms the injunction against eating the fruit of that tree in the middle (3.1–3.3).[24] Thus, says Dante, "We find that a woman spoke before anyone else, when the most presumptuous Eve responded thus to the blandishments of the Devil."

As far as Dante is concerned, that a woman speaks first will not do; no more can the first addressee be an animal—who, in fact, speaks before her. So he tidies scripture up a bit: "But although we find in scripture that a woman spoke first, I still think it more reasonable that a man should have done so; and it may be thought unseemly that so distinguished an action of the human race should first have been performed by a woman rather than a man. Therefore, it is reasonable to believe that the power of speech was given first to Adam, by Him who had just created him."[25] The first conversation occurs not between woman and animal, but, in a much more fitting primacy, between man and God.

At first, promisingly, Dante attributes language to need rather than to the superior power of reason: "Of all creatures that exist, only human beings were given the power of speech, because only to them was it necessary. It was not necessary that either angels or the lower animals should be able to speak; rather, this power would have been wasted on them, and nature, of course, hates to do anything superfluous."[26] Thomas Aquinas, on the other hand, did attribute speech to communication among angels. But theirs, he wrote, was an inward speech, the manifestation of mental concept; angels likewise can be said to speak to God both in praise and in seeking instruction.[27] The angels speak by breath, perhaps, only to share their concepts with human beings; speech that sounds still belongs only to those who need it. It is not long, though, before reason enters into Dante's explanation. Reason, too, is there to meet a requirement: humans need reason (and rational speech) because we lack the natural instincts of animals and the spiritually reflective capacities of angels.[28] The possibilities of thinking of reason as a faculty meant to meet or make up for a *deficit*, alas, do not seem to be developed—but we can keep them in mind as another way to view reason, a capacity based as much upon limitation as upon power, or upon the ever-present interplay between the two.

Despite his willingness to adapt scripture to accord better with what is reasonable, Dante does not want to stretch his interpretations *too* far from the text. He must acknowledge that God and animals are both said to speak in Genesis, the first in world-creation (and then in conversation with the humans), the second in discussion with the woman. Both modes of speaking, he declares, are indirect, and animal speaking is actually a sort of possession, a manipulation of the animal's body by an angel or demon.[29] Speaking is human and is a sign of man's rationality (I use the male possessive, of course, advisedly). While it seems to bear some relation to our embodiment, the limitations of which keep us from being angels, it is more firmly linked to reason—though it is interesting that even Dante, so invested here in reason and the rational, should still insist on the bodily nature of our speech.

For all of these writers, then—Ginzberg's collective narrators from whose stories he weaves his tale, the Qur'an itself, one of Judaism's most broadly influential philosophers, a Dominican priest whose work is more profoundly formative of Christian doctrine than almost any other, and a Renaissance linguist who interprets scripture in accordance with logic and nature (with its loathing of superfluity)—the first man is distinguished by his perfect mind. His capacity for reason sets him above all other animals, and the sign of that reason is language. For many, language and its superiority are especially shown in naming the animals, but even where that episode is not described, the superiority is evident. Thus the rather smug anthropocentrism of the Church fathers of late antiquity carries forward full force into at least the late Middle Ages, and it is linked to the human ability to speak.

Again, not all of these readings insist upon conflating the first and second creation stories in Genesis. All of those that do read the tale of naming, however, read the first man's ability to name the animals not as a sign of his capacity for relation to them, nor as showing the creative power of relationality as he breathes words among them, but as a sign of human superiority to the animals by virtue of a mental capacity limited rather than supplied by bodiliness: reason, knowledge, intellect, wisdom. Human reason is put into sharp contrast with animal irrationality, which is presented as pure instinctual carnality. As we know, the consequences of insisting upon human domination, the right to subdue or subordinate the rest of the world, have been ecologically disastrous, and it has become clear that those who might look to Genesis for instruction would do better to think about tilling and keeping, about stewardship rather than ownership. So there are some pieces of the story that one could pull out for what seem to us to be good ethical purposes. But still, what of the *saying* here? Is the naming story redeemable? Can it serve to do anything other than declare that humans rule? Can we, too, speak non-imperiously?

Dante himself has actually given us a possibility for so doing, in understanding speech as joyful response. "As to what was pronounced by the voice of the first speaker . . . I have no doubt that it was the name of God, or *El*. . . . [I]t is reasonable that he who existed before [the Fall] would have begun with a cry of joy; and, since there is no joy outside God, but all joy is in God, and since God Himself is joy itself, it follows that the first man to speak should first and before all have said 'God.'"[30] And why would this first speaker necessarily have cried "El!" *before* the woman spoke to the serpent? "Thinking, therefore . . . that the first man addressed his speech to God Himself, I say, equally reasonably, that this first speaker spoke immediately—as soon, indeed, as God's creative power had been breathed into him."[31] That breath breathed into the first man's nostrils is exhaled in the very joy that it names. Similarly, Cavarero notes that for Franz Rosenzweig,

> the bigram *Jah*—which can be traced back to a group of names for God that recall cultic invocations—corresponds "to one of those originary grids from which the language must have had its origins: speech at the original place of the encounter . . . pure vocative prior to any possibility of other cases of declension." Insofar as it is pure vocative, *Jah* is therefore also a pure vocal—an "originary cry," voice before speech. "The proper name of God, unlike all other proper names, not only had to have been at the beginning, but must always remain."[32]

From Dante's *El*, from Rosenzweig's *Jah*, come all words. The first word cries out a name for joy, in joy, in a perfect language. God gives humans breath; human breathing gives forth voice—glorious, really, but what happened to talking to the animals, among whom humans breathe?

Speaking Flesh

> [T]he question is . . . whether every relation between me and Being, even vision, even speech, is not a carnal relation, with the flesh of the world.
>
> MAURICE MERLEAU-PONTY, *The Visible and the Invisible*

Two possible first human speakings: the names of the animals, the name of God. Each is a response. Despite sharing the impatience that many of us must feel with Dante's fairly potent sexism, and a certain dubiousness as well as great readerly pleasure in his tendency to decide that scripture says what he thinks it should, I do find delightful the notion that the first movement of the divine breath once it has been given to humans (indeed, in the second creation story, the first time it is given to any animal) is an outcry of joy—that breath is drawn in as life and breathed out as joy in living. I have wondered elsewhere if every cry of joy might not harbor some trace of divine delight.[33] Perhaps because of this sense of multiplicity, though, and because of my lack of allegiance to some of the ideas that Dante held dear, I am still inclined to see the first human speaking, however indirectly cited, as the address to the animals. And I don't see why there should not have been great delight in it, too—perhaps even, from the lonely and singular human, a cry of joy, or of hope. Or perhaps every voicing must resonate with the divine voice, insofar as it names, insofar as naming creates—and can create only in responsiveness. Though the reading that puts the naming of the animals prior to the address to God is more clearly grounded in the text, we ought not forget the divine breath moving through the humans and the animals, forming them and enabling their answers—it is with God's breath that Adam names.

Whatever the first word may be, there is another naming to come. Returning to the Genesis story, we find that the call to the animals has not quite assuaged the first man's loneliness. Not that the man doesn't like the animals, so far as we are told, but they aren't of his kind, and so are not quite able to satisfy his need for companionship—as, we must realize, God also was not, so we should hesitate to assume that this is a sign of animal inferiority (again, the man in this story has been granted not the rights of dominance but the responsibilities of caretaking). One more act of creation takes place, this time out of the man's own living matter, to make a second human. (In a charming midrashic variant, the man becomes lonely when he sees that all the animals come to him in pairs, and so it is that God makes woman.[34]) How does the man respond? Just as he did to the animals: he calls—he names—the woman thus created ("This one shall be called 'woman'" [2:23]). But this call is differently heard, as communication within a species generally is, and the woman stays with him as one who is suitably companionate and helpful,[35] one who can be a good conversationalist.

We could read this with feminist indignation, and sometimes I find myself tempted to do so (turning in preference toward the dual creation of the first story), and we might not even be wrong: maybe the woman is just another animal under the dominion of the man (who will even, later on, rename her Eve [3:20]). But there are other readings of this combination of namings, and perhaps we might more hopefully say that the gift of companionship is rightly met when we call by name, when we acknowledge what the other is, human or not; that there is a special companionship among our own species, but that this does not exclude the possibility of calling across to others.

This is a possibility many have been eager to foreclose. One consequence of believing that speech demonstrates reason and therefore superiority is to incorporate the sense of dominance *into* human language itself, another move that continues to influence the thought of post-Patristic interpreters. Miller writes further,

> Chrysostom was especially enthusiastic about the exalted status of the human: "Do you see the unrivalled authority? Do you see [Adam's] lordly dominance?" Noting that Genesis specifies that Adam gave

names to all the cattle, all the birds of heaven and all the beasts of the earth, Chrysostom continues:

> The being that has the ability to put the right names on cattle, and birds, and beasts without getting the sequence mixed up, not giving to wild beasts the names suited to the tame ones nor allotting to the tame animals what belonged to the wild ones, but giving them all their right names—how could he not be full of intelligence and understanding?

Adam knew his animals! But in this kind of literal reading, the animals do not open on a depth shared by human beings but are reduced to an inferior reality.[36]

Might the animals, called by the man, call us to the depth of a shared world? (Might the man call the woman as well as the animals by name in the world they likewise share?) The realization that we need not conflate the stories of naming and dominion can allow us to reread the former, against the insistence on a natural domination granted by rationality. We have to go back to the point that, in Genesis, God does not know the names in advance, and this suggests that the animals are genuinely unnamed until the man encounters them. Adam does not *know* the names and get them right; either he makes them up, or he recognizes them in the animals themselves. There is no indication that the names preexist the calling. The God of Genesis does not instruct Adam to designate the animals so that a proper typology may be formed, or to enhance their use value, or to know which among them might be suited for food (in fact, the human beings in this story seem to be contentedly vegetarian or maybe vegan; it will only be after the Fall that God clothes them in leather [3:21]). Rather, God sends the animals and waits to see—to hear—how Adam calls them ("He brought them to the man to see what he would call them" [2:19]). What they are called will then be their names. There is no claim, even, of divine foreknowledge; God appears to be a little bit curious, interested in hearing how the animals are called, how the man will respond to their presence. The man in turn is not simply identifying, but calling; not simply designating, but naming, so that each animal may be called by name: a vocative as pure as the name of God. And God does not *instruct* the man to label the animals (though the stories of competition with the angels read Genesis thus), but sends the animals before them on the assumption that the man *will* respond to their presence by calling them—perhaps, though this exceeds the text, he will cry out in joy. God is not exercising dominion over this first human, nor giving him subjects for domination of his own, but offering him possible companions, helpers—friends, even—so that he will not be lonely; and the man is not exercising dominion over the animals, but responding to their presence, forming his breath into sounds among theirs. That he will still need a companion of his own species suggests a limit to this friendly possibility, but not its exclusion.

In his beautiful, angry, and elegiac text *The Animal Side*, Jean-Christophe Bailly views our own naming of animals, an echo of this first human naming, as itself something akin to a divine act. The divinity, however, is not so much (uniquely) ours as it is what permeates the language in which we are immersed (to turn back to Genesis, in the ever-speaking, word-made material world), and so does not at all grant superiority. Bailly reads the act of naming poetically and neoplatonically: "[T]he rain of the One, dispersed by language, drop by drop, is an infinite dissemination, and . . . with fingers pointed and names brandished, tentatively, as with the images we create, we lag behind and beneath all language, beneath its every modulation, its every utterance."[37] Humanity, following this first human speaking, points toward the animals and calls them by name, in a paradigmatic dispersal of language. But the pointing is *tentative*, awaiting and depending upon the response that will let us know if we have named rightly, the response that is the very meaning of right naming. The finger beckons as much as it indicates. In Genesis, the divine itself acknowledges the rightness of the call as it emerges into this relation.

Relation in words will, at some point, probably mean conversation. The first conversation in Genesis, the first *exchange* of words, is in the passage so indignantly noted by Dante, in which the woman speaks to the serpent. When she tells the serpent that she has been warned regarding the tree in the middle of the garden, he assures her that she can eat from it and will not find it fatal—an assurance, though tradition has tended to overlook the matter, that is in fact true.[38] (Thus it is that in some Gnostic traditions the serpent takes on the more positive and traditional valence of wisdom.[39]) After some discussion, the woman eats, and in her pleasure she persuades the man to do likewise (3:6).

It is seldom a good idea to defy a creator's direct orders, and most of the consequences that ensue are quite undesirable, including a dialogue between the humans and God, full of lying and accusation (3:9–13). This is followed by stern words in which punishment is meted out, both to the people and to the serpent, indeed to all future humanity and serpent-kind (3:14–19).[40] The people and the serpent are ousted from the garden, and nothing is ever the same.

Nothing, including words. After the human and serpentine condemnation and expulsion from peaceable harmony and immortality, interspecies communication will pretty much fall apart. This disintegration will be followed more explicitly by a disintegration we have already noted in considering the possibility of translation. Human communication falls apart in the stories of Noah's sons, divided "every one after his tongue" (Gen. 10:5; cf. 10:20 and 10:31), and, as we've seen, of Babel, in which human hubris is countered by division: when humans no longer speak the same language, they cannot cooperate on threateningly great projects such as building a tower to heaven (Gen. 11:1–9).[41] The perfection of prelapsarian speech is lost.[42] In looking at translation, we have already considered how that perfection might work in terms of words' physicality. But what does perfection mean when this first man talks to the animals, in the midst of the stories of creation?

With or without the presumption of rational dominance, linguists, semioticians, poets, and theologians have long turned to Genesis in their dreams of utterly perfect and transparent communication.[43] The episode of naming seems to bear this perfection; the names that Adam calls are so rightly the names of the animals that God accepts them without hesitation (perhaps the animals do as well, responding as they are called?). This is the language that falls apart after the Fall itself. But what was the nature of its holding together, when time was good? Could that goodness be anything other than the perfection of reason and the dominance it confers? (Are we finally going to answer that question about language's redemption?)

To review quickly: God speaks: to the formless and abyssal, to the animals, to the humans, to the multiplicity of itself. The world, the animals, the humans, and the self of God respond, in their widely varied fashions. The man speaks: to the animals, to the woman, to God. The woman speaks: to the serpent, to the man, to God. The serpent speaks to the woman, generating millennia of argument.

So what are we to make of all these stories, in all their diversity? The first man speaks, and those words *name*, and so call out rather than (simply) designate. But the call is not exegetically emphasized; interpretation has generally held that it is man's superiority, not connection, that is demonstrated in speaking: over woman, over animals, over angels. If we read the story of the animals as if the story itself really mattered, though, and mattered in the context of a responsive shaping breath that creates the world, perhaps we might let go a bit of the smugness even while we retain the astonished joy.

Was there a language in which the animals also spoke? Commentators have been somewhat invested in assuring us that whatever the serpent is up to here (and whoever or whatever speaks through him), the animals, generally, are speechless. Exceptions are few. There are some speaking animals in the Apocryphal Acts, and there is the charming, if noncanonical, tradition of talking animals at the Christian nativity, but canonically, the good animals are quiet, or at any rate without words.[44] Some mischievous composers have given them a musical vocabulary, as in Saint-Saëns's *The Carnival of the Animals* or Prokofiev's *Peter and the Wolf*, beloved works that, like the nativity animals, appeal through the ear to the spirits of children as well as to the minds of adults, offering us, perhaps, an especially pleased version of intersemiosis: the animals speak music. But the narrator retains a human voice.

Speaking-With: The Call of the World

> Yusef said that language comes between us and things, and that as soon as we had NAMES for what we saw, we experienced a certain degree of removal from the world. Thus, in Eden, appeared the serpent of divisive consciousness; if we could remove ourselves from kinship through the agency of language, then we could wreak havoc upon the world without feeling that we harmed ourselves.
>
> I said that the more we can name what we're seeing, the more language we have for it, the less likely we are to destroy it. . . .
>
> We're both right.
>
> MARK DOTY, *The Art of Description: World into Word*, describing a conversation with Yusef Komunyakaa

Even in the service of reading the creation stories for the possibility of speaking and song, I am not quite prepared to claim that the animals are word makers, any more than I would claim this of the world formed of matter and breath. Of course, there is a greater ambiguity about the issue, and greater proximity to language, in the animals' case, as their many modes of communication certainly do include sounds, even sounds intelligible to humans.[45] But let us look at an equally intriguing possibility, not one of animals making words, but one of a meaningful, significant appearance, a movement that is also a phrasing—like that of grammar or music, a speaking with the world in which humans are included.

I draw this possibility from Bailly. On the notion of meaningful animal phrasings, he quotes Maurice Merleau-Ponty:

> "A field of space-time has been opened: there is the beast there," [Merleau-Ponty] writes, and the whole animal realm is for him like the nonclosed sum of those fields of singularity, or like a grammar—in other words, a nonfinite possibility of phrasings. . . . Merleau-Ponty can say that "the form of the animal is not the manifestation of a finality, but rather of an existential value of manifestation, of presentation," that is, an appearance to be understood entirely as a language.[46]

For the animals, Bailly argues, that appearance is not other than reality or truth. Oddly to the human mind, there is no representation superadded to animal presence, unless that representation is ours—unless *we* make images, and words. But even before they are represented, before the word becomes a sign used for designation, the animal world is a space for this curious presentation. The animals in their own spaces are

> profoundly inscribed in the writing of their lives and in their material surroundings. . . . The expanse that is present, that responds "present," as it can do by leaving the scene, and by taking its leave, as it can do in Africa, with something tense and nonchalant at the same time, a sort of perfect harmony in the wake of a giraffe ambling along and living before our eyes in the other world of the film that it is making in slow motion. . . .
>
> The giraffe, for example, but also all the others, and each one in a unique film developed differently every day, a film whose scenario . . . has in any case no need for us in order to write itself.[47]

There is no separate representation here, no language animals have *about* what appears, what they are, what they do. Their film is not something they are thinking up and preserving for a later view. No book *about* the world, no song *about* creation: only the world in which animal tracks and motions, like our own, inscribe what is not quite a text, yet not quite other than textual; vibrate with divine breath; the book and the song and the speaking that *there is*, that is both matter and life. Theirs is *an appearance to be understood entirely as a language*. When in Genesis the animals appear before the man and he calls them by name, he exhibits his understanding of the appearance-language in the form of words, words that God likewise understands: he responds to the appearance understood as a language with words understood as names. He and the animals are matter with the breath of life, immersed in the same breath-blown world. "[T]heir form, like our own, is finite. . . . What surrounds it, welcomes it, threatens it, is infinite."[48] Their appearance in what is (like) a language, like our own emergence in(to) words, can never be narrowed down to those in it, but must consider the space as well, a space mutually made with those who move there.

Animals and humans share the breath of life, the divine breath that blows the world into habitable form. Animal materiality and responsivity mold that breath into a different, not a lesser, mode of living than our own. These modes, though, are harmoniously enfolded. In the very unfolding of their present and presence, they enact their own "texts," as if the division we must make between presentation and representation did not exist. As if, that is, animal language were a correspondence so pure that the very idea, the very distance necessary for one thing to correspond to (or with) another, ceased to be. As if *theirs* were the perfect language, the primal identity that Adam voiced, or echoed in vocalizing, when he first called them all by name, so rightly that the call belonged immediately to each of them—as if God saw, and heard, that this, too, was good. With the placement of the animals in the world, four different modes of meaning interact harmoniously: those of God, matter, human, animal. The goodness of language has to belong to, has to be breathed and sung by, all of them. Only the postlapsarian world brings dissonance and incomprehension. Language approaches perfection not in domination, but in harmony: the song of the world mirrors divine delight.

Miller raises the possibility of reading Adam among the animals, in this Edenic perfection, as something other than a force of domination.

> Does [Adam], like animals, exist in the world "like water in water," as Georges Bataille suggested? That is, is Adam's intimacy with the world so profound that there is a natural continuity between the human and the animal? As Bataille . . . remarked, "the animal opens before me a depth that attracts me and is familiar to me. In a sense, I know this depth: it is my own."[49]

On such an Orphic reading, language is made not to dominate, but to call and to harmonize, from the beginning in which matter and breath are given to one another. Adam is brought those animals not to show who is in charge, but because it is not good for him to be alone. In language, our own finite form reaches beyond itself. If there is a right name for each animal in the story, it cannot belong solely to humans. It must be right for the animals, too, and for God, who hears and acknowledges it; it must move rightly in the world of plants and waters and land. It must somehow belong to, somehow harmonize with, the animal phrasing; it must in sound be resonant with what appears, must ripple within it.

As I have noted, we should be careful not simply to presume that the first and second stories of creation in Genesis can be read as wholly compatible. There are respects, not least with regard to gender and to ecology, in which they are simply too different. We have seen with Miller the alarming possibilities of one such conflation, that of reading naming together with domination. But if we read in each story that of which it speaks in most detail—in the first, the speaking creation of the world that will be inhabited by the humans who come last in it; in the second, the creation and speaking-with of those humans in the world created around them—then a divine carnality of meaning does keep emerging as a way to play with the text. This is not simply a creation *by* voice, however allegorical its form. Creation *becomes* voice, the interaction of matter and breath. The world's movements continue the speaking, or even the song. And it is breath, too, that moves in, and moves, all animals (humans too), breath by which we live—but by which and as which we can only live as material. Humans are peculiar: we speak; we form breath into sound to make meaning. But other animals also mean, and they mean because they, too, form and phrase matter as they live—as they draw and release "the breath of life."

Despite the tendency to rejoice in human dominance and "natural" superiority, the hagiographic and ascetic traditions, Miller notes, sometimes give us richer options for understanding human–animal interaction. She describes one story in particular:

> The *Historia monachorum in Aegypto* tells the story of the holy anchorite Theon, who had practiced silence for thirty years. "One could see him with the face of an angel giving joy to his visitors by his gaze and abounding with much grace." "They say he used to go out of his cell at night and keep company with wild animals, giving them to drink from the water that he had. Certainly one could see the track of antelope and wild asses and gazelles and other animals near his hermitage. These creatures delighted him always." This was possibly a Christomimetic scenario, for it was when Christ was in the wilderness with wild beasts that angels ministered to him (Mk. 1:13). But perhaps . . . like Adam, Theon existed with the animals in the world like water in water, in an intimacy so profound that the animal and the angel were one.[50]

In such an intimacy, the joyful cry of "*El!*" and the calling of names to the animals are equally instances of perfect speech. Neither call leads to oneness nor even to partnership; the man, like the animals, will need another of his own species (though this pairing will not necessarily turn out all that well, and perhaps Adam, leaving Paradise, considers that he should have taken the dog, or Eve the helpful serpent). But they are harmonious in the world not yet out of tune with itself. A perfect language breathes in harmony with matter, with flesh and its meanings.

We humans still understand ourselves in relation to animal and divinity both, but we too often think of these relations in terms of differentiation rather than harmony, or in terms of hierarchy, where the classic view has the human halfway from god (or angel) to animal. More recently, we may reject the divine altogether to affirm our animal natures. But if the human is to live with the animal, and call to the divine, and live in the world like water in water, then the primally perfect humanity must be not suspended between, but alive among and drawn toward the divine and the animal too, without insisting upon their separation. Language must be as much polyphonic song as useful tool. And perhaps, in this world, the human not only exists, but speaks, like an animal and an angel: with a speech as world-suited as the animals to whom it calls, a speech as able to call the divine as the angels are, because that calling is in the very matter of the world, and because suitability to the world and to God are not so disharmonious after all. If this is speech without sin, it is also speech without lying—not because it tells the truth, but because, in the movement of its companionable evocation, truth status is not a relevant category.[51] And it is a speaking, and a meaning, wholly of the flesh—human, animal, world—all breathed through with divinity no longer separable from it. We call from body to body, breath to breath; to each other, to animals, to divinity, to the world.

Again, I have no wish to conflate animal inscription with human speaking, nor, as one who has been in love with language since before my first memories, to claim that there is nothing special about the latter. But, like others in love with words, I cannot help thinking of a perfect language. And when I look where others have looked, what I see is not perfect human control of words ("the question . . . [of] who is to be master, that's all"[52]) nor control of animals and the natural world either made or exhibited through words, but the sense of language transfigured, even when written, to the motility of speaking; of a body that breathes song, of divine animality, of continuous carnal creation; the breath of each material, animal, human body speaking its part in making the meaning of the world.

CHAPTER 6

The Meaning in the Music

The metaphysical prejudice according to which the spirit is necessarily aphonic, and all the more pure as it does not manifest itself, has, happily, never been enough to cause the human voice to fall silent.

—JEAN-LOUIS CHRÉTIEN, "The Wounded Word"

The preceding chapters might (broadly) be construed as philosophical theology. Modern and contemporary practitioners of both disciplines have tended not only to hear meaning aphonically, but to view themselves as ultimate arbiters of truth and meaning. Reemphasizing voice, returning sound to sense, might help us to undercut this particular arbitration.

Philosophy hears toward understanding—and is confident that it can, in fact, comprehend, perhaps more thoroughly than the speaker herself.[1] Nancy asks, at the beginning of his book *Listening*, "Is listening something of which philosophy is capable? Or . . . hasn't philosophy . . . substituted for listening, something else that might be more on the order of *understanding*?"[2] Perhaps it is even the case that a philosopher "cannot listen, or . . . , more precisely, neutralizes listening within himself, so that he can philosophize."[3] This is not an understanding that catches in the throat. As Cavarero argues, philosophy has long attempted to make meaning into something pure, distinct from voice, and voice, in turn, into nonrational and sometimes dangerous sound. This helps with the neutralization of voice, and lets us imagine concepts in abstract purity.

If we do not want to neutralize listening, then we have to allow our authors their animation, and listen not only to their ideas, but to their very voices. Thinking of voice and word (or, more exactly, of Voice and Word), Augustine beseeches his audience to *listen*, to hear a mystery. "In your patience, quiet eagerness, and attentive silence provide me with the chance to say, with the Lord's help, what he grants me to say; then your attention will undoubtedly profit you, and I shall be well paid for the pains I take in suggesting to your ears and minds something of the great mystery involved."[4] Silence here is an active and eager stance, not a wandering away, and it enables the voice to "suggest" to the ear as well as to the mind. Mind and ear, of course, are no more distinct than the single voice entering into them both.

Philosophy, all the more since it left ancient expansiveness and became reduced to a discipline, hasn't quite gotten over the notion that voice is irrelevant, that it does not matter who is speaking, so long as the speaker is sure of the universality of the truths he proclaims in his robust baritone.[5] Nothing to hear here, an undercurrent murmurs, only ideas to understand, all spoken in the same and therefore irrelevant voice. As we have already noted, voices from many margins have long encroached on this ideal, but they have only occasionally focused on sound. It turns out that theology, despite its not dissimilar masculine and antisensuous history, might help us to do that. Theology may actually listen better to voices because it is better attuned to silence. (Neither, of course, is true of deep dogmatism, but in this theology this is perhaps no worse than most fields of study.) And so now we turn explicitly not just to theological issues, such as those of creation, but to the issue of theology in its relation to philosophy, and the ways in which both can listen and speak.

Despite the dialogical nature of much early philosophy, thinkers have long valorized "a videocentric order of pure signifieds," one that may be contemplated in silence.[6] This contemplative silence, though, is a mere auditory absence, not the active attunement to voice for which Augustine hopes. We have undervalued silence as much as we have sound; we have undervalued the rhythm of their interplay. Socrates's death-bed considerations notwithstanding, philosophy has tried its best to keep out the music.

Plato warns us explicitly of the risks of musicality, even as he has Socrates revalue it. Most famously, in the *Republic*, he condemns poetry and the "weak" musical modes alike; they invite us to emotional excess, risk making us fluffy and feminine. Yet the *Republic*, too, is more complex than its reception. The tripartite, philosopher-ruled city described in the longer portion of the dialogue gets most of our attention. Yet Socrates in conversation with Adeimantus first creates an ideal city, where the well-balanced inhabitants "will serve noble cakes and loaves on some arrangement of reeds or clean leaves, and, reclined on rustic beds strewn with bryony and myrtle, they will feast with their children, drinking of their wine thereto, garlanded and singing hymns to the gods in pleasant fellowship" (372b). This is the healthy state, and the singing is good.

But the state does not stay in good health; excesses creep in and spill over. When Socrates converses with Glaucon about the "fevered state," they seem far more mistrustful of music. "Dirges and lamentations in words" having been briskly eliminated from this Republic, "dirgelike modes of music" must follow. These "are useless even to women who are to make the best of themselves, let alone to men." Similarly unmasculine are "the soft and convivial modes," also called "lax," which are useless to warriors especially. Despite admitting some ignorance regarding musical modes, Glaucon and Socrates nonetheless urge that in the Republic, rulers should "Leave us these two modes—the enforced and the voluntary—that will best imitate the utterances of men failing or succeeding, the temperate, the brave—leave us these."[7]

No soft words, no floppy emotional modes. We must be particular about our instrumentation, too. Lyres are acceptable. Flutes are not: "We are not innovating, my friend, in preferring Apollo and the instruments of Apollo to Marsyas and his instruments."[8] Socrates may resemble Marsyas and play his own voice like a flute, but the lyre—the very paradigm of music as *ratio*, with the tones of its strings determined by their mathematical proportion—is a more properly reasonable instrument. The dialogue goes on to determine proper harmonies (not too complex) and rhythms (orderly and brave).[9] Tempo is relevant, though Socrates is fuzzy on the details, which he breezily postpones for the consideration of an expert.[10] His very vagueness—from Socrates, who constantly and irritatingly demands more precision—must make us suspicious. The man is up to something.

Music is dangerous enough to require tight governmental control in every aspect—but only when things have gone wrong anyway, when the state is not in a state of health. When music goes bad, it is only along with the rest of the human world. All of this control is necessary only because even here music itself is necessary; it is what educates and forms the character of the guardians themselves, "imparting by the melody a certain harmony of spirit that is not science, and by the rhythm measure and grace."[11] The fears that music provokes are comic in their masculine stereotyping—we must not be soft, slow, or lax in our characters, but always firm and in control. Music is not eliminated in favor of reason, but it must be made to serve reason, to show only its rational side, and be kept away from the femininity and excess to which it seems suspiciously prone. Unless, of course, we were meant to be making music all along, seducing like flutes; unless our city is really ideal, filled with hymns of joy.

In the *Cratylus*, too, as Laura Odello points out, "The timbre and the voice—that is to say, the sonority—are subordinated to the logical ideality of things; the Platonic gesture is as obvious as it is decisive for philosophy." Reading the *Cratylus*, a dialogue that puzzles over names and the ways in which they might designate, imitate, or mean, Odello adds, "The philosopher does not want to know anything about listening: hearing is of no use to the philosopher because the end as well as the beginning of all philosophizing resides in the intellectual understanding: sonorities are superfluous, secondary, unnecessary for the silent vision of the *logos*, of the idea, of the ideal signified, which alone serves to grasp the truth."[12]

Yet music, she convincingly argues, returns, even *as silence(d)*. The philosophers' efforts to neutralize the voice fail; the very fact that voice is repressed alters what was never purely logical. Odello wonders if Socrates's deathbed worries that he should have made music represent "a return of the repressed, that is to say, of the music Plato strived to keep quiet: that excessive music which the platonic text seeks to reduce to silence, that music which lends itself to all and any transport, to all and any emotion, to anything which exceeds the *logos* and its ideal present." Perhaps not so repressed, either, but subtly interwoven; Socrates, at least, has a fine sense of irony. Socrates's *daimon* suspects what the text knows: Plato may have his characters do their best to make music the vehicle of reason, but music's tendency to passion and transport is essential to the transformative possibilities by which Socrates and his companions so strongly hope to make men rational. "It is no longer music that becomes philosophical; it is philosophy that turns into music: excessive and immoderate like music, philosophy here exposes itself to its own excess, the excess of an uncertain, lacking, or impertinent speech."[13] Every philosophical voice becomes like that of Hildegard's singers, full and even overfull of joyful lack. Unfortunately, philosophy, desiring to avoid desire, is out of harmony with itself, reasonably eliminating the excesses that made Socrates's voice so enduringly enticing, embracing the rigidity of the Republic in its disease.

Mladen Dolar, too, writes of voice as excessive, of "the voice in excess of speech and meaning, the voice as an excess."[14] Speaking is about signification, he says, but "[s]inging . . . turns the tables on the signifier; it reverses the hierarchy—let the voice take the upper hand, let the voice be the bearer of what cannot be expressed by words. . . . The voice appears as the surplus-meaning."[15]

Nevertheless, it means. Dolar may insist that music is insignificant; even Nancy may hear music in meaning more readily than meaning in music. But Kramer muses, "So what would happen, I wondered, if instead of treating the musical remainder as either an ineffable je ne sais quoi or as a negative principle, an abstract curb on articulate meaning, we tried to regard it as a positive phenomenon, a concrete involvement with the problem of meaning? The remainder in that case would not be what disqualifies me from speaking about music or from finding new contexts in which the music becomes meaningful."[16]

Though Kramer's interest, in the promise of meaning not yet given, differs slightly from mine here, I share his intuition that remainder is quite other than otherness altogether. In fact, a surplus of sayable meaning is not far from theological apophasis, meaning that can only be said-toward, never caught within words—but which needs words to try to say the unsaying. Can song, or the musicality of voice, be reincorporated into meaningfulness itself, or must the two, even found together in sung words, remain at odds?

For that matter, must they even remain distinct elements? Cavarero reminds us that the voice that Socrates hears, and knows to obey, is a *voice*, after all, and not an abstraction: "This is not an interior voice, nor is it a voice of the soul. It is the voice of the *daimon*, a divine, external, and imperative voice that neither develops arguments nor proceeds in a dialectical mode but rather commands. The fact that it is only audible to Socrates does not signal its general muteness, but rather signals the singular uniqueness that is part of the Greek meaning of *daimon*."[17]

What the daimon has to say tells us something of voicing, too. One of Plato's best-known instances of daimonic intervention occurs in *Phaedrus*, where, as we've seen, Socrates realizes that he has badly erred in dismissing the madness of love—and of poetry. Perhaps he has erred in beginning the dialogue, as he does, by claiming a fear of music. Socrates and Phaedrus engage in philosophical discussion at noon rather than napping under the trees, because if they were to nap, Socrates warns, they would risk falling under the spell of the cicadas' hum. Why would this matter? Because the cicadas are spies for the Muses, and the Muses will mock the nappers. But there is more: the cicadas, Socrates says, were once men. They were *too susceptible to music*, and let themselves be distracted by it from all other things, ultimately leading to their deaths (as men). Music was dangerous to them; their music poses a lesser but real danger to Socrates and Phaedrus. When

Socrates realizes that he has been wrong, when the *daimon* sternly reminds him to embrace the madness of poetry, the Muses and the cicadas alike are vindicated: listen, says the *daimon*, to the music, too. Even if listening is dangerous.

Risking the Fluffiness of Listening

pan tolmaton: all is to be dared

SAPPHO, translated by Anne Carson, in *Decreation*

Do we dare, now, to listen to the music in meaning, or is sound still too much a distraction, an excess to be expelled and not incorporated? Nancy is among those who want us to listen; he hopes, he says, "to *prick up the philosophical ear*: to tug at the philosopher's ear in order to draw it toward . . . accent, tone, timbre, resonance and sound."[18] The philosopher is thus drawn from analytical straightforwardness into Ariadne's labyrinthine web: hers, according to legends taken up and transformed by Friedrich Nietzsche, are the ears that hear even the things that are whispered in secret.[19] Nancy suggests that there is a "trembling discrepancy and dissymmetry"[20] between the two sides of the sense of the heard—between the sound and the truth. In this trembling, voice vibrates.

Philosophical rigor often entails a presumption that no other mode counts—that there is no poetic rigor, for instance, nor any other that we might see as proper to listening. In fact, it is sometimes a hallmark of philosophy that one's own confident position is best demonstrated by showing up the idiocy of others. Counterdemonstration is seldom useful—I once gave a talk on faith as other than propositional belief, only to have a student dismiss the arguments I drew from Augustine, Pseudo-Dionysius, and even Thomas Aquinas as "that fluffy stuff." Hearing toward understanding can impede understanding when it seeks not to reposition the listener, who might end up all fluffy or feminine or dwelling in mystery, but to find points of attack. Granted, most philosophers become a little better, and subtler, at doing so than this student was, but disciplinarily speaking, he was on the right track. He was able to resist, and specifically to resist music: the excessive, the feminine, the mobile, which might move him from the sturdy firmness of his position.

Femininity and fluff may be the lay senses of elusion and apophasis—or of music, as those ancient worries about weak modality return, stripped of their complex undertones. "Suppose truth is a woman?" says Nietzsche, a concept alarming (he hopes) to many of his contemporaries.[21] Like truth, voice has long been gendered, but not in straightforward ways. In the *Problems*, a text attributed, though likely misattributed, to Aristotle, we learn that women's voices are "shriller and smaller" than men's, because their vocal pipes are smaller, because women's throats are colder than those of men (their heat is weak). The voices of "young and diseased men" may also be shrill and small.[22] In "*The secrets of nature relating to physiognomy*," we learn that "A great and full voice in either sex shows them to be of a great spirit, confident, proud and willful"—but, of course, such voices are little found in women, as we've just read. In fact, "A full and yet mild voice, and pleasing to the hearer, shows the person to be of a quiet and peaceable disposition (which is a great virtue and rare to be found in a woman)."[23] Women's voices can show qualities as good as those of men—but mostly they don't; they are a little less feminine where they do. Women may be inferior for Aristotle or for this pseudo-Aristotle, but for Platonism it is the voice itself that is dangerous (though not every danger is the same thing as bad). Of course, the voices here are not a little problematized by probably not being Aristotle's, and by ignoring the complexity of Plato. The pseudonym, too, is dangerous, particularly where it appropriates a known name; it may speak in a voice that is not quite so much that of the name as it claims.

And Plato, though he writes under his own name (or by the name by which he was called), writes, nevertheless, in dozens of voices *except* his own. We do not learn from Plato how Socrates sounds; that is, whether his voice is high pitched or low, raspy or smooth—but we hear him endlessly, in his own voice or that of characters he creates (the *Symposium*'s Diotima, or the love-hating rhetorician of his first speech in *Phaedrus*, multiplying layer upon layer of remove from the name of the voice). He may generate, like Marsyas, seductive sounds. We sense, from the eagerness of so many to listen, that his voice is not matched to his famously homely appearance. But his *manly* emphasis, the one received down the centuries in the silence of his voice, remains firmly upon the truth, and this truth is no woman.

But might voice be? The association of femininity and voice shifts over the centuries, perhaps reflecting a desire to mitigate the threat posed by the power of both. Cavarero recounts, particularly, the fascinating trajectory of the story of the Sirens. In the *Odyssey*, she points out, the Sirens are to the eye true monsters, frightening and hideous; only their singing is attractive, and to a deadly extent. (Socratic monsters, perhaps: ugly to see, beautiful to hear?) Part of the attraction, however, is that with their beautiful voices they also tell beautiful, epic stories: "For Homer . . . the Sirens do not at all represent a presemantic vocality. Rather, they sing and narrate; or they sing narrating. The irresistible charm of the song is inextricably linked to the charm of the tale. . . . He is proud to trace the source of epic narration back to an omniscient female figure; the poet inherits from their song his own power to enchant."[24] The Sirens are frightening not only because they are ugly, but because they are all-knowing.[25] But gradually, as the story is retold,

> most Sirens sing, but they no longer narrate. Nor do they know all like their ancient mothers. They become sinuous, fishlike creatures—something that the Homeric monsters never were—who seduce men not only through their song, but also by their beauty. The charm of the voice, rendered even more disturbing by the absence of speech, still calls men to a pleasurable (and often explicitly erotic) death. . . . There is a feminine voice that seduces and kills, and that has no words.[26]

The omniscient monsters who command all aspects of language, its sound and song as well as its stories, become aquatic feminine beauties, lovely to look at and to hear, but without meaning. The masculine realm of meaningfulness is no longer threatened; women's only danger is that they are pretty. As women are reduced, so, too, is voice, with which they are linked—yet the restructuring of the myth cannot quite undo the sense of danger. And perhaps that danger, though Cavarero does not pursue the argument this way, might be that the sound itself sneaks into the meaning; when it is taken away, so too are the tales. The Sirens, all-knowing, knew what they were about, and Homer, epic poet, knew it too. And so, too, humming softly his final hymn to Apollo, did Socrates the philosopher.

Once the Sirens begin to sing nonsense, beauty and femininity uncoupled from significance remain dangerous, but they no longer endanger signification. In some traditions, they instead come to endanger those who sing, as if to undo the feminizing risk altogether: the carriers of that risk will (conveniently) end themselves. Stanley Cavell writes of his early fascination with Catherine Clément's *Opera, or the Undoing of Women*, in which "opera is about the death of women, and about the singing of women, and can be seen to be about the fact that women die because they sing."[27] Maybe this exaggerated feminine voice is too great a threat to masculine reason? Voices too near to song are silenced by the propriety of rational discourse.

There is reason to associate that voice with mystery, too. Wayne Koestenbaum remarks in *The Queen's Throat*, "One major reason voice has been marked as feminine is that the organs of its production are hidden from view."[28] This hiddenness allows both change and deception, by which what seems a simple dichotomy of feminine voice, masculine language,[29] turns out to be nothing of the sort: "[T]he singing throat is feminine, . . . it tends to wander and break, and . . . it has the mercurial ability to avoid gender."[30] Not only does Koestenbaum identify "hopelessly" with Tosca,[31] he is astonished by the lyric tenor of the Count in *The Barber of Seville*: "he wakes in me (and in other listeners?) an optimism: I didn't know men could sound like this, I didn't know masculinity could reveal itself."[32] Hiddenness and revelation, masculine and feminine, the seductive enticement of clear reason, all weave together in the singing voice. The singer's voice, as Michael Halliwell points out, "through individual vocal characteristics and perhaps a particular and recognizable vocal style, can suggest another layer of meaning or at least significance in the vocal performance, a layer in addition to that emerging from the sung text, orchestral music and mise-en-scène."[33] It is not just the fact of being voiced that adds to and alters meaning; it is *this* voice, singing. But however we try to ignore it, it is this voice, speaking, too.

The pure voice "possesses a dangerous attractive force," says Dolar, but "in itself it is empty and frivolous. The dichotomy of voice and logos is already in place."[34] Once they are fully dichotomized, ordering in a hierarchy becomes quite a bit easier. The Council of Trent, which was pretty good at hierarchizing, demanded intelligibility of the voice in speech or song: the *meaning*, the letter, is foremost.[35] Beauty is allowed only in meaning's service. This works best, of course, if the meaning is clear and not subject to question, if no contrary voicing passes through the throats of the devout and misdirects their desires. Where philosophy has suffered from letting the agonic become antagonistic, theology has sometimes cut off wonder by disallowing contrary perspective at all. The two need one another, to be sure; but both, a little desperately, need music.

Just as philosophy tries to understand meaning without listening to voices, theology works with ecclesial authority to keep the voices of the faithful speaking properly: speaking truth, and voicing, upon demand, their rejection of possible heresy. Musically, too, as Koestenbaum notes, "The throat, not the ears, receives the diva: the throat, organ from which 'I' speak."[36] The danger of hearing is that of speaking: we must either refuse to allow heresy to be spoken, or cut down contrary argument so decisively that it is silenced. The worry might be either that falsehoods (or demons) speak through us, or that we will become so trapped in the luxury of resonance that we forget the austere disciplines of meaning. Koestenbaum, however, suggests that sometimes opera can evade the trap set for intellectual disciplines: "which is primary, words or music? The listener must choose. And Strauss invites us to refuse the choice, to say, queerly, 'I choose ambiguity.'"[37] In Koestenbaum's terms, then, I might suggest that we listen a bit queerly to the voices speaking theories, speaking philosophically and theologically; then, too, that we let unfamiliar voices resound sometimes in our throats as in our ears, to see if they ring true, if our bodies can rightly speak them.

Where song is reintroduced to meaningful sense, language even now may read to us as feminine, or as queerly male. Think of some earlier examples: of Baldwin openly gay in his exile; of Joyce and Beckett, scarcely models of macho masculinity; of O'Connor, so seemingly asexual as to provoke speculation to this day. Vivid voice is unsettling—gratifyingly so, to some; worrisomely so, to others. The risk of fluff is at hand. What Hélène Cixous calls "l'ecriture feminine," feminine writing, "flows freely according to laws of resonance that constitute its meaning, and yet precisely because of this, it depends on a musical song that is its source."[38] Cixous identifies the source with the mother, but even that maternal voice resonates, not merely in a series of voices, but in a sea of meaningful sound, as if the song of the Sirens under the water still held far more *semantike* than a simple cry.[39] In Cixous's work, as Cavarero writes, we find "the proliferation of a sense that does not coincide with the phallogocentric dominion of the signified, but rather flows from the movement that combines words according to the laws of rhythm, echo, and resonance. The sound of one term calls another; the placement or displacement of a letter produces different names and generates neologisms." Its logic is inextricable from its sound, its reason from its music.[40]

As it listens for denotation, philosophy is distractedly drawn by the Siren of voice, and it worries about the possibility of moving outside the analytically rational. Because the rigor of Augustine or Dionysius is poetic as well as logical, it gives to the philosopher's ear things that it is unprepared to hear. Does theology listen better to that sensual side of speaking, the sternness after Trent (and the Reformation) notwithstanding? Theology is not music, and we know that it readily stalls in dogmatism—but there are reasons to suspect that it *has* to hear toward something other than the confidence of comprehension. It lives at a strange linguistic edge, and knows that it doesn't quite know what it is talking about. We logue away, without the illusion that we can thus define theos. To know that something in speaking eludes the words and the speaker alike is a step toward hearing voices.

Listening for Truth at the Edge of Sense

Questions are always a little more trustworthy than answers.

MARK DOTY, *The Art of Description*

The question does not come before there is a quotation.

GERTRUDE STEIN, *Tender Buttons*

I tell my first-year philosophy students (just before I make them start reading aloud) that philosophers are essentially sophisticated four-year-olds, people who like to keep asking *why*. But philosophy asks why in order to understand the answers, and stops at the edge of the incomprehensible. (Importantly, that *there is* the incomprehensible may nonetheless be acknowledged.) We have cut off the top step of Diotima's ladder of eros, the step on which we love incomprehensible beauty itself, and stopped at the level of loving wisdom.[41] To persist in asking once one hits the limits of language and understanding, right at the border of sense, trying to face down the fear of the nonsensical abyss and the silent spaces right before us—that seems to be something theology does a bit better. For that, one must listen, and be willing not to know. (Poetry does this awfully well, too.) And one must listen to what one *cannot* know, not only to the silence in language, but to sound, which gives to us something other than comprehension, something more physical. That something, the poetic voice, speaks with the resonance of premodern philosophy, before Plato and Platonism were simplified into the love of reason, before devocalization was quite *such* a success.

When we attend to speaking, even in reading, we must recognize the places that it stops and breaks. We recognize that silence separates meaning from a pure rush of sound, and that what is most meaningful may also be most elusive. We attend to music as something other than a topic, and to the poetics of language even when it plods.

The gaps in speaking and in meaning provide an avid philosopher with places to interrupt, even to dismantle an argument. Attentive hearing without grasping, without immediately seeking a firm control of the material, requires instead a kind of hospitality, a giving of space to speaking.[42] Perhaps, for example, those gaps are not errors, but paradoxes, pulls of tension that sustain our delight.[43] Perhaps they are wounds: to be healed or comforted, or to be astonishingly celebrated, as the gap in Christ's side, the swords through Mary's heart. Maybe they are gaps in the memory, pulling us inexplicably back. Maybe they are the memories of gaps: scars left on the glorified, or the mimesis of the stigmata. Maybe they are invitations: you may enter here; or: this is a conversational space. Maybe they are the spaces through which we lose ourselves. Maybe they are spots where the smoothness of time and space unfurling has given way to the disruptive jolt of enchantment or terror. Maybe they are those spaces in which language resonates, giving meaning to voice.

The willingness to dwell in those strange discursive places where theology happens requires a willingness to hear differently, to accept that language is doing something (rather than nothing) even as it struggles with its falls into silence. Into silence, and also into sound: wondering about saying requires attending to those who say, including the very strange (such as gods who somehow make by speaking) and the abjectly marginalized (such as criminals nailed up to die by suffocation); to the water in water movements of other animals; to the world itself, which might sign or sing or cry out; to citation as it edges into recitation as that in turn edges into liturgy, with its deliberately contagious quoting. If there is faith in theology, it is faith that we are not speaking *mere* nonsense, faith that there is something here worth listening to. That something is a very abstract something most of the time. But it is a very concrete something, too. It resounds. There is more to the voice than the letter.

Language must denote, of course, and we ought to be able to enjoy that—ideas can also proceed by pleasured skips. But at its most abstract and its most concrete, in apophatic ellipsis and vibratory voice, speech includes what eludes referential meaning but is nonetheless essential to it. Once we consider listening to language, in its stops and starts and runs and hesitations, we can also begin to think of listening to what else in it eludes strict denotation: we may listen to its music.

Attentiveness to the music of voice did not end when the Sirens became visually beautiful. We all know that Augustine heard, if not voices, at least a single voice: a child's, of indeterminate gender, directing him to a text, at an indeterminate passage. Take up and read, said the voice, and he did, and everything was different after that.[44]

And here another puzzle emerges, just because we do not know whose voice has called—nor whose voice speaks, exactly, when Augustine is converted by the Pauline words that he reads, that he puts on as his own, as the voice of the diva fills the opera queen's throat and makes him over. Have we been wrong all along to insist that it matters who is speaking, to insist on the materiality of the voice, when the *persona* that speaks through seems so capable of multiple embodiments?

At this late point in the text, the question is clearly rhetorical, but not altogether so. We have noted already that voice is acquired, formed in its accents and structures; it is artifice, especially when it is most marked in song—but artifice makes us, too. In that artifice we also see some of the complexity in the truth of voices. The opera diva is expected to live at an operatic scale: "Since Oscar Wilde, [the] confusion between mask and truth has been a cornerstone of gay culture," writes Koestenbaum.[45] This confusion, like the femininity of the voice, comes with a sense of danger: "The singer's face is called a mask, as if a voice were never capable of telling the truth."[46] The operatic voice speaks from a mask, but not to reveal the truth that the face conceals; rather, it speaks as a masked voice, a persona.

We might worry that the very notion of truth is undone here, not in a promising interpretive multiplicity but in a relativistic parody of the postmodern, where anything goes as well as anything else, and we are all just imitating voices not our own. But we might also consider that there are options other than this dichotomy of truth and falsehood; that notes likewise ring true—indeed, that truth is something that rings. "Whatever is profound loves masks," says Nietzsche, giving the mask not only to truth but to depth.[47] We might make use of masks or personae in words—of anonymity or pseudonym, or, in the premodern fashion, of a better-known name to make the voice audible. To speak from behind a mask, or in a new voice, might be not to lie about ourselves, but to expand the range of the truths that are possible to us. Koestenbaum writes that Søren Kierkegaard uses his *Either/Or* to "render . . . the unquenched desire of a man of words to cross over the border into the inaccessible fairyland of music."[48] This desire, though, might belong not only to the narrator, but also to Kierkegaard, who uses different names to allow different voices through the throat of his pen—to hear the different truths accessible to them, because, as Pranger firmly points out, "It is . . . not the sole privilege of descriptivity to be accurate. On the contrary. Performativity may have to contribute to further precision where the flatness of the descriptive falls short."[49] The performance of language is not simply in its words, but in its sound, its resonance, timbre, accent, theater.

Performing voice(s) can both create and convert. At his conversion, Augustine declares, "I sounded very strange," and "My uttered words said less about the state of my mind than my forehead, cheeks, eyes, colour, and tone of voice."[50] It is the sound that tells the truth in his words. The conversion scene, beginning with the childish song, "is operatic to the core," writes Pranger. "If we . . . take the *tolle lege, tolle lege* to be the (sung) command to Augustine to arrogate voice, we may catch a glimpse of that voice becoming momentarily his."[51] In our effort to understand this conversion, "All we can do to trace what really happened is to analyse the nature of the voices that have come together in the moment of conversion and to search for the way in which they are made to sound simultaneously."[52] The truth of the voice does not depend altogether upon its words, but upon those words being or becoming, for a moment or for good, our own. This means, for a moment or for good, that we are theirs. Augustine's faith emerges as he speaks the scriptural text as something more than nonsense.

Pranger adapts the notion of the arrogation of voice from Cavell, who uses it for philosophy's tendency to "claim to speak for the human . . . a certain universalizing of voice."[53] Cavell's term retains a sense of arrogance as well, as befits the claim to speak for all.[54] The sense in which Pranger attributes arrogation to Augustine is less prideful; Augustine's is a "hesitant" arrogation of the biblical text. "To introduce the arrogation of voice is another way of saying that . . . the text under consideration is, appearances notwithstanding, performative rather than descriptive."[55] Augustine's performance of conversion avoids arrogance because he claims no power of, or over, language; rather, "[p]rayer reflects exactly this process—or rather this ever repeated moment—of arrogating voice; and here we also find an explanation for Augustine arrogating the biblical voice. It is language (seemingly) external to himself which is proven to have been carrying and creating his self all along: 'before you were born I have chosen you.'"[56] Just as hearing or reading a voice can bring us to a sense of the possibilities not only of language but of ourselves (of who we might be, or even of the chance that we are not alone, that there are others who speak as we do, with whom we can speak), so speaking in a new voice can allow us the possibility of multiplying and complicating our truths, of saying what we found ourselves unable to say in our more established tones. Our voices are each choral, I argued earlier; to speak in new voices might add new sounds to the chorus of becoming ourselves. Even when we write under the name we were given, we may feel, as Cixous did, that "I" could not write such a thing, when a new voice emerges as our own.

The newness of voice calls like the song of a child. Though Augustine had previously dismissed Christianity for the childishness of its voices, for its simple silly stories, he became convinced by their depth and richness—as if he understood how many voices spoke through them (and, in fact, Ambrose's revelation of their multiple philosophical possibilities is essential to Augustine's change of heart). And as he awaited his Christian baptism in Milan, Augustine wrote about music.[57]

The Drumbeat of Words

> I live suspended in the shifting sands
> Of time measured
> Never on the 4/4.
>
> LAWRENCE BARRETT, *Yell Louder Please*

Augustine enters *De musica* to the drumbeats of words. "If I should strike a drum or a string at the same intensity and speed we pronounce '*modus*' or '*bonus*,'" Augustine writes, "would you recognize the times to be the same or not?"[58] Yes, of course his listener would. Augustine's choices here are hardly innocent; the music of language, the rhythm of style, is measure and good. In presenting his musilanguage hypothesis, Steven Brown writes that "in both language and music, the phrase is the basic unit of structure and function. It is what makes speaking and singing different from grunting and screaming."[59] We know the sound of speaking, the phrasing of *modus* on two beats. Brown elaborates:

> According to this view, music and language differ mainly in their emphasis rather than in their fundamental nature, such that language emphasizes sound reference while downplaying its sound emotion aspect (although it certainly makes use of sound emotion), whereas music's acoustic mode emphasizes sound emotion while downplaying its referential aspect (although it certainly makes use of referentiality). Language and music are essentially reciprocal specializations of a dual-natured precursor that used both sound emotion and sound reference in creating communication sounds.[60]

Levitin remarks on the neurological version of this anthropological claim, nothing that "music and speech, although they may share some neural circuits, cannot use completely overlapping neural structures."[61] More specifically, "Music appears to mimic some of the features of language and to convey some of the same emotions that vocal communication does, but in a nonreferential, and nonspecific way. It also invokes some of the same neural regions that language does, but far more than language, music taps into primitive brain structures involved with motivation, reward, and emotion."[62]

Susanne Langer, trained in both music and formal logic, offers a more philosophical version of this co-origin in her essay "The Origins of Speech and Its Communicative Function," which draws together some of the innovative concepts of her earlier books. She considers here the factors necessary for the emergence of speech:

> the power of elaborate vocalization, the discriminative ear that heard patterns of sounds, the nervous mechanisms that controlled utterance by hearing of inner and outer sounds, and the tendency to utter long passages of sound in gatherings of many individuals—that is, the habit of joint ululation—with considerable articulation that recurred at about the same point within every such occasion; and, in these same beings, the high mental activity that issued in visual image-making.

Song emerges, she argues, as "the vocal elements in primitive dance." Dance began as a communal protoritual. Gradually, the members of the community "became familiar with the vocal sounds that belonged to various sequences of steps and gestures. . . . The 'song,' or vocal part of the dance, became more and more differentiated with the evolution of the gestic patterns. At high points there were undoubtedly special shouts and elaborate halloos." While choreography might have required many bodies, sounds could be made with reasonably little effort by anyone in the group, and "[t]o remember the dance would bring the vocal element to [one's] throat."[63] Sound comes first, associated with movement; the rest of meaning emerges as denotations are fitted to the more inherent connotations.[64] And the voice remains, no matter what, "the bearer of musical ideas."[65]

In both Brown's anthropological and Langer's philosophical versions, music and language do not perfectly part. Not only does music add to words, but, as Langer insightfully notes, words add musicality, too:

> Words may enter directly into musical structures without being understood; the *semblance of speech* may be enough. The most striking illustration of this principle is found in plain-song. . . . Play such a line on the piano or on any melody instrument, it sounds poor and trivial, and seems to have no particular motion. But as soon as the words are articulated it moves, its wandering rhythmic figures cease to wander as they incorporate intoned speech rhythms, and the great Latin words fill the melodic form exactly as chords and counterpoints would fill it. . . . It is not the sentiment expressed in the words that makes them all-important to Gregorian chant; it is the cohesion of the Latin line.[66]

Langer goes on to argue that early song is incantation, designed to extend the power of prayer[67]—a suspicion she shares with Nietzsche, who declares, "one tried to *compel* the gods by using rhythm and to force their hand: poetry was thrown at them like a magical snare. . . . The magical songs in the spell seem to be the primeval form of poetry."[68]

Language and music may well emerge in tandem, with a difference in emphasis, not in kind. And this is compatible, I think, with the notion of sound nonetheless in excess of denotation: there are acoustic attributes that overflow even after meaning has been made, but there are also sounds that add sense. Though the emotive-referential distinction may be a bit too simple for the nuances of language that we are considering here, the sense of interwovenness and commonality is no less important. What if music is not just that which is left over when sense is done, or a dangerous distraction to be taken out of meaning as well as possible, but part of what meaning is? Suppose truth is a Siren? All language phrases; moreover, as Brown notes, most of the world's languages have been tonal.[69] Languages' phrases "are melodorhythmic as well as semantic structures."[70] Even non-tonal languages tend to have tonal indicators, such as the rising pitch of the English question.[71]

Augustine did not get around to melody, but the completed books of *De Musica* deal with rhythm—reaching back through his ambivalently beloved Platonists to the Pythagoreans, for whom proportion structures in beautiful harmony the very cosmos, from divinity to brute matter. Marvelously, we know rhythmic proportion (good measure) through *pleasure*, as Philipp Jeserich writes: "The thesis that is perhaps most momentous for the later argumentation in *De musica* and its 'aesthetic' implication remains implicit: the 'rightly measured' is *eo ipso pleasing*. Number is the condition of possibility . . . of giving pleasure."[72] We take this pleasure in ideas and in listening and in dancing; in the rhythms that we *feel*, even if we do not know the theory behind the numbers.[73] The move from arithmetic to music is the move from number to numerical relation. Like those who thought before him, Augustine sees in these relations the harmony of divine creation.[74] Verse, particularly, makes concrete the abstraction of God's own order.[75] Delight tugs at our ears and so pulls on our souls, thereby orienting them to the truth[76]—the pleasure in listening is downright conversionary. Before we take up and read, we hear children singing.

In the *Confessions*, Augustine declares that the beauty—that is, the well-proportioned forms—of worldly things tells him of God.[77] In *De musica*, the beauty of sound does much the same thing, not by a logical deduction, not even by an argument from creation, but by the pervasiveness of beauty itself. The *music* of language already tells us divinity.[78] This idea is older than Augustine, as Jeserich points out: "The historically specific profile of this theory follows from the relation between this concept of form and the theological concept of order indebted to Neoplatonism that constitutes 'musical' form as a 'sign of truth.'"[79] I will not rehearse here my own obsessions with Augustinian semiotics, but I will note that for him a sign of truth is all that the world's beauty is; the sign is how the world gives us God. Augustine grants not only the beauty and the analogical function of proportion, but the *truth* of modulation and harmony.[80]

Here let me take one last step, one that Augustine will not take with me, no matter how enticingly I may try to read him. I want to attend just a little bit more to another who has been tugging all along at our ears. Augustine's sense of music is Apollonian: the god of the lyre is the god of light, of order and exactitude. His is the oracle that praises Socrates and calls him the wisest of men; his are the musical instruments permitted in the imperfect but just city. But ancient music as *rhythm* has another patron deity, the very Dionysus who in Nietzsche's tale pulls, drunkenly perhaps, at Ariadne's ears, and at our own. In *The Birth of Tragedy*, Nietzsche puts the Apollonian and Dionysian into sharp contrast, as the measured and the ecstatic, the collected and the passionate. Less often noticed is that both retain, for him, their importance and their beauty as art: they are joined together in a third distinction, against the rationality of Plato's Socrates (whom Nietzsche, for all his ironic sense, seems to read straightforwardly). Truth comes in both musical proportion and the seductive hint of dissonance and madness. For Nietzsche, music retains its essential connection with dance; his particular interest is the movement that rhythm invokes; he loathes the static quality too often adhering to philosophical Truth.

But Nietzsche is never uncomplicated in his attitudes. Trying to figure out how a figure so famously ugly as Socrates could nonetheless fascinate so many, Nietzsche decides, "He fascinated by appealing to the competitive impulse of the Greeks—he introduced a variation into the wrestling match between young men and youths. Socrates was a great erotic."[81] This great erotic's greatest test of truth is not reason, but the agreement of the *daimon*—Socrates, too, hears voices, and he pays attention to them, not least when they tell him that his rationality has dishonored the divine madness of poetry and love: of rhythmic speech and desire. The beauty of the world is dissonance as well as harmony, unintended as well as carefully formed: the scrape in the throat, the unexpected accent, the pace and the tone of the truth, the grain of the voice; it is the art and the eros that sustain even the driest rationality.

Truth is not restricted to reason, but belongs as well to sound, to tones. That voices will give away any lies that words try to keep is a commonplace, though not altogether true—good liars are good at tone and pacing, and we know, too, the suspicion of the trained operatic voice. The early actor—who must also be a musician—likewise intones from behind a mask. The music of a voice may even alter a language to make it tell new truths, like the roar of Kamau Brathwaite's Caribbean hurricane.[82]

Still, voices can be more difficult to disguise than some sensory elements; they may tell lying words, but it is harder, at least, for them to lie in tone. Cavarero notes the Biblical tale of the misrecognition of Jacob when he seeks to steal the blessing rightly belonging to his older brother, Esau, from his blind father, Isaac. Isaac is fooled by the hairy shirt that Jacob wears, which has both the texture and the scent of Esau; he is fooled by Jacob's words—but he is puzzled, declaring nonetheless that "the voice is the voice of Jacob." Though Isaac will finally go against the evidence of his ears, it is the voice that tells the truth.[83] Cavell declares of this story, "I find I do not believe that a father can fail to know the origin of his son's voice, however at variance their accents."[84] There is a limit to the arrogation of voice, and Jacob has crossed it, crossed the boundary between influence, or even imitation, into theft. That line, of course, is never so crystalline as we might like. Lines seldom are.

Against that blurred quality, Cavell quotes "the terrible, ungrantable wish Theseus madly expresses to Hippolytus":

> All men should have two voices, one the just voice,
> and one as chance would have it. In this way
> the treacherous scheming voice would be confuted
> by the just, and we should never be deceived. (II.924–31).[85]

What is true in tone is not identical with what is true in fact, and we run into trouble when we conflate them—and when we simply separate them, too.

They come closest to harmony when we find the meaning in the music: the truth and the rightness of the tone to that of which the words tell, surely one of the most difficult aspects of speaking and writing alike. This demands, as we saw earlier, that we listen for the way that things want to be said, that we allow receptivity into our voices. Dolar writes that "words fail us when we are faced with the infinite shades of the voice, which infinitely exceed meaning," but which uniquely among acoustic phenomena points toward meaning, having some special relationship with it.[86] I would argue that this special relationship is not simply one of exceeding meaning, but rather one of greatly complicating meaning, sometimes by adding to the kinds of meaning that are available, and the ways of communicating it; less often by undercutting the denotation. This is sensory and carnal knowing, but it is entangled with the knowledge of ideas: each enhances the other, until they are no longer separate things. Dolar insists that the voice "is the material element recalcitrant to meaning, . . . the voice is precisely that which cannot be said."[87] I do not think that this recalcitrance is exhaustive. There is sonorous meaning and meaningful sound; the two are entangled with one another—not simply because sound is our medium for voicing—*and* there are sound and meaning distinct from one another, the acoustic and the ideal as each eludes and overflows any chance of full containment. The voice is not precisely uncanny—that is, we are not unacquainted with it—but it is the bearer of a kind of knowledge that many intellectuals and theorists have forgotten how to know, an aesthetic knowledge that does not leave language alone—as if omniscient Sirens still sang epic tales.

The divine voice, Cavarero writes, "is divine precisely because it precedes and generates the semantic register of speech. In the Greece of the philosophers, there is no space for reflection on the voice as voice, no room for the reverberation of language as the unexpressed within expression. If anything, in language there reverberates only the mute order of thought."[88] Of course, we have seen that a stubborn undercurrent of poetry keeps working itself back into the most determinedly bare philosophies. Caverero beautifully describes the possibility contrary to the devocalization of language, and though she does not specifically evoke the divinity of speaking flesh, it is hard not to hear it in the music of her words:

> From a vocal perspective, the reciprocal communication of the speakers lies in the symphony of a double relationality. One regards the uniqueness of a voice that is for the ear; the other resounds in the musicality of language itself. Both have a physical, corporeal substance. The logos that is shared in the voices . . . is a logos that vibrates in throats of flesh. In this sense, the distinction between the semantic and the vocalic alludes to the ineludible bond between the universality of a linguistic register, which organizes the disembodied substance of signifieds, and the particularity of an embodied existence, who makes herself heard in voice. Speech . . . bridges these two shores. Even when it begins to communicate something, obeying the universal codes of language, it still communicates singular voices and, at the same time, the rhythmic cadence of a resonance that links these voices.[89]

Voices resonate and share by a sameness that is never simply the same, never simply the one voice ever again. Augustine's gaze is drawn through the beauty of the world straight to that of his God, "in the flash of a trembling glance." He is more hesitant with his hearing, worrying that his love of beautiful voices might make him neglect the ideational meaning in the words of hymns.[90] He hesitates, though, precisely because he knows how strongly music draws him—all the way back, if Langer and Brown are right, to a primal meaningfulness of sound as song, to a beginning of word indistinct from the flesh.

Music is the sound of order and reason, but of desire directed infinitely too, at the beauty that is divine. In the trembling dissymmetry between sense and sense, sound and pure abstraction, we hear that beauty; we hear truth, in all its complication. Rather than hearing what cannot be cognized as if it were antithetical to meaning, we listen to the silence and the sound, and between them the speaking voice that vibrates, giving flesh to words.

The materiality of language is easy to ignore, because language and matter are both so very complicated already. When we do not ignore it, though, the complications may be delightful. They may enrich our reading, as we hear the lively accented voices of writers and pass that pleasure on to other readers. They may add carnality to our myths of first speaking, and so to the ways we translate from one language to another, as if we crossed the threshold of a medieval church. They may shape the world by song, and tell us that it sings.

Always beginning, God speaks, breath vibrating the responsive waters. Listening to voice, we learn in our bodies to think. Learning to hear, to sing along, we hope to teach. We reach back to a word that was purely made flesh, to a sense that is bursting with sound. And inconvenient authors stir to life. Their sentences give us a thrill.

Acknowledgments

I should begin acknowledging all of the help I've received with this book, directly and indirectly, by thanking the wide variety of relatives who read to me more or less constantly at my imperious infantile demand, giving me a love for the sound of books from the very beginning. I owe gratitude as well to all of the undoubtedly overburdened schoolteachers who did their best to feed the word-hungry mind that was thus created. I cannot send a book on voice into the world without thanks to my mother, as by all accounts we sound remarkably alike, which fact long ago prompted me to start thinking about what voices are.

More immediately or recently, I owe great thanks to the friends who put up with my preliminary, never very coherent ramblings and provided me with invaluable feedback about what became *The Matter of Voice*, especially Jennifer Glancy, Virginia Burrus, and Patricia Cox Miller. All are members of LARCeNY (Late Antique Religion in Central New York), a smart and inspiring discussion group, where I was able to talk about some of the ideas that make their way into the concluding chapter here. Musicologist Anne Yardley gave up most of a day to take me through "O Magne Pater," from which I benefited beyond words. Among them, I owe a special debt to

Patricia Cox Miller, who pointed out to me that I had just spent a few years writing on voice and had in fact generated a book—something one might think I'd have realized on my own, but which I had not.

The essays that eventually became that book were solicited and accepted by a wide range of sources. None of the chapters appears in quite the same form as any of the original essays, but some are quite close, and in each case the solicitation was an inspiration as well. Thus my deep thanks to:

Jana Schmidt, who allowed me to write an essay called "The Matter of Voice" for "The Word Flesh," a special issue of *theory@buffalo* (issue 17) that she co-edited with Brian O'Neil. That essay is broken up and put into various places here, but working it through was valuable, and the editors were very patient.

Wilson Dickinson, who edited a special issue of the *Journal of Cultural and Religious Theory* on "Pedagogical Exercises and Theories of Practice" (12.2), drawing forth a version of "Speaking to Learn to Listen."

Elaine Miller and Emily Zakin, who organized the PhiloSophia conference on "Translating the Canon" and, in the issue of *philoSophia* coming out of that conference (3.1), published a version of "Thou Art Translated!"

Nicola Masciandaro, who edited issue 7 of *Glossator*, "The Mystical Text (Black Clouds Course Through Me Unending)," providing me with an excuse to write "The Voice in the Mirror."

Richard Kearney and Brian Treanor, editors of *Carnal Hermeneutics* (Fordham, 2015), for which "Original Breath" emerged.

I owe gratitude to Alan Griffin, who is forever disrupting my procrastination with a stern "Shouldn't you be writing?" If I really listened to him, my books would emerge much sooner.

While Fordham's former editor Helen Tartar is not replaceable, she is successible, and in Tom Lay Fordham has found a worthy successor indeed. It has been a real pleasure to work with him. Part of that pleasure has been his brilliant selection of readers for the manuscript: In addition to Patricia Cox Miller, I am much indebted to Mark Jordan, Kim Haines-Eitzen, and Lawrence Kramer for their insights. Besides Tom, I am grateful to all the staff at Fordham University Press, who are invaluable to and gentle with those whose understanding of books really ends with reading and writing. This book is very much improved by the work and the suggestions of everyone I have mentioned. Its remaining flaws are entirely of my own making.

NOTES

INTRODUCTION: HEARING VOICES

1. Roland Barthes, "The Death of the Author," in *Image, Music, Text*, trans. Stephen Heath (New York: Hill and Wang, 1977), 142–48.

2. "The 'grain' of the voice is not—or not only—its timbre; the *signifying* ['significance'] it affords cannot be better defined than by the *friction* between music and something else, which is the language (and not the message at all)." *The Grain of the Voice*, trans. Richard Howard, in *The Responsibility of Forms* (Berkeley: University of California Press, 1982/1985), 273. Thus cited in Laura Wahlfors, "Resonances and Dissonances: Listening to Waltraud Meier's Envoicing of Isolde," in *On Voice*, ed. Walter Bernhart and Lawrence Kramer (Amsterdam: Rodopi, 2014), 57–76, at 61.

3. Barthes, *Image, Music, Text*, and *A Lover's Discourse: Fragments*, trans. Richard Howard (New York: Hill and Wang, 2010). See also Adriana Cavarero, *For More than One Voice*, trans. Paul A. Kottman (Stanford: Stanford University Press, 2005), 15: "According to Barthes, what is proper to voice is what he calls its *grain*. Rather than appertain to breath, the voice concerns 'the materiality of the body that springs from the throat, there where the phonic metal is forged.'" Citing Barthes, in collaboration with Roland Havas, "Ascolto," in *Encyclopedia Einaudi* (Turin: Einaudi, 1977), 1:247. Cavarero continues: "His attention, in short, falls on the oral cavity, the quintessential erotic locus. The grain of the voice has to do above all with the way in which the voice, through the pleasure of sonorous emission, works in language. What interests Barthes is 'song' as a primary place of phonic and musical texture from which language grows" (247).

4. Samuel Beckett, *Stories and Texts for Nothing* (New York: Grove Press, 1967), Text 3, 85–91, at 85.

5. Beckett, *Stories and Texts for Nothing*, 85.

6. Michel Foucault, "What Is an Author?" in *Language, Counter-Memory, Practice*, ed. and trans. Donald F. Bouchard and Sherry Simon (Ithaca, NY: Cornell University Press, 1977), 124–27.

7. Foucault, "The Order of Discourse," inaugural lecture at the Collège de France, 1970, in *Untying the Text: A Post-Structuralist Reader*,

ed. Robert Young (London: Routledge and Kegan Paul, 1981), 48–78, at 48.

8. Stanley Cavell, *A Pitch of Philosophy: Autobiographical Exercises* (Cambridge, MA: Harvard University Press, 1994), 24.

9. Foucault, "The Order of Discourse," 48. Citing Samuel Beckett, "The Unnamable," in *Trilogy* (London: Calder and Boyars, 1959), 418.

10. Anne Carson, "Foam," in *Decreation: Poetry, Essays, Opera* (New York: Vintage Books, 2005), 45.

11. Ibid.

12. Lawrence Kramer, introduction, in Bernhart and Kramer, *On Voice*, vii–xv, at vii. Cf. Lawrence Kramer, "The Voice of/in Opera," 43–55, at 45, in *On Voice*: "In speaking the voice exceeds and extends speech through tone, tempo, volume, timbre, and contour. The force of any speech act is as much melodic as it is social."

13. Lawrence Kramer, *Expression and Truth: The Music of Knowledge* (Berkeley: University of California Press, 2012), Kindle Edition, location 2104.

14. I should note that not everyone agrees. Michael Halliwell, for instance, writes, "The novel is not an aural genre and it is obvious that it is only in some form of adaptation that the words on the page are given actual sonorous presence." Halliwell is very engaged in questions of vocal sound, but does not find them in reading, whereas I am unable not to do so. Halliwell: "'Her throat, full of aching, grieving beauty': Reflections on Voice in Operatic Adaptations of *The Great Gatsby* and *Sophie's Choice*," in *On Voice*, 1–27, at 2.

15. Birgitte Stougaard Pedersen, "Voice and Presence in Music and Literature: Virginia Woolf's *The Waves*," in *On Voice*, 117–28, at 123. Citing "Stilen og lykken," *Den Blå Port* (n.p., 1993), 27f.

16. Beckett, *Stories and Texts*, 85.

17. Mladen Dolar, *A Voice and Nothing More* (Cambridge, MA: MIT Press, 2006), Kindle Edition, locations 259–63. "We can almost unfailingly identify a person by the voice, the particular individual timbre, resonance, pitch, cadence, melody, the peculiar way of pronouncing certain sounds. The voice is like a fingerprint, instantly recognizable and identifiable. This fingerprint quality of the voice is something that does not contribute to meaning, nor can it be linguistically described, for its features are as a rule not linguistically relevant, they are the slight fluctuations and variations which do not violate the norm—rather, the norm itself cannot be implemented without some 'personal touch,' the slight trespassing which is the mark of individuality." While I would agree with Dolar regarding the "fingerprint quality," it will become increasingly clear that I *do* regard that quality, and other sonorous qualities, as part of meaning.

18. Cavarero, *For More than One Voice*, 173. Cf. Kramer, who writes in *Expression and Truth* of speaking melody, "who is it that speaks? The voice, which is unheard, has no tone, no timbre, no material identity; it belongs to no one, especially not to the one who hears it." Location 875.

19. Karmen MacKendrick, *Divine Enticement: Theological Seductions* (New York: Fordham University Press, 2013), 141–68. Cf. Jean-Louis Chrétien, "The Wounded Word: The Phenomenology of Prayer," in *Phenomenology and the Theological Turn: The French Debate*, ed. Dominique Janicaud (New York: Fordham University Press, 2001), 147–75, at 158: "Prayer appears to be always surpassed and preceded by the one to whom it is addressed. It does not begin, it *responds*," and 159: "The silence of prayer is here a silence *heard* by God; it is still and always dialogue, and can be so only because a first silence, different and purely privative, was broken."

20. Dolar, locations 710–11. Citing Larousse, no further citation.

21. Ovid, *Metamorphoses*, trans. A. D. Melville (Oxford: Oxford University Press, 1998), 152.

22. The Cave of the Sibyl was rediscovered in May 1932 by Italian archaeologist Amedeo Maiuri.

23. T. S. Eliot opens "The Waste Land" with an epigraph from the version of this story in Gaius Petronius's *Satyricon*, which he translates: "I saw with my own eyes the Sibyl at Cumae hanging in a cage, and when the boys said to her: 'Sibyl, what do you want?' she answered: 'I want to die.'" In Eliot, *The Annotated Waste Land and Eliot's Contemporary Prose* (New Haven: Yale University Press, 2005). From Gaius Petronius, *Satyricon*, available at http://www.thelatinlibrary.com/petronius1.html. Translation by Alfred R. Allinson, available at http://www.sacred-texts.com/cla/petro/satyr/.

24. Dolar, *A Voice*, locations 827–30.

25. Ibid., locations 701–703: "There is no voice without a body, but yet again this relation is full of pitfalls: it seems that the voice pertains to the wrong body, or doesn't fit the body at all, or disjoints the body from which it emanates."

26. I do not take on here the argument as to whether writing or voice is more philosophically valued. Jacques Derrida has famously insisted that philosophy is focused on the voice (see *Signature Event Context*), but the relevant sense of voice in that text seems simply to entail a kind of unmediated production of meaning rather than to focus on sound or embodiment.

27. I am unable to resist recounting an unusual event. I sometimes perform as a *palmera*—one who keeps tempo by clapping—with a local flamenco group. At the end of one performance in which the audience had sung along at times, an elderly woman asked me if I also sang. I told her ruefully that I did not, as I have a terrible singing voice. She shook her head and put a hand

on my arm. “All voices,” she said firmly, “are good for singing.” And despite my own inabilities, I cannot shake the sense that in some way she must be right.

1. THE MATTER OF VOICE

1. Cavarero, *For More than One Voice*, 89.

2. Theresa MacPhail, “The Art and Science of Finding Your Voice,” *Chronicle of Higher Education*, August 8, 2014 (accessed at chroniclevitae.com). For the latter two, the ease of a Google search obviates the value of a list of references.

3. I understand that many people think in images or spatial forms. This is so foreign to me, however, that I have not been able to explore it further.

4. Cf. Ursula LeGuin, “Off the Page: Loud Cows (A Talk and a Poem about Reading Aloud)” in *A Wave in the Mind: Talks and Essays on the Writer, the Reader, and the Imagination* (Boston: Shambhala, 2012), Kindle edition, locations 1876–77: “What happened to stories and poems after the invention of printing is a strange and terrible thing. Literature lost its voice. Except on the stage, it was silenced. Gutenberg muzzled us. By the time I got born the silence of literature was considered an essential virtue and a sign of civilisation. Nannies and grannies told stories aloud to babies, and ‘primitive’ peoples spoke their poems, poor illiterate jerks, but the real stuff, literature, was literally letters, letterpress, little black noiseless marks on paper. And libraries were temples of the goddess of silence attended by vigilant priestesses going Shhhh.”

5. Wayne Koestenbaum, *The Queen’s Throat: Opera, Homosexuality And The Mystery Of Desire* (Jackson, TN: Decap Press, 1993), Kindle Edition, location 187.

6. Koestenbaum, *The Queen’s Throat*, locations 547–48.

7. Kramer, *Expression*, location 2046.

8. Richard Wilbur, in *Writers: Writers on the Art of Writing*, ed. Nancy Compton (New York: Quantuck Lane Press, 2005), 52.

9. Le Guin, “Old body not writing,” in *The Wave in the Mind*, locations 4374–75.

10. Virginia Woolf, *The Letters of Virginia Woolf Volume 3: 1923–1928*, ed. Nigel Nicolson and Joanne Trautmann (New York: Harcourt, Brace, Jovanovich, 1980), 247.

11. Jean-Luc Nancy, “Récit Recitation Recitative,” trans. Charlotte Mandell, in *Speaking of Music: Addressing the Sonorous*, eds. Keith Chapin and Andrew H. Clark (New York: Fordham University Press, 2013), 242–55, at 245.

12. Nancy, "Récit," 243.

13. Cavell, *A Pitch of Philosophy*, 24.

14. This line occurs in a 1998 *New York Times* interview with Jacques Derrida, in which he defends the notions of deconstruction and interpretation. "'Everything is a text; this is a text,' he said, waving his arm at the diners around him in the bland suburbanlike restaurant, blithely picking at their lunches, completely unaware that they were being 'deconstructed.'" Dinitia Smith, "Philosopher Gamely in Defense of His Ideas," *New York Times*, May 30, 1998, archived at http://www.nytimes.com/1998/05/30/arts/philosopher-gamely-in-defense-of-his-ideas.html.

15. Kramer, *Expression*, location 2083. Kramer cites Derrida, *Of Grammatology*, trans. Gayatri Chakravorty Spivak (Baltimore: Johns Hopkins University Press, 1976), 1–65.

16. Pedersen, "Voice and Presence," 122. Pedersen cites Barthes's *The Grain of the Voice* and Derrida's *Voice and Phenomenon: Introduction to the Problem of the Sign in Husserl's Phenomenology* (Evanston, IL: Northwestern University Press, 2011).

17. Kramer, *Expression*, location 2091. Cf. "The phonocentric bias is maybe not the whole story of the metaphysical treatment of the voice. There exists a metaphysical history of the voice, where the voice, far from being the safeguard of presence, is considered dangerous, threatening, and possibly ruinous." Dolar, "The Object of Voice," in *Gaze and Voice as Love Objects*, eds. Renata Salecl and Slavoj Žižek (Durham, NC: Duke University Press, 1996), 7–31, at 16; cited thus in Pedersen, 123.

18. Patricia T. Clough, "The Affective Turn: Political Economy, Biomedia, and Bodies," in *The Affect Theory Reader*, eds. Melissa Gregg and Gregory J. Seigworth (Durham, NC: Duke University Press, 2010), 206–24, at 206.

19. Anna Gibbs, "After Affect: Sympathy, Synchrony, and Mimetic Communication," in Gregg and Seigworth, *The Affect Theory Reader*, 186–205, at 200.

20. Friedrich Nietzsche, *The Will to Power*, trans. Walter Kaufmann (New York: Vintage Books, 1967), §481, translation slightly modified.

21. Allowances must be made for Tom Lehrer's spirited version of the periodic table, sung to the tune of Gilbert and Sullivan's "I Am the Very Model of a Modern Major-General," though it is a listing rather than a formula. Tom Lehrer, "The Elements," from *An Evening Wasted with Tom Lehrer*, Reprise/Warner Brothers Records, 1959.

22. Seigworth and Gregg, "An Inventory of Shimmers," in Gregg and Seigworth, 1–25, at 1.

23. Ferdinand de Saussure, *Course in General Linguistics*, trans. Wade Baskin (New York: Columbia University Press, 2011).

24. Cf. Kramer, *On Voice*, Introduction: "Voice, then, arises at the crossroads of words and music not because it can, or may, do so but because voice in general just is that which arises at that crossroads," vii.

25. Jacob Rogozinski, *The Ego and the Flesh: An Introduction to Ego Analysis*, trans. Robert Vallier (Stanford: Stanford University Press, 2010), esp. ch. 9.

26. Philippe Lacoue-Labarthe, *Phrase* (Paris: Christian Bourgois, 2000), 130; cited in Nancy, "Récit," 255.

27. Kramer, *On Voice*, Introduction, viii. Kramer cites Martin Heidegger, "Language," in *Poetry Language Thought*, trans. Albert Hofstadter (New York: HarperCollins, 1971), 185–208.

28. Kramer, *On Voice*, Introduction, vii.

29. Michel de Certeau, *The Mystic Fable, Vol. One: The Sixteenth and Seventeenth Centuries*, trans. Michael B. Smith (Chicago: University of Chicago Press, 1992), 187.

30. Jean-Louis Chrétien, *The Ark of Speech*, trans. Andrew Brown (London: Routledge, 2004), 9.

31. Anna Gibbs, "After Affect: Sympathy, Synchrony and Mimetic Communication," in Gregg and Seigworth, *The Affect Theory Reader*, 186–205, at 191.

32. Music is intriguing in this regard, as being both affectively potent and immensely contagious. Neurologist and popular science writer Oliver Sacks remarks that "rhythm binds together the individual nervous systems of a human community," a more biological way of putting a widespread observation about the power of sound, especially its temporal elements. Oliver Sacks, *Musicophilia: Tales of Music and the Brain* (New York: Knopf, 2008), Kindle Edition, location 3149.

33. Chrétien, *Ark*, 50.

34. Pedersen, "Voice and Presence," 120.

35. Maurice Blanchot, *A Voice from Elsewhere*, trans. Charlotte Mandel (Stanford: Stanford University Press, 2007), 46.

36. Cavarero, *For More than One Voice*, 90, citing Nancy, "Sharing Voices," trans. Gayle Ormiston, in *Transforming the Hermeneutic Context: From Nietzsche to Nancy*, eds. Ormiston and Alan D. Schrift (Albany: State University of New York Press, 1990), 211–59, at 221.

37. Certeau, *The Mystic Fable*, 175–76.

38. Derrida, *The Animal That Therefore I Am*, ed. Marie-Louise Mallet, trans. David Wills (New York: Fordham University Press, 2008), 60.

39. Blanchot, *Voice*, 41.

40. Blanchot, *Voice*, 38. Here is the passage more fully (37–38): "Socrates, who rejects the impersonal knowledge of the book, rejects no less forcefully—but with more reverence—another impersonal language, the

pure speech that seeks to articulate the sacred. [. . .] So that everything that is said against writing would serve, as well, to discredit the recited speech of the hymn, where the speaker, whether he is the poet or the echo of the poet, is nothing more than the irresponsible organ of a language that infinitely surpasses him.

"In that way, mysteriously, although writing is linked to the development of prose, when verse stops being an indispensable tool for memory, the written thing seems essentially close to sacred speech, whose strangeness it seems to carry into the written work, and whose excessiveness, risk, and power that evades all calculation and refuses any guarantee, it inherits."

41. Chrétien, *Ark*, 75.

42. Blanchot, *Voice*, 25.

43. Rogozinski, *The Ego and the Flesh*, 297.

44. Nancy, *Listening*, 142.

45. Blanchot, *Voice*, 26; des Forêts uncited.

46. Blanchot writes of Paul Celan: "And what is speaking to us, in these poems that are often very short, where words and phrases seem, by the rhythm of their undefined brevity, surrounded with white space, is that this white space, these stops, these silences, are not pauses or intervals that allow the reader to breathe, but belong to the same rigor, one that authorizes only a little relaxation, a nonverbal rigor that is not supposed to convey meaning, as if the void were less a lack than a saturation, an emptiness saturated with emptiness." Blanchot, *Voice*, 57.

47. Blanchot, *Voice*, 10.

48. V. S. Naipaul, in Compton, *Writers*, 186.

49. Cavell, *A Pitch of Philosophy*, 69.

50. Roger Boylan, "Samuel Beckett: The Early Years," *Boston Review*, July 8, 2014, accessed at http://www.bostonreview.net/books-ideas/roger-boylan-samuel-beckett-echos-bones.

51. "There are no white spaces unless there is black, no silence unless speech and noise are produced, in order to cease." Blanchot, *Voice*, 12.

52. Blanchot, *Voice*, 20; des Forêts uncited.

53. Nancy, *Listening*, 6.

54. We can fall silent and leave unsaid, but we cannot, as Blanchot points out, keep silence: "Silence cannot be kept. . . . It demands a wait which has nothing to await, a language which, presupposing itself as the totality of discourse, would spend itself all at once, disjoin and fragment endlessly." Maurice Blanchot, *The Writing of the Disaster*, trans. Ann Smock (Lincoln: University of Nebraska Press, 1995), 29.

55. Certeau, *The Mystic Fable*, 78.

56. Dolar, *The Object of Voice*, locations 238–41.

57. James Baldwin, *Sonny's Blues* (New York: Penguin, 1995).

58. Jorge Luis Borges, in Compton, *Writers*, 74.

59. Will Stockton and D. Gilson, *Crush* (Brooklyn, NY: Punctum Books, 2014), 66.

60. Harold Bloom, in Compton, *Writers*, 102.

61. Carson, *Decreation*, 176–77, citing Marguerite Porete, *The Mirror of Simple Souls*, trans. and introduction by Edmund Colledge, Judith Grant, and J. C. Marler (Notre Dame, IN: University of Notre Dame Press, 1999), 135.

62. John Ashbery, in Compton, *Writers*, 94.

63. Anne Carson, cited in Emilia Brockes, "A Life in Writing: Magical Thinking," *The Guardian*, December 29, 2006, accessed at http://www.theguardian.com/books/2006/dec/30/featuresreviews.guardianreview7.

64. Carson, cited in Brockes.

65. Ibid.

2. Speaking to Learn to Listen

1. Motoko Rich, "Pediatrics Group to Recommend Reading Aloud to Children from Birth," *New York Times*, June 24, 2014. Accessed at http://www.nytimes.com/2014/06/24/us/pediatrics-group-to-recommend-reading-aloud-to-children-from-birth.html?smid=tw-nytimes&_r=0.

2. I currently teach undergraduate required courses and the occasional undergraduate elective. While some of what I say here would apply to graduate teaching as well, some of it would not; graduate students tend bring with them, if not a love of a particular course, at least a desire for long-term engagement with a given intellectual discipline.

3. N. Kapur and N. F. Lawton, "Dysgraphia for Letters: a Form of Motor Memory Deficit?" *Journal of Neurological Psychiatry* 46:6 (1983): 573–75, at 573; emphasis added.

4. Kapur and Lawton, "Dysgraphia for Letters," 573.

5. A time use study by the US Bureau of Labor Statistics found that college students averaged 3.3 hours a day engaged in educational activities, 3.1 hours working, 8.3 hours sleeping, and 3.7 hours in leisure and sports activities. "American Time Use Survey," U.S. Department of Labor, Bureau of Labor Statistics, 2013, at http://www.bls.gov/tus/datafiles_2013.htm. Another study, noting how little students learn, particularly during their first two years of college, manages to blame both the students' use of time and their professors' research work. Kayla Webley, "$80,000 for Beer Pong? Report Shows College Students Learn Little during First Two Years (Except Party Skills)," *Time*, January 18, 2011, archived and accessed at http://newsfeed.time.com/2011/01/18/what-do-college-students-learn-in-the-first-two-years-not-a-whole-lot/#ixzz1Y3aERA5k.

6. Augustine, *Confessions*, trans. Henry Chadwick (Oxford: Oxford University Press, 1991), 11.39.

7. Teresa of Avila, *The Life of Teresa of Avila, by Herself*, trans. J. M. Cohen (London: Penguin Books, 1957), 101.

8. Catherine Conybeare, "Beyond Word and Image: Aural Patterning in Augustine's *Confessions*," in *Envisioning Experience in Late Antiquity and the Middle Ages*, ed. Giselle de Nie and Thomas F. X. Noble (Aldershot: Ashgate, 2012), 143–64, at 145.

9. The following retelling is taken from Plato, *Phaedo*, trans. Benjamin Jowett, in *Six Great Dialogues* (New York: Dover, 2007), 57a–61c.

10. 60e. I am very grateful to Mark Jordan for pointing out the Greek *musikein* here, which is not well captured in Jowett's translation.

11. Plato, *Phaedrus*, trans. Alexander Nehamas and Paul Woodruff (Indianapolis: Hackett Publishing, 1994), 242c and following.

12. Laura Odello, "Waiting for the Death Knell," in Chapin and Clark, *Speaking of Music*, 39–48, at 45.

13. Cavarero, *For More than One Voice*, 46.

14. Ibid.

15. Evidence of the problematizing of this intersection may be found, for example, in Jane Gallop, *Feminist Accused of Sexual Harassment* (Durham, NC: Duke University Press, 1997); bell hooks, "Eros, Eroticism and the Pedagogical Process," in *Teaching to Transgress* (New York: Routledge, 1995), 191–200.

16. Cavarero, *For More than One Voice*, 70–71.

17. Gerald W. Gruber, "Voice and Voices in Oratorios: On Sacred and Other Voices," in Bernhart and Kramer, *On Voice*, 149–60, at 149.

18. Athanasius, "A Letter of Athanasius, Our Holy Father, Archbishop of Alexandria, to Marcellinus on the Interpretation of the Psalms," in *Athanasius: The Life of Antony and The Letter to Marcellinus*, trans. Robert C. Gregg, Classics of Western Spirituality (Mahwah, NJ: Paulist Press, 1980), 101–29, sec. 14–15.

19. Athanasius, "Letter," 27.

20. Ibid., 28.

21. Ibid.

22. See Björn Vickhoff, Helge Malmgren, Rickard Åström, Gunnar Nyberg, Seth-Reino Ekström, Mathias Engwall, Johan Snygg, Michael Nilsson, and Rebecka Jörnsten, "Music structure determines heart rate variability of singers," *Frontiers of Psychology*, July 2013, at http://journal.frontiersin.org/Journal/10.3389/fpsyg.2013.00334/full. I am grateful to Anne Yardley for alerting me to this reference.

23. Daniel J. Levitin, *This Is Your Brain on Music: The Science of a Human Obsession* (New York: Penguin Books, 2006), Kindle Edition, location 1633.

24. M. B. Pranger, *The Artificiality of Christianity: Essays on the Poetics of Monasticism* (Stanford: Stanford University Press, 2003), 286.

25. "When cenobitic monasticism developed in the early fourth century, monks were assisted toward literacy. Here too the ability to read was linked with religious vocation, as the spiritual exercises prescribed for monks included reading and meditating on scripture (though eremitic monks might or might not have been literate)." Harry Y. Gamble, *Books and Readers in the Early Church: A History of Early Christian Texts* (New Haven, CT: Yale University Press, 1995), 10.

26. Gamble, *Books and Readers*, 233. Gamble cites *De Laz.* (available in John Chrysostom, *Four Discourses, Chiefly Concerning the Rich Man and Lazarus*, Discourse 3, trans. F. Allen (London: Longmans, Green, Reader and Dyer, 1869), also at http://www.tertullian.org/fathers/chrysostom_four_discourses_00_intro.htm); *Homilies on Genesis 21* (available in *The Fathers of the Church: John Chrysostom*, Homilies on Genesis 18–45, Washington, DC: Catholic University of America Press, 1990); and *Homilies on the Gospel of St. Matthew* 2 (available in *Nicene and Post-Nicene Fathers*, Series 1, Volume 10, Peabody, MA: Hendrickson Publishers, 1994), 2.

27. Pranger, *The Artificiality of Christianity*, 41.

28. Brian Stock, *After Augustine: The Meditative Reader and the Text* (Philadelphia: University of Pennsylvania Press, 2001), 18.

29. Pranger, *The Artificiality of Christianity*, 23. "The monastery, for its part, is purposely artificial. As such it is small and intense."

30. Ibid., 22. "From the patristic-era sources of medieval literature until the high Middle Ages (twelfth century), the slowest movement imaginable of life, language, and thought is to be found. . . . The monastery's is a triple fixity: the fixity of classical genres as part of the monk's basic training, a more extensive fixity of the sermon (*collatio*) and the rumination on Scripture reflecting a continuing and uneventfulness unknown to the world in which the monk had been living previously, and, finally, the all-embracing fixity of his lifestyle."

31. Cf. Pranger, *The Artificiality of Christianity*, 21. "In order to meet the requirement just formulated to produce an alternative concept of time, my focus will be . . . on slowing down, on retardation verging on immobility, and, indeed, on eternity."

32. This is not an accusation against my students but an admission of one of my own weaknesses.

33. Pranger, *The Artificiality of Christianity*, 87.

34. I am particularly grateful to Lawrence Kramer for his comments in his review of this manuscript, which helped me to think through vital qualifications here.

35. Pranger, *The Artificiality of Christianity*, 89.

36. Studying and testing a variety of rhythmic "skilled sequential finger movements," John W. Krakauer and Rheza Shadmehr found that learning movement series in immediate sequence resulted in interference of one with the other and consequent forgetfulness, but allowing six hours between learning series let subjects remember without such interference. J. W. Krakauer and R. Shadmehr, "Consolidation of Motor Memory," in *Trends in Neurosciences*, 29 (2006): 58–64, at 58–60.

37. Stock, *After Augustine*, 52. Stock cites Seneca, *Moral Epistles*, 15.2–6. The text is available at http://www.stoics.com/seneca_epistles_book_1.html#%E2%80%98XV1: "Of course I do not command you to be always bending over your books and your writing materials; the mind must have a change,—but a change of such a kind that it is not unnerved, but merely unbent."

38. Speed reading is, for example, part of the "mind flow" techniques offered by TestPrepNY as a way to improve SAT, GRE, and similar scores.

39. http://www.spreeder.com/.

40. Deniz Peters, "Gesture, Empathy, Affect: The Adverbial Expression of Emotion in Music," presented April 19, 2014, at "Sound and Affect" conference, Stony Brook University.

41. Cf. Pedersen, "Voice and Presence in Music and Literature," 120: "We listen to the voice with the ear and the body. You both listen and hear through the use of your own voice."

42. Thus Pranger notes, for instance, of the monastic sermon, "On the one hand, there is retardation, as, for example, in the endless amplifications of allegory that are part of the sermon genre; retardation becomes so prominent as to make motion indistinguishable from motionlessness. On the other hand, there is an undeniable sense of urgency, produced . . . by the inner workings—and turmoil—of the monastic memory." Pranger, *The Artificiality of Christianity*, 88.

43. Pranger, *The Artificiality of Christianity*, 25.

44. Ibid.

45. Rebecca Krawiec, "Evagrius, Text, and Memory: Writing and Tradition in the Egyptian Desert" (presented at Oxford Classics Conference, 2011).

46. Pranger, *The Artificiality of Christianity*, 192–94.

47. See Maurice Merleau-Ponty, *The Visible and the Invisible*, trans. Alphonso Lingis (Evanston, IL: Northwestern University Press, 1969).

48. Pranger, *The Artificiality of Christianity*, 25, citing Robert Musil, *The Man Without Qualities*, vol. 2, trans. Eithne Wilkins and Ernst Kaiser (London: Secker and Warburg, 1967), 336.

49. Friedrich Nietzsche, *On the Genealogy of Morals*, trans. Douglas Smith (Oxford: Oxford University Press, 2009), essay 3, 77–136.

50. Stephen Mitchell, *Gilgamesh: A New English Version* (New York: Free Press, 2004), 69–70.

51. I cannot resist pointing out that this is not the odd notion it might seem. It is quite pleasant for the upper back, but note taking is rendered difficult. Regrettably, the position is not workable with a Kindle or similar device.

52. Italo Calvino, *If on a Winter's Night a Traveler* (1979), trans. William Weaver (New York: Harcourt Brace & Company, 1981), 3.

53. I am grateful to my colleague Jennifer Glancy for reminding me of this.

54. Glancy cites the text, from 2 Thessalonians, and summarizes Irenaeus's worries. First, the text: "And then will be revealed the Lawless One, whom the Lord Jesus will kill with the breath [spiritus] of his mouth . . . , he whose coming will take place by the working of Satan with all power and signs and portents of falsehood." Glancy writes, "On one reading—in fact on the easier reading—it seems that the coming of the Lord Jesus will take place by the working of Satan. Irenaeus insists that in the corporal reading of the text the reader should make clear that the working of Satan leads instead to the coming of the Lawless One." Jennifer Glancy, "Reading Bodies, Reading Scripture" (delivered at the July 2011 International Society for Biblical Literature meeting, London).

55. Irenaeus, *Against Heresies* (electronic version, Wyatt North Publishing, 2012), 3.7.

56. Glancy, "Reading Bodies."

57. Gamble, *Books and Readers*, 205.

58. Pranger, *The Artificiality of Christianity*, 284.

59. "Deus per angelum loquebatur et Virgo per aurem impraegnebatur." St. Augustine: *Sermo de Tempore*, xxii. Cited in Ernest Jones, *The International Psycho-Analytical Library No. 5: Essays in Applied Psycho-Analysis* (London: International Psycho-Analytical Press, 1923), chapter 8: "The Madonna's Conception through the Ear: A Contribution to the Relation between Aesthetics and Religion," 261–309. Jones also cites other early Christian hymns to echo this point.

60. American English may make the pun, which hinges on pence and pounds, obscure. Lewis Carroll, *Alice's Adventures in Wonderland*, in *The Annotated Alice: The Definitive Edition*, ed. and annotated Martin Gardner (New York: W. W. Norton and Co., 1999), 3–128, at 92.

61. See an informational website on the notion: Brendan Clifford, "Introduction to Lectio Divina," accessed at http://www.goodnews.ie/lectio.shtml.

62. "Lectio Divina has been likened to 'Feasting on the Word.' The four parts are first taking a bite (Lectio), then chewing on it (Meditatio). Next is the opportunity to savor the essence of it (Oratio). Finally, the Word is digested and made a part of the body (Contemplatio)." Luke Dysinger, "Lectio Divina," in *The Oblate Life*, ed. Gervase Holdaway (London: Canterbury Press Norwich, 2008), 107–17, at 109.

63. Julia Kristeva gives this quotation as an epigraph on page 133 of *Powers of Horror: An Essay on Abjection*, trans. Leon D. Roudiez (New York: Columbia University Press, 1982). ("Se méprendre sur le rythme d'une phrase, c'est se méprendre sure le sens meme de la phrase." Kristeva citing Nietzsche, *Pouvoirs de l'horreur: Essai sur l'abjection* [Paris: Éditions du Seuil, 1980], 156.) Kaufmann renders the sentence somewhat differently: "A misunderstanding about its tempo, for example—and the sentence itself is misunderstood." Friedrich Nietzsche, *Beyond Good and Evil: Prelude to a Philosophy of the Future*, trans. Walter Kaufmann (New York: Vintage Books, 1966), §246. Kaufmann's translation comes closer to the German: "Ein Missverständniss über sein Tempo zum Beispiel: und der Satz selbst ist missverstanden!" Friedrich Nietzsche, *Jenseits von Gut und Böse* (Stuttgart: Reclam, 1998), §246. I have cited Kristeva's version because it makes the musical element more vivid; in context it is clear that the tempo Nietzsche had in mind is musical as well.

64. Aniruddh Patel, "Syntactic Processing in Language and Music: Different Cognitive Operations, Similar Neural Resources?" In *Music Perception*, 16:1 (Fall 1998): 27–42, at 28.

65. Aniruddh Patel, *Music, Language, and the Brain* (Oxford: Oxford University Press, 2010), 3.

3. THOU ART TRANSLATED!

1. Cavarero, *For More than One Voice*, 148; see Edward Kamau Brathwaite, *History of the Voice: The Development of a Nation Language in Anglophone Caribbean Poetry* (London: New Beacon Books, 1984), 10.

2. Steven Brown, "The 'Musilanguage' Model of Music Evolution," in *The Origins of Music*, ed. N. L. Wallin, B. Merker, and S. Brown (Cambridge, MA: MIT Press), 271–300.

3. William Shakespeare, *A Midsummer Night's Dream* (New York: Washington Square Press Folger Shakespeare Library, 2004), Act 1, scene 2, ll 68–70.

4. Shakespeare, *Midsummer Night's Dream*, Act 3, scene 1, l 114.

5. Ibid., l 118.

6. "I will get Peter Quince to write a ballad of this dream: it shall be called Bottom's Dream, because it hath no bottom; and I will sing it in the

latter end of a play, before the duke. . . . " Shakespeare, *Midsummer Night's Dream*, Act 4, scene 1, ll 224–26.

7. John Parker, "What a Piece of Work Is Man: Shakespearean Drama as Marxian Fetish, the Fetish as Sacramental Sublime," *Journal of Medieval and Early Modern Studies*, 34:3 (Fall 2004): 643–72, at 661–62. I am indebted to Tom Lay for bringing this article to my attention.

8. For more detail on this very complex subject, see my *Fragmentation and Memory* (New York: Fordham University Press, 2008), 102–31.

9. Cavell, *A Pitch of Philosophy*, 69.

10. Walter Benjamin, "The Task of the Translator: An Introduction to the Translation of Baudelaire's *Tableaux Parisiens*," trans. H. Zohn, in *Illuminations: Essays and Reflections* (New York: Routledge, 2000), 69–82, at 78.

11. Benjamin, "The Task of the Translator," 78.

12. Ibid., 76.

13. Jacques Derrida, *The Ear of the Other: Otobiography, Transference, Translation*, trans. Peggy Kamuf and Avital Ronell, ed. Christie McDonald (Lincoln: University of Nebraska Press, 1988), 29.

14. Umberto Eco, *Mouse or Rat? Translation as Negotiation* (London: Weidenfeld and Nicolson, 2003), 56.

15. Pedersen, "Voice and Presence," 117. Pedersen adopts the term "transmedial" from Lars Elleström, "The Modalities of Media: A Model for Understanding Intermedial Relations," in Lars Elleström, ed., *Media Borders, Multimodality and Intermediality* (Basingstoke: Palgrave Macmillan, 2010), 11–50.

16. This is not a hypothetical example. Stéphane Mallarmé's poem "Afternoon of a Faun" (1865) inspired or was intersemiotically translated into Claude Debussy's musical "Prelude to an Afternoon of a Faun" (1894), to which Vaslav Nijinsky choreographed a famous avant-garde ballet by the same name (1912).

17. See Eco, *Mouse*, 158f.

18. Thomas Carl Wall, *Radical Passivity: Levinas, Blanchot and Agamben* (Albany: State University of New York Press, 1999), 9–10.

19. Joseph Brodsky, in Compton, *Writers*, 88.

20. Eco, *Mouse*, 136–37.

21. Choreographers will often speak of "choreographing on" a particular dancer to fit the movements to her or his body, as one writes on a page; the "same" movements on a different bodily form can become quite different in appearance.

22. Hélène Cixous, *Three Steps on the Ladder of Writing*, trans. Sarah Cornell and Susan Sellers (New York: Columbia University Press, 1993), 64.

23. Benjamin, "The Task of the Translator," 78. The quotation is from the prologue to the fourth canonical Christian gospel, which retells in more

overtly philosophical terms the Genesis story, in which "God said . . . " functions as the creative move: "In the beginning was the Word (Logos), and the Word was with God, and the Word was God." *Oxford Catholic Study Bible: New American Bible* (Oxford: Oxford University Press, 1990), John 1:1. The continuation in the paragraph refers to verse 14 of the same book: "And the Word became flesh, and made his dwelling among us."

24. Cixous, *Three Steps*, 22–23.

25. Anonymous, *Sefer Yizira: The Book of Creation*, trans. Irving Friedman (New York: Weiser, 1977), 2.5. Cited in Umberto Eco, *The Search for the Perfect Language*, trans. James Fentress (Oxford: Blackwell, 1995), 29.

26. Abraham Abulafia, Perush Havdalah de-Rabbi 'Akivà. Cited and glossed in Eco, *Search*, 30. This infinite unfolding of meaning, with each letter in turn a whole word, even a whole book, is intriguingly similar to that of Valentinian Christianity, a second-century variant with a strong verbal focus. See especially "The Gospel of Truth," trans. Einar Thomassen and Marvin Meyer, in *The Nag Hammadi Scriptures: International Edition* (New York: HarperCollins, 2007), 36–47.

27. Eco, *Search*, 30, citing Moshe Idel, *The Mystical Experience of Abraham Abulafia* (Albany: State University of New York Press, 1988), 21.

28. Virginia Burrus notes that for Jewish religious scholar Franz Rosenzweig, translation is essential to reception. She quotes an early letter from Rosenzweig to demonstrate that "for Rosenzweig the Bible is not the Bible—Homer is not Homer—until it has been received by another language." This insight runs, as she shows, throughout Rosenzweig's work. Virginia Burrus, "Augustine's Bible," in *Ideology, Culture, and Translation*, ed. Scott Elliott and Roland Boer (Semeia Studies, Society of Biblical Literature, 2012), 69–82, at 80. Burrus cites Franz Rosenzweig, Letter to Rudolf Ehrenberg, October 1, 1917, as cited by Seidman, *Faithful Renderings*, 156, from the translation of Barbara Ellen Galli, *Franz Rosenzweig and Jehuda Halevi: Translating, Translations, and Translators* (Montreal and Kingston: McGill-Queen's University Press, 1995), 322, and Galli's commentary at ibid.

29. Eco, *Search*, 53.

30. Ibid., 133.

31. Ibid., 132f. Eco writes specifically of Renaissance thinker Giordano Bruno, a brilliant Dominican whose unorthodox cosmology, in particular, got him burned at the stake in 1600.

32. Cixous, *Three Steps*, 4.

33. Ibid., 25.

34. Alexander Gross, "Hermes: God of Translators and Interpreters," presented at Translation2000, New York University, 2000. http://language.home.sprynet.com/trandex/hermes.htm.

35. See David Robson, "Power of Babel: Why One Language Isn't Enough," *New Scientist*, 2842:14 (December 2011), 34–47, accessed at http://www.newscientist.com/article/mg21228421.200-power-of-babel-why-one-language-isnt-enough.html. See also Anonymous, "Myths Surrounding Language," accessed at http://aberwiki.org/Myths_surrounding_language. Eco points out the very brief and often overlooked earlier mention of linguistic division in Genesis at Genesis 10:5, a description of the fate of Noah's sons: "By these [sons] were the isles of the Gentiles divided in their lands; every one after his tongue, after their families, in their nations." Oxford Catholic Study Bible. Cf. Genesis 10:20 and 10:31. Eco, *Search*, 9–10. As I shall note again in chapter five, little attention is paid to this verse as compared to that given to the Babel story at Genesis 11:1–9.

36. Eco, *Search*, 345.

37. Maurice Blanchot, "Translating," trans. Elizabeth Rottenberg, in *Friendship* (Stanford: Stanford University Press 1997), 57–61, at 61.

38. Eco, *Search*, 111.

39. For example, "'It's a compelling idea,' says Sohini Ramachandran of Brown University in Providence, Rhode Island, who studies population genetics and human evolution. 'Language is such an adaptive thing that it makes sense to have a single origin before the diaspora out of Africa. It's also a nice confirmation of what we have seen in earlier genetic studies. The processes that shaped genetic variation of humans may also have shaped cultural traits.'" Ferris Jabr, "Evolutionary Babel was in southern Africa," *Science* 19 (April 14, 2011), accessed at http://www.newscientist.com/article/dn20384-evolutionary-babel-was-in-southern-africa.html.

40. See Julia Parish-Morris, Roberta Michnick Golinkoff, and Kathryn Hirsh-Pasek, "From Coo to Code: A Brief Story of Language Development," in Philip David Zelazo, ed., *The Oxford Handbook of Developmental Psychology*, vol. 1 (Oxford: Oxford University Press 2013), 867–908, at 871–72. This is complicated, to be sure, by recent research indicating that there is some prenatal familiarizing with language (see Christine Moon, Hugo Lagercrantz, and Patricia K. Kuhl, "Language experienced in utero affects vocal perception after birth: a two-country study," in *Acta Paediatrica* 102:2 [February 2013], 156–60). Somewhat relatedly, sounds and intonations that children learn young and then lose, as in the case of some adoptees, may retain their familiarity long after the designation of the words themselves has fled. Lara J. Pierce, Denise Klein, Jen-Kai Chen, Audrey Delcenserie, and Fred Genesee, "Mapping the Unconscious Maintenance of a Lost First Language," *Proceedings of the National Academy of Sciences of the United States of America* 111:48 (October 2014): 17314–19.

41. Levitin, *This Is Your Brain*, location 1671.

42. Benjamin, "Task of the Translator," 82.

43. Blanchot, "Translating," 58.

44. Eco, *Search*, 26: "Had it not been for Adam's sin, these letters [of the Torah] might have been joined differently to form another story. For the kabbalist, God will abolish the present ordering of these letters, or else will teach us how to read them according to a new disposition, only after the coming of the Messiah."

45. Eco, *Search*, 40–41.

46. Jacques Derrida, "Des tours de Babel," in *Differences in Translation*, ed. J. Graham (Ithaca, NY: Cornell University Press, 1985), 209–48. As cited in Eco, *Mouse*, 2003, 175.

47. Plato, *Symposium*, trans. Alexander Nehamas and Paul Woodruff (Indianapolis, IN: Hackett Publishing, 1989), 202D–203B.

48. Umberto Eco, *Interpretation and Overinterpretation*, ed. Stefan Collini (Cambridge: Cambridge University Press, 1992), 52.

49. In Derrida's gloss: "A sacred text is untranslatable, says Benjamin, precisely because the meaning and the letter cannot be dissociated. The flow of meaning and the flow of literality cannot be dissociated, because the sacred text is untranslatable. The only thing one can do is to read between the lines, between its lines. Benjamin says that this reading or this intralinear version of the sacred text is the ideal of all translation: pure translatability." Reply in "Roundtable on Translation," trans. Peggy Kamuf, in *The Ear of the Other*, 91–161, at 103.

50. As Eco points out, "It can happen that certain more or less esoteric interpretive practices recall those of certain deconstructionist critics. But in the shrewdest representatives of this school the hermeneutic game does not exclude interpretive rules." Eco, *Interpretation*, 60.

51. Eco, *Interpretation*, 32.

52. Derrida, *Ear*, 115.

53. Ibid.

54. Wall, *Radical Passivity*, 5.

55. Cixous, "Three Steps," 21.

56. Ibid., 102–103.

57. Derrida, *Ear*, 51.

58. Benjamin, "Task of the Translator," 75.

59. Andrew Robinson, *Lost Languages: The Enigma of the World's Undeciphered Scripts* (New York: Nevramont Publishing, 2002), 140–81.

60. A particularly intriguing instance of this hope is presented by the centuries-long efforts to decipher the very strange fifteenth-century Voynich manuscript. In February 2014, the first steps toward a successful translation may have been made. In the same year, the linguist responsible for the

possible breakthrough won international recognition for his work on eye tracking in reading, suggesting a gratifying ability on his part to attend to the matter of texts. "600 Year Old Mystery Manuscript Decoded by University of Bedfordshire Professor," University of Bedfordshire, http://www.beds.ac.uk/news/2014/february/600-year-old-mystery-manuscript-decoded-by-university-of-bedfordshire-professor.

4. THE VOICE IN THE MIRROR

1. Kramer, *On Voice*, Introduction, xii.

2. Bruce Holsinger, "The Flesh of the Voice: Embodiment and the Homoerotics of Devotion in the Music of Hildegard von Bingen (1098–1179)," *Signs: Journal of Women in Culture and Society* 19 (1993): 92–125, at 94.

3. Barbara Newman in Hildegard of Bingen, *Symphonia*, critical edition with introduction, translations, and commentary by Barbara Newman (Ithaca, NY: Cornell University Press 1998), 13; Carmen Acevedo Butcher, *Hildegard of Bingen: A Spiritual Reader* (Brewster, MA: Paraclete Press 2007), 24–25.

4. Hildegard, *Symphonia*, 104.

5. Ibid., 105.

6. On the vocative strength of prayer, see my *Fragmentation and Memory: Meditations on Christian Doctrine* (New York: Fordham University Press, 2008), and "When You Call My Name," *Glossator* 5 (2011): 57–67.

7. In fact, tempo is harder for a choral director to change than other musical elements; music is recalled and recreated as a whole, and not simply in series. This observation, too, I owe to Anne Yardley. In *This Is Your Brain on Music*, Daniel Levitin makes a similar point: "The average person seems to have a remarkable memory for tempo. In an experiment that Perry Cook and I published in 1996, we asked people to simply sing their favorite rock and popular songs from memory and we were interested to know how close they came to the actual tempo of the recorded versions of those songs. As a baseline, we considered how much variation in tempo the average person can detect; that turns out to be 4 percent. In other words, for a song with a tempo of 100 bpm, if the tempo varies between 96 and 100, most people, even some professional musicians, won't detect this small change (although most drummers would—their job requires that they be more sensitive to tempo than other musicians, because they are responsible for maintaining tempo when there is no conductor)." Location 928; cf. 934.

8. The exception is lines 6–7; 6 (*plenos quibus indigemus*) ends on a C and 7 (*Nunc placeat tibi, Pater*) begins on the D just above it.

9. As epigraph, Hildegard, *Symphonia*, 1. The *Causes and Cures* is available in English translation by Priscilla Throop (Charlotte, VT: Lulu Books, 2008).

10. *Magne Pater* is not one of her widest-ranging pieces, covering about one and a half octaves, but is still somewhat unusual in comparison to music contemporary with it.

11. Hildegard, in *The Book of Divine Works: Ten Visions of God's Deeds in the World and Humanity*, ed. Matthew Fox (Santa Fe, NM: Bear and Company, 1987), 4.105.

12. Hildegard, letter to the Prelates of Mainz, in *Divine Works*, 358.

13. Augustine, Sermon 288, in *The Works of Saint Augustine: A Translation for the 21st Century*, Vol. 3.8, Sermons 273–305A, trans. Edmund Hill, OP; ed. John E. Rotelle, OSA (Hyde Park, NY: New City Press, 1994), sec. 2: "*I am a voice crying in the desert* (Jn 1:22–23). He called himself a voice. You have John as a voice; what have you got Christ as, if not as a word. The voice is sent on ahead, so that the Word later on may be understood."

14. Augustine, Sermon 288, sec. 2.

15. Ibid., sec. 4.

16. Ibid.

17. Hildegard, *Divine Works*, Part 1, Vision 4, 128.

18. Augustine, *Confessions*, 1.1.1.

19. See Lewis Mackey, *Peregrinations of the Word* (Ann Arbor: University of Michigan Press, 1997), especially 19.

20. Particularly through analysis of Hildegard's Marian hymn "Ave Generosa," Bruce Holsinger argues that her music expresses, to a subversive degree, the desire and delight of the female body. "In the fifth verse, however, Hildegard turns her attention away from God and Christ and toward the body of the Virgin herself, and, just as she does so, she mentions music for the first time in the hymn: 'For your womb held joy, when all the celestial symphonia rang out from you.' . . . Just as music is the medium of gaudium in the fifth verse, the liquid of dew is its bearer in the sixth: 'Your flesh held joy, just as grass on which dew falls when greenness is poured into it.' . . . In the text to the fifth verse, music fills the Virgin's womb with delight and causes her body to resound in sonorous joy. And it is just at this point, on the word symphonia, that the music of the hymn reaches its highest point. . . . This immense gap of an octave and a sixth is augmented in the culminating phrase itself: the highest note is approached by a leap of a fourth, a gesture emphasizing openness and breadth." Holsinger, *The Flesh of the Voice*, 101–102.

21. Hildegard, *Divine Works*, Part 1, Vision 4, 129.

22. Ibid., 100, 122.

23. Hildegard, *Liber Divinorum Operum* (Brepolis, 1996), Visio Quarta, c. 100, 243.

24. For a much longer and more involved meditation on this curious duality, see the chapter "Fold" in my *Word Made Skin*.

25. As Nicola Masciandaro reminds me, Hildegard's *aspicias in nos* may also be rendered *gaze into us*, by which the Word is invited to see into the heart. We might add that when the Word sees word within, the mirroring and echoing effect is further multiplied.

26. There are websites that disagree with me on this matter; they appear to be more devout than scholarly, however.

27. Hildegard, *Divine Works*, Vision 4, 128–29.

28. Ibid., Vision 1, 11.

29. Evidence for this sense of entanglement in Hildegard is too widespread in various works to be given a precise source; however, for her comments on cosmology in *Divine Works*, see especially Vision 2, Sections 32–46.

30. The Online Etymology Dictionary is typically helpful here, defining *mystery*: "from Anglo-Fr. *misterie (O.Fr. mistere), from L. mysterium, from Gk. mysterion (usually in pl. mysteria) 'secret rite or doctrine,' from mystes 'one who has been initiated,' from myein 'to close, shut,' perhaps referring to the lips (in secrecy) or to the eyes (only initiates were allowed to see the sacred rites)." http://www.etymonline.com/index.php?term=mystery&allowed_in_frame=0.

31. Nancy, "Récit," 244.

32. Augustine, *The Teacher*, in Against Academicians *and* The Teacher, trans. Peter King (Indianapolis: Hackett Publishing, 1995), 98, 102.

33. Lewis Carroll, *Through the Looking-Glass*, in Carroll, *The Annotated Alice: The Definitive Edition*, ed. and annotated Martin Gardner (New York: W. W. Norton and Company, 1999), 225.

34. Nicola Masciandaro, "What Is This that Stands before Me? Metal as Deixis," in Niall Scott, ed., *Reflections in the Metal Void* (Oxford: Inter-Disciplinary Press, 2012) 3–17, at 4–5.

35. Masciandaro, "What Is This," 5.

36. Cf. T. S. Eliot, "Burnt Norton": "I can only say, there we have been: but I cannot say where. / And I cannot say, how long, for that is to place it in time." In Eliot, *Four Quartets* (San Diego, CA: Harcourt Brace Jovanovich, 1943), II.68–69.

37. John 8:58.

38. Of course, we may answer in the negative, but when we do so, we are generally assuming that the question is actually misdirected. That is, if someone asks me, "Is that you?" and I answer "No," what I mean is approximately, "I think you are looking for someone else," even though the correct answer to "Is that you?" would have to be "Yes." "You" picks out any addressee, but when it is used in a question, we may reasonably assume that a *particular* addressee is implicitly intended—the deixis is standing in for ostension.

39. David Markson, *Wittgenstein's Mistress* (Elmwood Park, IL: Dalkey Archive Press, 1988), 47.

40. Ibid., 48.

41. Rainer Maria Rilke, *New Poems (1907)*, trans. Edward Snow (New York: North Point Press, 1990), 40; 39: "und warum willst Du, daß ich sagen muß/Du seist, wenn ich Dich selber nicht mehr finde . . . Ich bin allein mit aller Menschen Gram,/den ich durch Dich zu linern unternahm,/der Du nicht bist."

42. Eliot, "Little Gidding," in *Four Quartets*, II.86–102.

43. Jean-Luc Nancy, *Dis-Enclosure: The Deconstruction of Christianity*, trans. Bettina Bergo, Gabriel Malenfant, and Michael B. Smith (New York: Fordham University Press, 2008), 6.

44. Nancy, *Listening*, trans. Charlotte Mandell (New York: Fordham University Press, 2007), 67.

45. Marianne Richert Pfau, "Music and Text in Hildegard's Antiphons," in Hildegard of Bingen, *Symphonia*, 74–94, at 75.

46. In Hildegard, *Symphonia*, 94.

47. Levitin points out that not only are other animals often at least as sensitive as we are to sound, but other "species—monkeys and cats, for example—show octave equivalence, the ability to treat as similar, the way that humans do, tones separated by this amount." Levitin, *This Is Your Brain*, location 483.

48. See Augustine, *City of God*, trans. Henry Bettenson (London: Penguin, 2003), especially 14.24. The emphasis on Adam rather than Eve in the reading of the Genesis story is not simple sexism, though it is not unreasonable to suspect that sexism is active as well. Augustine, in keeping with the medical knowledge of his time, understood human heritage to be entirely seminal (with the sperm as homunculus). If original sin is to be inherited, as he believed it was, it would have to come through the father.

49. Hildegard, letter to the Prelates of Mainz, 356.

50. Ibid.

51. Ibid., 357.

52. Ibid., 358.

53. Brendan Doyle notes that the deep physicality of Hildegard's music "makes wonderful sense if we realize that she was a physical scientist as well as a musician." "Introduction to the Songs," in Hildegard, *Divine Works*, 364.

54. Cavarero, *For More than One Voice*, 161, "On each of the celestial spheres, [Plato] says, there lies a Siren 'who emits a single voice [*phone*], a single note. But from all these eight voices resounds the concord [*symphonein*] of a single harmony.'" Plato, *Republic*, 617b.

55. Gershom Scholem, "Walter Benjamin and His Angel," in Werner J. Dannhauser, ed., *On Jews and Judaism in Crisis* (New York: Schocken, 1976), 212–13. Cited in Cavell, *A Pitch of Philosophy*, xii.

5. ORIGINAL BREATH

1. Except where otherwise noted, I have used the New American Bible translation (in *Catholic Study Bible* [Oxford University Press, 2011]).

2. For an important discussion of the "face of the deep" over which this wind sweeps, in contradistinction to the insistence on creation *ex nihilo*, see Catherine Keller, *Face of the Deep: A Theology of Becoming* (New York: Routledge, 2002).

3. The Spirit is said to *move* in the American Standard Version, Bible in Basic English, Douay-Rheims, Good News Translation, King James Version, New American Standard, New Century, Webster, Third Millennium, and Tyndale Bible. It *hovers* in the New International Version, Complete Jewish Bible, English Standard Version, God's Word Translation, Hebrew Names Version, Lexham English Bible, New International Reader's Version, New King James Version, New Living Translation, Darby, Today's New International, and World English translations. The Common English Bible and the New Revised Standard both translate *ruach elohim* as "a wind from God," which in both instances *sweeps* over the waters. Finally, in Young's Bible the Spirit *flutters*; the Wycliffe Bible offers the waters more agency as the Spirit is *borne upon* them, and The Message reads, perhaps a bit freely and, to my mind, a little terrifyingly, "Earth was a soup of nothingness, a bottomless emptiness, an inky blackness. God's Spirit brooded like a bird above the watery abyss." All of these are available at the highly useful Online Parallel Bible at http://www.biblestudytools.com/parallel-bible/.

4. Christian interpreters tend to be tempted to read the Trinitarian "Holy Spirit" here. Despite the ambiguous numbering of God, it is challenging to justify this reading textually.

5. Cavarero, *For More than One Voice*, 20.

6. William Chittick clarifies the workings of this connection in Islam, where the loveliness of divine self-disclosure is perhaps mitigated somewhat by anthropocentrism: "The hadith of the Hidden Treasure tells us that God loved to be known. The Qur'an and the tradition in general make it clear that the knowledge that God desired to actualize through creation can be achieved only by human beings, who are God's chosen representatives. Since God created only human beings among all creatures in His own image, they alone are able to know God's self-disclosure in a full sense." William Chittick, "The Divine Roots of Human Love," at http://www.ibnarabisociety.org/

articles/divinerootsoflove.html. We might note here some closeness to Hildegard, for whom God knows God through human reflection and resonance.

7. Oddly, though marine life and birds are given this instruction, and then "God made all kinds of wild animals, all kinds of cattle, and all kinds of creeping things of the earth" and "saw how good it was" (1:25), and humanity is next created and given the same instruction to fertility, we are not told that the land animals are to multiply fruitfully. Still, this omission does not seem to carry the weight of intent, since the text gives no reason that there shouldn't be more cattle. I have assumed that we are to read the story as if these animals are similarly instructed to reproduce, because it seems that an exception would be more likely to be noted in the text.

8. This is not clear in the NAB: "And to all the animals of the land, all the birds of the air, and all the living creatures that crawl on the ground, I give all the green plants for food," but emerges in the NRSV: "And to every beast of the earth, and to every bird of the air, and to everything that creeps on the earth, everything that has the breath of life, I have given every green plant for food" (Gen 1:30). Here the NAB is closer to the original, but I have included the NRSV not only as suiting my purposes, but more defensibly because it is clear that the animals that creep, crawl, or otherwise move upon the earth are in this context living beings.

9. Cavarero, *For More than One Voice*, 21, citing Walter Benjamin, "Language as Such and on the Language of Man," in *Selected Writings*, ed. Marcus Bullock and Michael W. Jennings (Cambridge, MA: Harvard University Press, 1996), vol. 1, 62–74, 67.

10. Animals born from eggs actually breathe slightly through the delicately porous eggshell.

11. In the first *Duino Elegy*, Rainer Maria Rilke writes strikingly of this difference: "already the knowing animals are aware / that we are not really at home in / our interpreted world." ("die findigen Tiere merken es schon, / daß wir nicht sehr verläßlich zu Haus sind / in der gedeuteten Welt.") In *The Selected Poetry of Rainer Maria Rilke*, ed. and trans. Stephen Mitchell (New York: Vintage, 1982), 150–51. In a text that extensively considers Rilke, Jean-Christophe Bailly writes, "[Animals] all have it, this precedence, an air of seniority, the look of having been there before, and this is what we see when we see them looking at us and when we see them simply being among themselves, in their own domains. Although the pretentious ideology of humankind as the pinnacle of creation implies the destruction of all the respect for this precedence that would normally be due . . . we recognize the seniority of animals at least implicitly." Jean-Christophe Bailly, *The Animal Side*, trans. Catherine Porter (New York: Fordham University Press, 2011), 62.

12. Patricia Cox Miller, "Adam, Eve, and the Elephants: Asceticism and Animality," in *Ascetic Culture: Essays in Honor of Philip Rousseau*, ed. Blake Leyerle and Robin Darling Young (Notre Dame, IN: University of Notre Dame Press, 2013), 255.

13. Miller, "Adam, Eve," 255.

14. "The angels were not all of one opinion. The Angel of Love favored the creation of man, because he would be affectionate and loving; but the Angel of Truth opposed it, because he would be full of lies. And while the Angel of Justice favored it, because he would practice justice, the Angel of Peace opposed it, because he would be quarrelsome. To invalidate his protest, God cast the Angel of Truth down from heaven to earth, and when the others cried out against such contemptuous treatment of their companion, He said, 'Truth will spring back out of the earth.' The objections of the angels would have been much stronger, had they known the whole truth about man. God had told them only about the pious, and had concealed from them that there would be reprobates among mankind, too." In Louis Ginzberg, *The Legends of the Jews* (1901–1938), vol. 1, trans. Henrietta Szold; *From the Creation to Jacob* (Digireads.com, 2004), vol. 1, "The Angels and the Creation of Man." See also vol. 5, *From the Creation to the Exodus: Notes for Volumes One and Two* (Baltimore: Johns Hopkins University Press, 1998), 69n12.We read in the Qur'an, "And when your Lord said to the angels, I am going to place in the earth a khalif, they said: What! wilt Thou place in it such as shall make mischief in it and shed blood, and we celebrate Thy praise and extol Thy holiness? He said: Surely I know what you do not know." Qur. 2.30. Citations from the Qur'an from *The Holy Qur'an*, trans. M. H. Shakir (Tahrike Tarsile Qur'an, Inc., 1983). Via Online Book Initiative at http://quod.lib.umich.edu/k/koran/.

15. Ginzberg, *The Legends of the Jews*, vol. 1, "The Ideal Man." See vol. 5, 83nn29–30.

16. "He said: O Adam! inform them of their names. Then when he had informed them of their names, He said: Did I not say to you that I surely know what is *ghaib* in the heavens and the earth and (that) I know what you manifest and what you hide?" Qur. 2.33. "And when We said to the angels: Make obeisance to Adam they did obeisance, but Iblis (did it not). He refused and he was proud, and he was one of the unbelievers." Qur. 2.34.

17. Dag Nikolaus Hasse, "Influence of Arabic and Islamic Philosophy on the Latin West," *Stanford Encyclopedia of Philosophy*, 2008, at http://plato.stanford.edu/entries/arabic-islamic-influence/.

18. Chittick, "The Divine Roots of Human Love."

19. Hasse, "Arabic and Islamic Philosophy."

20. Moses Maimonides, *The Guide for the Perplexed*, trans. M. Friedländer (London: Routledge and Kegan Paul, 1904), available at http://www.sacred-texts.com/jud/gfp/gfp012.htm, 1.2.

21. Ibid.

22. Hasse, "Arabic and Islamic Philosophy."

23. Thomas Aquinas, *The Summa Theologica of St. Thomas Aquinas*, trans. Fathers of the English Dominican Province, 1920, accessed at http://www.newadvent.org/summa/1094.htm; Kevin Knight, 2008, Part 1, Question 94, Article 3, "On the Contrary." In this article, the "I answer that" agrees with the "on the contrary": "the first man was established by God in such a manner as to have knowledge of all those things for which man has a natural aptitude." Thus, Thomas both grants the first man perfect human knowledge and keeps that knowledge distinct from divine omniscience.

24. "The serpent asked the woman, 'Did God really tell you not to eat from any of the trees in the garden?' The woman answered the serpent: 'We may eat of the fruit of the trees in the garden; it is only about the fruit of the tree in the middle of the garden that God said, 'You shall not eat it or even touch it, lest you die.' But the serpent said to the woman: 'You certainly will not die! No, God knows that the moment you eat of it your eyes will be opened and you will be like gods who know what is good and what is bad'" (3:1–5).

25. Dante Alighieri, *De Vulgari Eloquentia*, ed. and trans. Steven Botterill (Cambridge: Cambridge University Press, 1996), 1.4.2–3.

26. Dante, *De Vulgari*, 1.2.1–2. On angels, 1.2.3. On animals' shared instincts, 1.2.5. Cutting off in advance the possible argument that the animals might have wanted to speak outside their own kind, Dante adds, "Between creatures of different species, on the other hand, not only was speech unnecessary, but it would have been injurious, since there could have been no friendly exchange between them" 1.2.5. Dante's notion that "nature hates to do anything superfluous" echoes the more famous injunction of the roughly contemporary philosopher William of Ockham (1287–1347), whose declaration that explanatory "entities should not be multiplied unnecessarily" becomes within a few centuries one of the central principles of modern science.

27. Thomas Aquinas, *Summa Theologica*, 1.107, "The Speech of Angels," Art. 1, Reply to Objection 2; Art. 3, Replies to Objections 1 and 2. From *The Summa Theologica of St. Thomas Aquinas*. Accessed at http://www.newadvent.org/summa/1107.htm.

28. "Since, then, human beings are moved not by their natural instinct but by reason, and since that reason takes diverse forms in individuals, according to their capacity for discrimination, judgment, or choice . . . I hold that

we can never understand the actions or feelings of others by reference to our own, as the baser animals can. Nor is it given to us to enter into each other's minds by means of spiritual reflection, as the angels do, because the human spirit is so weighed down by the heaviness and density of the mortal body." Dante, *De Vulgari*, 1.3.1.

29. "[If] the air can be moved at the command of the lesser nature which is God's servant and creation . . . can it not also, at God's command, so be moved as to make the sound of words?" Dante, *De Vulgari*, 1.4.6; on animals as something like ventriloquists' dummies, see Dante, 1.2.6.

30. Dante, *De Vulgari*, 1.4.4.

31. Ibid., 1.5.1.

32. Cavarero, *For More than One Voice*, 23. Citing Emanuel Levinas, *Philosophical Writings*, ed. Adrian Peperzak, Simon Critchley, and Robert Bernasconi (Indianapolis: Indiana State University Press, 1996), 201, 223.

33. *Seducing Augustine: Bodies, Powers, Confessions*, with Virginia Burrus and Mark Jordan (New York: Fordham University Press, 2010), conclusion, 115–27; *Divine Enticement: Theological Seductions* (New York: Fordham University Press, 2013), esp. chapter 4, 141–67.

34. Ginzberg, *The Legends of the Jews*, vol. 1, "Woman": "The Divine resolution to bestow a companion on Adam met the wishes of man, who had been overcome by a feeling of isolation when the animals came to him in pairs to be named."

35. Actually, in the same story in which the animals come forward in pairs, the first woman, Lilith, turns out to be not so helpful at all, but quite unsatisfactory as a spouse. The second woman, Eve, is therefore created not from the dust of the earth like Adam and Lilith, but from Adam's own body, providing for a closer and more enduring union. Ginzberg, *The Legends of the Jews*.

36. Miller, "Adam, Eve," 255–56. Citing John Chrysostom, *Saint John Chrysostom: Homilies on Genesis 1–17*, trans. Robert C. Hill, in *Fathers of the Church* 74 (Washington, DC: The Catholic University of America Press, 1986), 14.19–20 (*Patrologia Graeca* 53.116; *Fathers of the Church*, 191).

37. Bailly, *The Animal Side*, 60–61.

38. It is the case that the penalty for eating the fruit is death in the form of mortality; before disobedience, humans were immortal. Because death is not immediate but at the end of a lifetime, it is arguable whether the imposition of mortality legitimately constitutes a fulfillment of that sentence, or whether the serpent is telling the truth.

39. See particularly "The Hypostasis of the Archons":

> Then the female spiritual principle came in the snake, the instructor; and it taught them, saying, "What did he say to you? Was it, 'From every tree in the garden shall you eat; yet—from the tree of recogniz-

> ing good and evil do not eat?'" The carnal woman said, "Not only did he say 'Do not eat,' but even 'Do not touch it; for the day you eat from it, with death you are going to die.'" And the snake, the instructor, said, "With death you shall not die; for it was out of jealousy that he said this to you. Rather your eyes shall open and you shall come to be like gods, recognizing evil and good." [This, too, is borne out by the text; see Gen. 3:22.]

"The Hypostasis of the Archons," trans. Bentley Layton, in *The Nag Hammadi Library*, ed. James M. Robinson (New York: HarperCollins, 1990), 160–69, at 164–65.

40. If we follow Dante, this last would be unjust; because animals cannot speak, their apparent speech is only a matter of their bodies being used and manipulated by angels or demons. Perhaps the serpent somehow agreed to demonic possession. Here again, the Qur'an makes an interesting addition to the story: though they are tempted, eat, and are driven from the garden, the man "received (some) words from his Lord, so He turned to him mercifully; surely He is Oft-returning (to mercy), the Merciful" (Qur. 2.37). The speech that curses is followed by words of more merciful speech, by which mercy and the return of divine presence are possible.

41. Umberto Eco points out the very brief and often overlooked mention of linguistic division at Genesis 10:5, a description of the fate of Noah's sons: "By these [sons] were the isles of the Gentiles divided in their lands; every one after his tongue, after their families, in their nations." Cf. Genesis 10:20 and 10:31. Umberto Eco, *The Search for a Perfect Language*, trans. James Fentress (Oxford: Blackwell, 1995), 9–10. As noted in chapter three in this volume, little attention is paid to this verse as compared to that given to the Babel story at Genesis 11:1–9.

42. For tenth- or eleventh-century Arab writer Ibn Hazm, this first language is one that grasps essences, as we saw earlier in the naming episode. "In the beginning there existed a single language given by God, a language thanks to which Adam was able to understand the quiddity of things. It was a language that provided a name for every thing . . . and a thing for every name." Eco, *Perfect Language*, 352.

43. Genesis is not the only site of such a myth; stories of a language once whole and then scattered appear in a wide range of cultures. See chapter 3 in this volume.

44. For the reminder of both of these, I am grateful to my colleague Jennifer Glancy, who also alerted me to Judith Perkins, "Animal Voices," *Religion & Theology* 12:3–4 (2006), 385–96.

45. A particularly interesting case of such a sound is the domestic cat's "soliciting purr." What makes the soliciting purr so intriguing in this context

is that it functions very specifically as a mode of interspecies communication: "Researchers at the University of Sussex have discovered that cats use a 'soliciting purr' to overpower their owners and garner attention and food. Unlike regular purring, this sound incorporates a 'cry,' with a similar frequency to a human baby's. The team said cats have 'tapped into' a human bias—producing a sound that humans find very difficult to ignore." Victoria Gill, "Cats 'Exploit' Humans By Purring," BBC News Online, July 13, 2009, archived and accessed at http://news.bbc.co.uk/2/hi/science/nature/8147566.stm.

46. Thus in Bailly, *The Animal Side*, 49. Citing Maurice Merleau-Ponty, *Nature: Course Notes from the Collège de France*, ed. Dominique Seglard, trans. Robert Vallier (Evanston, IL: Northwestern University Press, 2003), 155, 188.

47. Bailly, *The Animal Side*, 70.

48. Ibid., 55.

49. Miller, "Adam, Eve," 254–55, citing Georges Bataille, *Theory of Religion*, trans. Robert Hurley (New York: Zone Books, 1989), 24, 22.

50. Miller, "Adam, Eve," 265, citing *Historia monachorum in Aegypto*, 6, "On Theon," ed. A.-J. Festugière, *Subsidia Hagiographica* 34 (Brussels: Société des Bollandistes, 1961), 44; English translation in *The Lives of the Desert Fathers*, trans. Norman Russell (Kalamazoo, MI: Cistercian Press, 1981), 68.

51. We might note in this context that humans begin lying, and it seems in fact that human lying only becomes possible, upon the consumption of the fruit of knowledge of good and bad—and that this is the beginning of the disintegration of language. This may suggest a closer affinity between true-false and good-bad than Maimonides had argued, though in fairness I think the affiliation is not the conflation that he rejects.

52. Humpty Dumpty to Alice, in Lewis Carroll, *Through the Looking-Glass and What Alice Found There*, 213: "'The question is,' said Alice, 'whether you *can* make words mean so many different things.' 'The question is,' said Humpty Dumpty, 'which is to be master—that's all.'"

6. THE MEANING IN THE MUSIC

1. There are exceptions, of course, particularly once we get to the post-Heideggerians, such as Emmanuel Levinas and Jacques Derrida, who emphasize the wholly otherness across us.

2. Nancy, *Listening*, 1.

3. Ibid.

4. Augustine, Sermon 288, sec. 1, at 110.

5. Perhaps you are wondering whether this is a real problem. At least some major philosophers believe that it is. See, for example, Eleonore Stump and Helen De Cruz, Open letter to the American Philosophical Association,

at http://www.change.org/petitions/the-american-philosophical-association-through-its-board-of-officers-to-undersign-an-open-letter-to-the-apa-asking-them-to-produce-a-code-of-conduct-and-a-statement-of-professional-ethics-for-the-academic-discipline-of-philosophy?utm_campaign=petition_created&utm_medium=email&utm_source=guides.

6. Both the quotation and the summary of Aristotle are from Cavarero, *For More than One Voice*, 40.

7. Plato, *Republic*, in *Plato in Twelve Volumes*, vols. 5 and 6, trans. Paul Shorey (Cambridge, MA: Harvard University Press; London: William Heinemann Ltd., 1969), 398d–399c.

8. Ibid., 399e.

9. Ibid., 400a–b.

10. Ibid., 400c.

11. Ibid., 522a.

12. Odello, "Waiting for the Death Knell," 41.

13. Ibid., 47.

14. Dolar, *A Voice and Nothing More*, locations 127–28.

15. Ibid., locations 366–69.

16. Kramer, *Expression*, 836–37.

17. Cavarero, *For More than One Voice*, 73.

18. Nancy, *Listening*, 3.

19. See Friedrich Nietzsche, *Twilight of the Idols*, in *Twilight of the Idols and the Anti-Christ*, trans. R. J. Hollingdale (New York: Penguin Books, 2003), 89; see also Robert Graves, *The Greek Myths*, vol. 1 (Baltimore: Penguin Books, 1955), 282.

20. Nancy, *Listening*, 3.

21. Friedrich Nietzsche, *Beyond Good and Evil*, trans. Walter Kaufmann (New York: Vintage Books, 1989), 1: "Suppose truth is a woman: what then? Are there not grounds for the suspicion that all philosophers, insofar as they were dogmatists, have been very inexpert about women?"

22. Aristotle (Attributed), "Of the Roof of the Mouth"; see also "Of Divers Matters," both in *Aristotle's Book of Problems*, in *The Works of Aristotle the Famous Philosopher Containing his Complete Masterpiece and Family Physician; his Experienced Midwife, his Book of Problems and his Remarks on Physiognomy*, available via Project Gutenberg, at http://www.gutenberg.org/ebooks/12699?msg=welcome_stranger#BOOK_OF_PROBLEMS.

23. Aristotle (Attributed), "Of the Judgment of Physiognomy," ch. 2 of *The secrets of nature relating to physiognomy*, in *The Works of Aristotle the Famous Philosopher*.

24. Cavarero, *For More than One Voice*, 114.

25. Ibid., 104–6.

26. Ibid., 106.

27. Catherine Clément, *Opera, or the Undoing of Women*, trans. Betsy Wing (Minneapolis: University of Minnesota Press, 1999); in Cavell, *A Pitch of Philosophy*, 132.

28. Koestenbaum, *The Queen's Throat*, locations 1836–38.

29. "[I]t's a commonplace idea that language is masculine and that music is feminine." Koestenbaum, *The Queen's Throat*, locations 2017–18.

30. Ibid., locations 1860–61.

31. Ibid., locations 2332–33.

32. Ibid., location 2528.

33. Halliwell, "Reflections on Voice," 4.

34. Dolar, *A Voice and Nothing More*, locations 507–509. "Already" is impressive in this instance; Dolar cites a text from the Chinese emperor Chun, written about 2200 BCE.

35. Dolar, *A Voice and Nothing More*, locations 584–87: "All the documents seem to have been written by the same hand and guided by the same single obsession: to pin down the voice to the letter, to limit its disruptive force, to dissipate its inherent ambiguity." Dolar cites Michel Poizat, *La voix du diable: La jouissance lyrique sacrée* (Paris: Metailie, 1991).

36. Koestenbaum, *The Queen's Throat*, location 187.

37. Ibid., locations 2240–41.

38. Cavarero, *For More than One Voice*, 145.

39. Cf. Koestenbaum: "Joan Sutherland copied her mother's scales and exercises; Clara Butt said, 'I believe that I owe my voice to the fact that my mother had a beautiful voice but did not sing'; Ernestine Schumann-Heink said, 'I sang what my mother sang.' But if the diva sings by imitating her mother, eventually the voice itself becomes a demanding child, and the diva must, as Galli-Curci phrases it, 'mother the insistent flow' of the voice." *The Queen's Throat*, locations 1125–27.

40. Cavarero, *For More than One Voice*, 141.

41. See Plato, *Symposium*, 210a–212c, for Diotima's ladder.

42. Though it dates from 1994, Norman Swartz's essay "Philosophy as a Blood Sport" still receives attention and does not seem to have diminished in relevance. http://www.sfu.ca/~swartz/blood_sport.htm.

43. Though I first heard the line "A paradox is just a contradiction in the hands of a theologian" from a divinity student, my interest in paradox derives first from my own graduate readings in Nietzsche and Deleuze. Cavarero points out, "With the advent of the era of philosophers, the divine aura that characterizes the enigma dissolves. Significantly, this is not a simple liquidation of the enigma; rather, it is a reductive understanding of this enigma that

makes it into a mere 'contradictory discourse.'" Cavarero, *For More than One Voice*, 77.

44. Augustine, *Confessions*, 8.12.

45. Koestenbaum, *The Queen's Throat*, locations 1609–10.

46. Ibid., locations 1770–71.1.

47. Nietzsche, *Beyond Good and Evil*, section 40.

48. Koestenbaum, *The Queen's Throat*, locations 2190–92.

49. M. B. Pranger, *Eternity's Ennui: Temporality, Perseverance and Voice in Augustine and Western Literature* (Leiden: Brill, 2010), 87.

50. Augustine, *Confessions*, 8.8.19; also cited in Pranger, *Eternity's Ennui*, 78.

51. Pranger, *Eternity's Ennui*, 86.

52. Ibid., 87–88.

53. Cavell, *A Pitch of Philosophy*, vii.

54. Ibid., 3: "The arrogance of philosophy is not one of its best kept secrets."

55. Pranger, *Eternity's Ennui*, 76.

56. Ibid., 89.

57. Philipp Jeserich, *Musica Naturalis: Speculative Music Theory and Poetics, from Saint Augustine to the Late Middle Ages in France*, trans. Michael J. Curley and Steven Rendall (Baltimore: Johns Hopkins University Press, 2013), 52.

58. Augustine, *De musica*, trans. Robert Catesby Taliaferro, in *The Fathers of the Church* vol. 4 (Washington, DC: Catholic University of America Press, 1977), 153–379, 1.1, p. 170.

59. Steven Brown, "The 'Musilanguage' Model of Music Evolution," in *The Origins of Music*, ed. N. L. Wallin, B. Merker, and S. Brown (Cambridge, MA: MIT Press), 271–300, at 273.

60. Brown, "Musilanguage," 278. See also 273: "both speech phrases and musical phrases are melodorhythmic structures in which melody and rhythm are derived from three sources: acoustic properties of the fundamental units (pitch sets, intensity values and duration values in music; phonemes and phonological feet in speech); sequential arrangement of such units in a given phrase (combinatorial rules in both domains); and expressive phrasing mechanisms that modulate the basic acoustic properties of the phrase for expressive emphasis and intention (phrasing rules in both domains)."

61. Levitin, *This Is Your Brain*, location 1913.

62. Ibid., location 2934.

63. Susanne K. Langer, "The Origins of Speech and Its Communicative Function," *The Quarterly Journal of Speech* 46:2 (1960), 121–34, at 132.

64. Langer, "Origins," 128.

65. Langer, *Feeling and Form: A Theory of Art* (New York: Charles Scribner's Sons, 1953), 141. See also Levitin, *This Is Your Brain*, location 144: "The Sesotho verb for singing (ho bina), as in many of the world's languages, also means to dance; there is no distinction."

66. Langer, *Feeling and Form*, 151.

67. Ibid., 149.

68. Nietzsche, *The Gay Science*, sec. 84.

69. Brown, "Musilanguage," 281, citing Victoria Fromkin, ed., *Tone: A Linguistic Survey* (New York: Academic, 1978). As Brown points out, "the notion of lexical tone implies that pitch can and does play an essential role in language, not just as a prosodic or paralinguistic device, but as a semantic device."

70. Brown, "Musilanguage," 279.

71. With exceptions, of course. There are portions of Maryland and southern Pennsylvania where the rising intonation is not used—a peculiarity that drove me mad when I lived there. The much-parodied uptalking of the 1980s "Valley girls" ends all sentences with the rising tone so that one cannot actually distinguish which are questions.

72. Jeserich, *Musica Naturalis*, 59.

73. Augustine, *De musica*, 1.13, p. 203.

74. Jeserich, *Musica Naturalis*, 65: "The unification of the different through *proporitio* or *analogia* is, as a formal principle, valid beyond arithmetic: the transition from 'pure' arithmology to music theory corresponds to the transition from number theory as such to the theory of numerical relationships." (Jeserich notes: cf. Gyburg Radke, *Die Theorie der Zahl im Platonismus. Ein systematisches Lehrbuch* [Tübingen, 2003], 250ff. and 231.)

75. Jeserich, *Musica Naturalis*, 82, notes that God's right ordering reaches all through earth and even into hell to govern. See Augustine, *De musica*, 6.17, p. 378; 6.12, p. 361.

76. "Therefore, delight orders the soul." Augustine, *De musica* 6.11, p 355.

77. Augustine, *Confessions*, 10.6.

78. Jeserich, *Musica Naturalis*, 104: "*De musica* teaches . . . the systematic disregard of the referential dimension of versified language, without making assertions about the status of reference as such. In particular, the concept of the 'musicality' of verse developed in *De musica* does not stand in contradiction to referentiality."

79. Jeserich, *Musica Naturalis*, 105. Cf. 55, "The *musica disciplina* that figures in the canon of the *artes liberals* and that was the subject of Augustine's work is thus said to be no less than the preparation for the 'recognition of the true.'" Jeserich cites Heinz Edelstein, *Die Musikanschauung Augustins nach seiner Schrift De musica* (Ohlau: 1929), 46.

80. As Jeserich rather elegantly summarizes, "[d]espite Platonism's and Christianity's depreciation of this world, which is subject to change, the dependency of the whole theory on musical acoustics lends the concept a significant advantage in clearness and plausibility. To the proportions as the basal elements of the numerical-harmonic order corresponds, with the symphonic interval, a form perceptible by the senses. The arithmetically based abstract 'science' and the simplest music represent a relation of mutual confirmation that provides the latter with relevance, the former with increased plausibility and clarity." Jeserich, *Musica Naturalis*, 138.

81. Nietzsche, *Twilight of the Idols*, "The Problem of Socrates," section 8. Koestenbaum notes that the seductively voiced opera diva is likewise construed as visually unappealing, even problematically gendered: "The beauty and magnitude of a diva's voice resides, so the iconography suggests, in her deformity. Her voice is beautiful because she herself is not—and her ugliness is interpreted as a sign of moral and social deviance. . . . For example, Benedetta Pisaroni's 'features horribly disfigured by small-pox,' prompting spectators to shut their eyes 'so as to hear without being condemned to see.' Audiences speculated that Maria Malibran was not anatomically a woman, but an androgyne or hermaphrodite—an aberrant physique to match her voice's magic power." Koestenbaum, *The Queen's Throat*, locations 1226–29.

82. Cavarero, *For More than One Voice*, 148.

83. Ibid., 24.

84. Cavell, *A Pitch of Philosophy*, 38.

85. Ibid., 101, citing Euripides, *Hippolytus*, trans. Michael R. Halleran (Newburyport, MA: Focus Publishing, 2001).

86. Dolar, *A Voice and Nothing More*, locations 159–61.

87. Ibid., locations 173–74.

88. Cavarero, *For More than One Voice*, 24.

89. Ibid., 198.

90. Augustine, *Confessions*, 11.35f.

BIBLIOGRAPHY

7SpeedReading, Spreeder, at http://www.spreeder.com/.

Dante Alighieri. *De Vulgari Eloquentia*. Edited and translated by Steven Botterill. Cambridge: Cambridge University Press, 1996.

Anderson, Ben. "Modulating the Excess of Affect: Morale in a State of 'Total War.'" In *The Affect Theory Reader*, edited by Melissa Gregg and Gregory J. Seigworth, 161–85. Durham, NC: Duke University Press, 2010.

Anonymous. "600 Year Old Mystery Manuscript Decoded by University of Bedfordshire Professor." University of Bedfordshire. http://www.beds.ac.uk/news/2014/february/600-year-old-mystery-manuscript-decoded-by-university-of-bedfordshire-professor.

———. "The Gospel of Truth." Translated by Einar Thomassen and Marvin Meyer. In *The Nag Hammadi Scriptures: International Edition*, 36–47. New York: Harper Collins, 2007.

———. "Myths Surrounding Language." Accessed at http://aberwiki.org/Myths_surrounding_language.

———. *Sefer Yizira: The Book of Creation*. Translated by Irving Friedman. New York: Weiser, 1977.

———. *The Holy Qur'an*. Translated by M. H. Shakir. Tahrike Tarsile Qur'an, Inc., 1983. Accessed via Online Book Initiative at http://quod.lib.umich.edu/k/koran/.

———. "The Hypostasis of the Archons." Translated by Bentley Layton. In *The Nag Hammadi Library*, edited by James M. Robinson, 160–69. New York: HarperCollins, 1990.

———. *Historia monachorum in Aegypto*. Edited by A. J. Festugière. *Subsidia Hagiographica* 34. Brussels: Société des Bollandistes, 1961. English translation in *The Lives of the Desert Fathers*, translated by Norman Russell. Kalamazoo, MI: Cistercian Press, 1981.

Aquinas, Thomas. *The Summa Theologica of St. Thomas Aquinas*. Translated by the Fathers of the English Dominican Province, 1920. Accessed at http://www.newadvent.org/summa/1094.htm. Electronic copyright Kevin Knight, 2008.

Aristotle (Attributed). *Aristotle's Book of Problems*, in *The Works of Aristotle the Famous Philosopher Containing his Complete Masterpiece and Family Physician; his Experienced Midwife, his Book of Problems and his Remarks on Physiognomy*. Available via Project Gutenberg, at http://www.gutenberg.org/ebooks/12699?msg=welcome_stranger#BOOK_OF_PROBLEMS.

Athanasius. "A Letter of Athanasius, Our Holy Father, Archbishop of Alexandria, to Marcellinus on the Interpretation of the Psalms." In *Athanasius: The Life of Antony and The Letter to Marcellinus*, translated by Robert C. Gregg, 101–29. Mahwah, NJ: Paulist Press, 1980.

Augustine of Hippo. *City of God*. Translated by Henry Bettenson. London: Penguin, 2003.

———. *Confessions*. Translated by Henry Chadwick. Oxford: Oxford University Press, 1991.

———. *De musica*. Translated by Robert Catesby Taliaferro. In *The Fathers of the Church*, volume 4, 153–379. Washington, DC: Catholic University of America Press, 1977.

———. *The Teacher*. In Against Academicians *and* The Teacher, translated by Peter King. Indianapolis, IN: Hackett Publishing, 1995.

———. *The Works of Saint Augustine: A Translation for the 21st Century*. Volume 3.8, Sermons 273–305A. Translated by Edmund Hill, OP, and edited by John E. Rotelle, OSA. Hyde Park, NY: New City Press, 1994.

Augustine (Attributed). Sermo de Tempore Barbarico. In *Patrologia Latina*, volume 38, 699–708, edited by J. P. Migne. (Paris: Migne, 1844–1855).

Bailly, Jean-Christophe. *The Animal Side*. Translated by Catherine Porter. New York: Fordham University Press, 2011.

Baldwin, James. *Sonny's Blues*. New York: Penguin Books, 1995.

Barthes, Roland, in collaboration with Roland Havas. "*Ascolto*." In *Encyclopedia Einaudi*. Turin: Einaudi, 1977.

———. *Image, Music, Text*. Translated by Stephen Heath. New York: Hill and Wang, 1977.

———. *A Lover's Discourse: Fragments*. Translated by Richard Howard. New York: Hill and Wang, 2010.

———. *The Responsibility of Forms*. Translated by Richard Howard. Berkeley: University of California Press, 1982.

Bataille, Georges. *Theory of Religion*. Translated by Robert Hurley. New York: Zone Books, 1989.

Beckett, Samuel. *Stories and Texts for Nothing*. New York: Grove Press, 1967.

———. *Trilogy*. London: Calder and Boyars, 1959.

Benjamin, Walter. "Language as Such and on the Language of Man." In *Selected Writings, Part 1*, 62–74, edited by Marcus Bullock and Michael W. Jennings. Cambridge, MA: Harvard University Press, 1996.

———. "The Task of the Translator: An Introduction to the Translation of Baudelaire's *Tableaux Parisiens*." Translated by H. Zohn. In *Illuminations: Essays and Reflections*, 69–82. New York: Routledge, 2000.

Bernhart, Walter, and Lawrence Kramer, eds. *On Voice*. Amsterdam: Rodopi, 2014.

Blanchot, Maurice. "Translating." In *Friendship*, translated by Elizabeth Rottenberg, 57–61. Stanford: Stanford University Press, 1997.

———. *A Voice from Elsewhere*. Translated by Charlotte Mandel. Stanford: Stanford University Press, 2007.

———. *The Writing of the Disaster*. Translated by Ann Smock. Lincoln: University of Nebraska Press, 1995.

Boylan, Roger. "Samuel Beckett, the Early Years." *Boston Review*, July 8, 2014. Accessed at http://www.bostonreview.net/books-ideas/roger-boylan-samuel-beckett-echos-bones.

Brathwaite, Edward Kamau. *History of the Voice: The Development of a Nation Language in Anglophone Caribbean Poetry*. London: New Beacon Books, 1984.

Brockes, Emilia. "A Life in Writing: Magical Thinking." Interview with Anne Carson. *The Guardian*, December 29, 2006. Accessed at http://www.theguardian.com/books/2006/dec/30/featuresreviews.guardianreview7.

Brown, Steven. "The 'Musilanguage' Model of Music Evolution." In *The Origins of Music*, edited by N. L. Wallin, B. Merker, and S. Brown, 271–300. Cambridge, MA: MIT Press, 1999.

Burrus, Virginia. "Augustine's Bible." In *Ideology, Culture, and Translation*, edited by Scott Elliott and Roland Boer, 69–82. Atlanta: Society of Biblical Literature, 2012.

Calvino, Italo. *If on a Winter's Night a Traveler*. Translated by William Weaver. New York: Harcourt Brace & Company, 1981.

Carroll, Lewis. *Alice's Adventures in Wonderland*. In Lewis Carroll, *The Annotated Alice: The Definitive Edition*, edited and annotated by Martin Gardner, 3–128. New York: W. W. Norton and Company, 1999.

———. *Through the Looking-Glass and What Alice Found There*. In *The Annotated Alice: The Definitive Edition*, 129–274.

Carson, Anne. *Decreation: Poetry, Essays, Opera*. New York: Vintage Books, 2005.

Cavell, Stanley. *A Pitch of Philosophy: Autobiographical Exercises*. Cambridge, MA: Harvard University Press, 1994.

Cavarero, Adriana. *For More than One Voice*. Translated by Paul A. Kottman. Stanford: Stanford University Press, 2005.

Certeau, Michel de. *The Mystic Fable, Vol. One: The Sixteenth and Seventeenth Centuries*. Translated by Michael B. Smith. Chicago: University of Chicago Press, 1992.

Chittick, William. "The Divine Roots of Human Love." Accessed at http://www.ibnarabisociety.org/articles/divinerootsoflove.html.

Chrétien, Jean-Louis. *The Ark of Speech*. Translated by Andrew Brown. London: Routledge, 2004.

———. *The Call and the Response*. Translated by Anne A. Davenport. New York: Fordham University Press, 2004.

———. "The Wounded Word." In Dominique Janicaud, Jean-François Courtine, Jean-Louis Chrétien, Michel Henry, Jean-Luc Marion, and Paul Ricoeur, *Phenomenology and the "Theological Turn": The French Debate*, 147–75. New York: Fordham University Press, 2000.

Cixous, Hélène. *Three Steps on the Ladder of Writing*. Translated by Sarah Cornell and Susan Sellers. New York: Columbia University Press, 1993.

Clément, Catherine. *Opera, or the Undoing of Women*. Translated by Betsy Wing. Minneapolis: University of Minnesota Press, 1999.

Clifford, Brendan. "Introduction to Lectio Divina." Accessed at http://www.goodnews.ie/lectio.shtml.

Clough, Patricia T. "The Affective Turn: Political Economy, Biomedia, and Bodies." In Gregg and Seigworth, *The Affect Theory Reader*, 206–28.

Compton, Nancy, ed. *Writers: Writers on the Art of Writing*. New York: Quantuck Lane Press, 2005.

Conybeare, Catherine. "Beyond Word and Image: Aural Patterning in Augustine's *Confessions*." In *Envisioning Experience in Late Antiquity and the Middle Ages*, edited by Giselle de Nie and Thomas F. X. Noble, 143–64. Aldershot: Ashgate, 2012.

Derrida, Jacques. *The Animal That Therefore I Am*. Edited by Marie-Louise Mallet. Translated by David Wills. New York: Fordham University Press, 2008.

———. *Of Grammatology*. Translated by Gayatri Chakravorty Spivak. Baltimore: Johns Hopkins University Press, 1976.

———. "Signature Event Context." In *Limited Inc.*, 1–23. Evanston, IL: Northwestern University Press, 1977.

———. "Des tours de Babel." In *Differences in Translation*, edited by J. F. Graham, 209–48. Ithaca, NY: Cornell University Press, 1985.

———. *Voice and Phenomenon: Introduction to the Problem of the Sign in Husserl's Phenomenology*. Evanston, IL: Northwestern University Press, 2011.

Derrida, Jacques, et al. *The Ear of the Other: Otobiography, Transference, Translation*. Translated by Peggy Kamuf and Avital Ronell, edited by Christie McDonald. Lincoln: University of Nebraska Press, 1988.

Dolar, Mladen. "The Object of Voice." In *Gaze and Voice as Love Objects*, edited by Renata Salecl and Slavoj Žižek, 7–31. Durham, NC: Duke University Press, 1996.

———. *A Voice and Nothing More*. Cambridge, MA: MIT Press, 2006. Kindle Edition.

Dysinger, Luke. "Lectio Divina." In *The Oblate Life*, edited by Gervase Holdaway, 107–17. London: Canterbury Press Norwich, 2008.

Eco, Umberto. *Experiences in Translation*. Translated by Alastair McEwen. Toronto: University of Toronto Press, 2001.

———. with Richard Rorty, Jonathan Culler, and Christine Brooke-Rose. In *Interpretation and Overinterpretation*, edited by Stefan Collini. Cambridge: Cambridge University Press, 1992.

———. *Mouse or Rat? Translation as Negotiation*. London: Weidenfeld and Nicolson, 2003.

———. *The Search for the Perfect Language*. Translated by James Fentress. Oxford: Blackwell, 1995.

Edelstein, Heinz. *Die Musikanschauung Augustins nach seiner Schrift De musica*. Ohlau in Schlesien: H. Eschenhagen, 1929.

Eliot, T. S. *The Annotated Waste Land and Eliot's Contemporary Prose*. New Haven: Yale University Press, 2005.

———. *Four Quartets*. San Diego: Harcourt Brace Jovanovich, 1943.

Elleström, Lars. "The Modalities of Media: A Model for Understanding Intermedial Relations." In *Media Borders, Multimodality and Intermediality*, edited by Lars Elleström, 11–50. Basingstoke: Palgrave Macmillan, 2010.

Engdahl, Horace. "Stilen og lykken." *Den Blå Port*, 27–28, 1993.

Euripides. *Hippolytus*. Translated by Michael Halleran. Newburyport, MA: Focus Publishing, 2001.

Foucault, Michel. "The Order of Discourse," Inaugural lecture at the Collège de France, 1970. In *Untying the Text: A Post-Structuralist Reader*, edited by Robert Young, 48–78. London: Routledge and Kegan Paul, 1981.

———. "What Is an Author?" Translated by Donald F. Bouchard and Sherry Simon. In *Language, Counter-Memory, Practice*, edited by Donald F. Bouchard, 124–27. Ithaca, NY: Cornell University Press, 1977.

Fromkin, Victoria, ed. *Tone: A Linguistic Survey*. New York: Academic, 1978.

Gaius Petronius. *Satyricon*. Available at http://www.thelatinlibrary.com/petronius1.html. English translation by Alfred R. Allinson available at http://www.sacred-texts.com/cla/petro/satyr.

Galli, Barbara Ellen. *Franz Rosenzweig and Jehuda Halevi: Translating, Translations, and Translators*. Montreal and Kingston: McGill-Queen's University Press, 1995.

Gallop, Jane. *Feminist Accused of Sexual Harassment*. Durham, NC: Duke University Press, 1997.

Gamble, Harry Y. *Books and Readers in the Early Church: A History of Early Christian Texts*. New Haven, CT: Yale University Press, 1995.

Gibbs, Anna. "After Affect: Sympathy, Synchrony and Mimetic Communication." In Gregg and Seigworth, *The Affect Theory Reader*, 186–205.

Gibbs, Raymond W. "Metaphor Interpretation as Embodied Simulation." *Mind and Language* 21:3 (2006), 434–58.

Gill, Victoria. "Cats 'Exploit' Humans by Purring." BBC News Online, July 13, 2009. Archived and accessed at http://news.bbc.co.uk/2/hi/science/nature/8147566.stm.

Ginzberg, Louis. *The Legends of the Jews*. Volume 1, *From the Creation to Jacob*. Translated by Henrietta Szold. Philadelphia: The Jewish Publication Society of America, 1969.

———. *The Legends of the Jews*. Volume 5, *From the Creation to the Exodus: Notes for Volumes One and Two*. Baltimore: Johns Hopkins University Press, 1998.

Glancy, Jennifer. "Reading Bodies, Reading Scripture." Paper delivered at the International Society for Biblical Literature meeting, London, July 2011.

Graves, Robert. *The Greek Myths*, volume 1. Baltimore: Penguin Books, 1955.

Gross, Alexander. "Hermes: God of Translators and Interpreters." Paper presented at Translation2000, New York University, 2000. Accessed at http://language.home.sprynet.com/trandex/hermes.htm.

Gruber, Gerald W. "Voice and Voices in Oratorios: On Sacred and Other Voices." In Bernhart and Kramer, *On Voice*, 149–60.

Halliwell, Michael. "'Her throat, full of aching, grieving beauty': Reflections on Voice in Operatic Adaptations of *The Great Gatsby* and *Sophie's Choice*." In Bernhart and Kramer, *On Voice*, 1–27.

Hasse, Dag Nikolaus. "Influence of Arabic and Islamic Philosophy on the Latin West." *Stanford Encyclopedia of Philosophy*, 2008. Accessed at http://plato.stanford.edu/entries/arabic-islamic-influence/.

Heidegger, Martin. "Language." In *Poetry Language Thought*, translated by Albert Hofstadter, 185–208. New York: HarperCollins, 1971.

Hildegard of Bingen. *The Book of Divine Works: Ten Visions of God's Deeds in the World and Humanity*, edited by Matthew Fox, translated by Robert Cunningham, 5–266. Santa Fe: Bear and Company, 1987.

———. *Causes and Cures*. Translated by Priscilla Throop. Charlotte, VT: Lulu Books, 2008.

———. *Hildegard of Bingen: A Spiritual Reader*. Edited by Carmen Acevedo Butcher. Brewster, MA: Paraclete Press, 2007.

———. Letter 41, to the Prelates of Mainz. Translated by Ronald Mille. In Fox, *The Book of Divine Works*, 354–59.

———. *Ordo Virtutum*. Audio. Sequentia, 1998.

———. *Scivias*. Translated by Columba Hart and Jane Bishop. Mahwah, NJ: Paulist Press, 1990.

———. *Symphonia*. Critical edition with introduction, translations, and commentary by Barbara Newman. Ithaca, NY: Cornell University Press, 1998.

Holsinger, Bruce. "The Flesh of the Voice: Embodiment and Homoerotics of Devotion in the Music of Hildegard von Bingen (1098–1179)." *Signs: Journal of Women, Culture and Society*, 19 (1993): 92–125.

hooks, bell. "Eros, Eroticism and the Pedagogical Process." In *Teaching to Transgress*, 191–200. New York: Routledge, 1995.

Idel, Moshe. *The Mystical Experience of Abraham Abulafia*. Albany: State University of New York Press, 1988.

Irenaeus. *Against Heresies*. Wyatt North Publishing, 2012.

Jabr, Ferris. "Evolutionary Babel was in southern Africa." In *Science* 19 (April 14, 2011). Accessed at http://www.newscientist.com/article/dn20384-evolutionary-babel-was-in-southern-africa.html.

Jeserich, Philipp. *Musica Naturalis: Speculative Music Theory and Poetics, from Saint Augustine to the Late Middle Ages in France*. Translated by Michael J. Curley and Steven Rendall. Baltimore: Johns Hopkins University Press, 2013.

John Chrysostom. *Four Discourses, Chiefly Concerning the Rich Man and Lazarus*. Translated by F. Allen. London: Longmans, Green, Reader and Dyer, 1869.

———. *The Fathers of the Church: John Chrysostom, Homilies on Genesis 1–17*. Translated by Robert C. Hill. Washington, DC: Catholic University of America Press, 1986.

———. *The Fathers of the Church: John Chrysostom, Homilies on Genesis 18–45*. Translated by Robert C. Hill. Washington, DC: Catholic University of America Press, 1990.

———. *Homilies on the Gospel of St. Matthew* 2. In *Nicene and Post-Nicene Fathers*, Series 1, Volume 10. Peabody, MA: Hendrickson Publishers, 1994.

Jones, Ernest. "The Madonna's Conception through the Ear: A Contribution to the Relation between Aesthetics and Religion." In *The International Psycho-Analytical Library* 5. London: International Psycho-Analytic Press, 1923.

Kapur, N., and N. F. Lawton. "Dysgraphia for Letters: a Form of Motor Memory Deficit?" *Journal of Neurological Psychiatry*, 46:6 (1983): 573–75.

Keller, Catherine. *Face of the Deep: A Theology of Becoming*. New York: Routledge, 2002.

Koestenbaum, Wayne. *The Queen's Throat: Opera, Homosexuality, and the Mystery of Desire*. Jackson, TN: Dacap Press, 1993. Kindle Edition.

Krakauer, J. W., and R. Shadmehr. "Consolidation of Motor Memory." *Trends in Neurosciences* 29:1 (January 2006): 58–64.

Kramer, Lawrence. *Expression and Truth: The Music of Knowledge*. Berkeley: University of California Press, 2012.

Krawiec, Rebecca. "Evagrius, Text, and Memory: Writing and Tradition in the Egyptian Desert." Presented at Oxford Classics Conference, 2011.

Kristeva, Julia. *Powers of Horror: An Essay on Abjection*. Translated by Leon D. Roudiez. New York: Columbia University Press, 1982. From *Pouvoirs de l'horreur: Essai sur l'abjection*. Paris: Éditions du Seuil, 1980.

Lacoue-Labarthe, Philippe. *Phrase*. Paris: Christian Bourgois, 2000.

Lakoff, George and Mark Johnson. *Philosophy in the Flesh: The Embodied Mind and Its Challenge to Western Thought*. New York: Basic Books, 1999.

Langer, Susanne K. *Feeling and Form*. New York: Scribner's, 1953.

———. "The Origins of Speech and its Communicative Function." *The Quarterly Journal of Speech* 46:2 (1960): 121–34.

LeGuin, Ursula. "Old Body not Writing." In *The Wave in the Mind: Talks and Essays on the Writer, the Reader, and the Imagination*, 283–88. Boston: Shambhala, 2004.

Lehrer, Tom. "The Elements." From *An Evening Wasted with Tom Lehrer*. Reprise/Warner Brothers Records, 1959.

Levinas, Emanuel. *Philosophical Writings*. Edited by Adrian Peperzak, Simon Critchley, and Robert Bernasconi. Indianapolis: Indiana State University Press, 1996.

Levitin, Daniel J. *This Is Your Brain on Music: The Science of a Human Obsession*. New York: Penguin Books, 2006. Kindle Edition.

MacKendrick, Karmen. *Divine Enticement: Theological Seductions*. New York: Fordham University Press, 2013.

———. *Fragmentation and Memory: Meditations on Christian Doctrine*. New York: Fordham University Press, 2008.

———. "When You Call My Name." *Glossator*, 5 (2011): 57–67.

———. *Word Made Skin*. New York: Fordham University Press, 2004.

MacKendrick, Karmen, with Virginia Burrus and Mark Jordan. *Seducing Augustine: Bodies, Powers, Confessions*. New York: Fordham University Press, 2010.

Mackey, Lewis. *Peregrinations of the Word*. Ann Arbor: University of Michigan Press, 1997.

MacPhail, Theresa. "The Art and Science of Finding Your Voice." *Chronicle of Higher Education*, August 8, 2014. Accessed at chroniclevitae.com.

Markson, David. *Wittgenstein's Mistress*. Elmwood Park, IL: Dalkey Archive Press, 1988.

Masciandaro, Nicola. "What Is This that Stands before Me?: Metal as Deixis." In *Reflections in the Metal Void*, edited by Niall Scott, 3–17. Oxford, UK: Inter-Disciplinary Press, 2012.

Merleau-Ponty, Maurice. *Nature: Course Notes from the Collège de France*. Edited by Dominique Seglard, translated by Robert Vallier. Evanston, IL: Northwestern University Press, 2003.

———. *The Visible and the Invisible*. Translated by Alphonso Lingis. Evanston, IL: Northwestern University Press, 1969.

Miller, Patricia Cox. "Adam, Eve, and the Elephants: Asceticism and Animality." In *Ascetic Culture: Essays in Honor of Philip Rousseau*, edited by Blake Leyerle and Robin Darling Young. Notre Dame, IN: University of Notre Dame Press, 2013.

Mitchell, Stephen. *Gilgamesh: A New English Version*. New York: Free Press, 2004.

Moon, Christine, Hugo Lagercrantz, and Patricia K. Kuhl. "Language Experienced *in utero* Affects Vocal Perception after Birth: A Two-Country Study." *Acta Paediatrica* 102:2 (February 2013): 156–60.

Moses Maimonides, *The Guide for the Perplexed*. Translated by M. Friedländer. London: Routledge and Kegan Paul, 1904. Accessed at http://www.sacred-texts.com/jud/gfp/gfp012.htm, 1.2.

Musil, Robert. *The Man Without Qualities*, volume 2. Translated by Eithne Wilkins and Ernst Kaiser. London: Secker and Warburg, 1967.

Nancy, Jean-Luc. *Dis-Enclosure: The Deconstruction of Christianity*. Translated by Bettina Bergo, Gabriel Malenfant, and Michael B. Smith. New York: Fordham University Press, 2008.

———. *Listening*. Translated by Charlotte Mandell. New York: Fordham University Press, 2007.

———. "Of Divine Places." Translated by Michael Holland. In *The Inoperative Community*, edited by Peter Connor, 110–50. Minneapolis: University of Minnesota Press, 1991.

———. "Récit Recitation Recitative." Translated by Charlotte Mandell. In *Speaking of Music: Addressing the Sonorous*, edited by Keith Chapin and Andrew H. Clark, 242–55. New York: Fordham University Press, 2013.

———. "Sharing Voices." Translated by Gayle Ormiston. In *Transforming the Hermeneutic Context: From Nietzsche to Nancy*, edited by Gayle Ormiston and Alan D. Schrift, 211–59. Albany: State University of New York Press, 1990.

Nietzsche, Friedrich. *Beyond Good and Evil: Prelude to a Philosophy of the Future*. Translated by Walter Kaufmann. New York: Vintage Books, 1966.

———. "Notebooks." In *The Portable Nietzsche*, edited and translated by Walter Kaufmann. New York: Penguin Books, 1977.

———. *The Gay Science*. Translated by Walter Kaufmann. New York: Vintage Books, 2010.

———. *On the Genealogy of Morals*. Translated by Douglas Smith. Oxford: Oxford University Press, 2009.

———. *Twilight of the Idols*. In *Twilight of the Idols and the Anti-Christ*, translated by R. J. Hollingdale. New York: Penguin Books, 2003.

———. *The Will to Power*. Translated by Walter Kaufmann. New York: Vintage Books, 1967.

Odello, Laura. "Waiting for the Death Knell," in Chapin and Clark, *Speaking of Music*, 39–48.

Online Etymology Dictionary. http://www.etymonline.com.

Online Parallel Bible. http://www.biblestudytools.com/parallel-bible/.

Ovid. *Metamorphoses*. Translated by A. D. Melville. Oxford: Oxford University Press, 1998.

Oxford Catholic Study Bible: New American Bible. Oxford: Oxford University Press, 1990.

Parish-Morris, Julia, Roberta Michnick Golinkoff, and Kathryn Hirsh-Pasek. "From Coo to Code: A Brief Story of Language Development." In *The Oxford Handbook of Developmental Psychology*, volume 1, edited by Philip David Zelazo, 867–908. Oxford: Oxford University Press, 2013.

Parker, John. "What a Piece of Work Is Man: Shakespearean Drama as Marxian Fetish, the Fetish as Sacramental Sublime." *Journal of Medieval and Early Modern Studies* 34:3 (Fall 2004): 643–72.

Patel, Aniruddh D. *Music, Language, and the Brain*. Oxford: Oxford University Press, 2010.

———. "Syntactic Processing in Language and Music: Different Cognitive Operations, Similar Neural Resources?" *Music Perception* 16:1 (Fall 1998): 27–42.

Patel, Aniruddh D., with John R. Iversen and Peter Hagoort. "Musical Syntactic Processing in Broca's Aphasia: A Preliminary Study." In *Proceedings of the 8th International Conference on Music Perception and Cognition in Evanston, IL, 2004*, edited by D. Lipscomb, R. Ashley, R. O. Gjerdingen, and P. Webster. Adelaide: Causal Productions, 2004.

Pedersen, Birgitte Stougaard. "Voice and Presence in Music and Literature: Virginia Woolf's *The Waves*. In Bernhart and Kramer, *On Voice*, 117–28.

Perkins, Judith. "Animal Voices." *Religion & Theology* 12:3–4 (2006): 385–96.

Peters, Deniz. "Gesture, Empathy, Affect: The Adverbial Expression of Emotion in Music." Presented at Sound and Affect, Stony Brook University, 2014.

Pfau, Marianne Richert. "Music and Text in Hildegard's Antiphons." In Hildegard of Bingen, *Symphonia*, 74–94.

Pierce, Lara J., Denise Klein, Jen-Kai Chen, Audrey Delcenserie, and Fred Genesee. "Mapping the Unconscious Maintenance of a Lost First Language." *Proceedings of the National Academy of Sciences of the United States of America*, 111:48 (October 2014): 17314–319.

Plato, *Phaedo*. Translated by Benjamin Jowett. In *Six Great Dialogues*. New York: Dover, 2007.

———. *Phaedrus*. Translated by Alexander Nehamas and Paul Woodruff. Indianapolis, IN: Hackett Publishing, 1994.

———. *Republic*. In *Plato in Twelve Volumes*, Volumes 5 and 6. Translated by Paul Shorey. Cambridge, MA: Harvard University Press; London: William Heinemann Ltd., 1969.

———. *Symposium*. Translated by Alexander Nehamas and Paul Woodruff. Indianapolis, IN: Hackett Publishing, 1989.

Poizat, Michel. *La voix du diable: La jouissance lyrique sacrée*. Paris: Metailie, 1991.

Porete, Marguerite. *The Mirror of Simple Souls*. Translated and introduced by Edmund Colledge, Judith Grant, and J. C. Marler. Notre Dame, IN: University of Notre Dame Press, 1999.

Pranger, M. B. *The Artificiality of Christianity: Essays on the Poetics of Monasticism*. Stanford: Stanford University Press, 2003.

———. *Eternity's Ennui: Temporality, Perseverance and Voice in Augustine and Western Literature*. Leiden: Brill, 2010.

Radke, Gyburg. *Die Theorie der Zahl im Platonismus. Ein systematisches Lehrbuch*. Tübingen: A. Francke, 2003.

Rich, Motoko. "Pediatrics Group to Recommend Reading Aloud to Children From Birth." *New York Times*, June 24, 2014. Accessed at http://www.nytimes.com/2014/06/24/us/pediatrics-group-to-recommend-reading-aloud-to-children-from-birth.html?smid=tw-nytimes&_r=0.

Rilke, Rainer Maria. *New Poems (1907)*. Translated by Edward Snow. New York: North Point Press, 1990.

———. *The Selected Poetry of Rainer Maria Rilke*. Edited and translated by Stephen Mitchell. New York: Vintage Books, 1982.

Robinson, Andrew. *Lost Languages: The Enigma of the World's Undeciphered Scripts*. New York: Nevramont Publishing, 2002.

Robson, David. "Power of Babel: Why One Language Isn't Enough." *New Scientist*, 2842:14 (December 2011): 34–47. Accessed at http://www.newscientist.com/article/mg21228421.200-power-of-babel-why-one-language-isnt-enough.html.

Rogozinski, Jacob. *The Ego and the Flesh: An Introduction to Ego Analysis*. Translated by Robert Vallier. Stanford, CA: Stanford University Press, 2010.

Rosenzweig, Franz. Letter to Rudolf Ehrenberg, October 1, 1917. Translated by Barbara Ellen Galli. *Franz Rosenzweig and Jehuda Halevi: Translating, Translations, and Translators*. Montreal and Kingston: McGill-Queen's University Press, 1995.

Sacks, Oliver. *Musicophilia: Tales of Music and the Brain*. New York: Knopf, 2008. Kindle Edition.

Saussure, Ferdinand de. *Course in General Linguistics*. Translated by Wade Baskin. New York: Columbia University Press, 2011.

Scholem, Gershom. *On Jews and Judaism in Crisis*. New York: Schocken Books, 1989.

Seigworth, Gregory J., and Melissa Gregg. "An Inventory of Shimmers." Introduction in Gregg and Seigworth, *The Affect Theory Reader*, 1–25.

Lucius Annaeus Seneca. *Moral Epistles*, Volume 1. Translated by Richard M. Gummere. Cambridge, MA: Harvard University Press, 1917–1925. Accessed at http://www.stoics.com/seneca_epistles_book_1.html#%E2%80%98XV1.

Shakespeare, William. *A Midsummer Night's Dream*. New York: Washington Square Press Folger Shakespeare Library, 2004.

Smith, Dinitia. "Philosopher Gamely In Defense of His Ideas." *New York Times*, May 30, 1998. Accessed at http://www.nytimes.com/1998/05/30/arts/philosopher-gamely-in-defense-of-his-ideas.html?pagewanted=all&src=pm.

Stock, Brian. *After Augustine: The Meditative Reader and the Text*. Philadelphia: University of Pennsylvania Press, 2001.

Stockton, Will, and D. Gilson. *Crush*. Brooklyn, NY: Punctum Books, 2014.

Stump, Eleonore, and Helen De Cruz, Open letter to the American Philosophical Association. Accessed at http://www.change.org/petitions/the-american-philosophical-association-through-its-board-of-officers-to-undersign-an-open-letter-to-the-apa-asking-them-to-produce-a-code-of-conduct-and-a-statement-of-professional-ethics-for-the-academic-discipline-of-philosophy?utm_campaign=petition_created&utm_medium=email&utm_source=guides.

Swartz, Norman. "Philosophy as a Blood Sport." Accessed at http://www.sfu.ca/~swartz/blood_sport.htm.

Teresa of Avila. *The Life of Teresa of Avila, by Herself*. Translated by J. M. Cohen. London: Penguin Books, 1957.

U.S. Department of Labor, Bureau of Labor Statistics. "American Time Use Survey," 2013. Accessed at http://www.bls.gov/tus/datafiles_2013.htm.

Vickhoff, Björn, Helge Malmgren, Rickard Åström, Gunnar Nyberg, Seth-Reino Ekström, Mathias Engwall, Johan Snygg, Michael Nilsson, and Rebecka Jörnsten. "Music structure determines heart rate variability of singers." *Frontiers of Psychology*, July 2013. Accessed at http://journal.frontiersin.org/Journal/10.3389/fpsyg.2013.00334/full.

Wahlfors, Laura. "Resonances and Dissonances: Listening to Waltraud Meier's Envoicing of Isolde." In Bernhart and Kramer, *On Voice*, 57–76.

Wall, Thomas Carl. *Radical Passivity: Levinas, Blanchot and Agamben*. Albany: State University of New York Press, 1999.

Watkins, Megan. "Desiring Recognition, Accumulating Affect." In Gregg and Seigworth, *The Affect Theory Reader*, 269–88.

Webley, Kayla. "$80,000 for Beer Pong? Report Shows College Students Learn Little during First Two Years (Except Party Skills)." *Time*, January 18, 2011. Accessed at http://newsfeed.time.com/2011/01/18/what-do-college-students-learn-in-the-first-two-years-not-a-whole-lot/#ixzz1Y3aERA5k.

Woolf, Virginia. Letter to Vita Sackville-West, March 16, 1926. In *The Letters of Virginia Woolf*, vol. 3, 1923–1928, edited by Nigel Nicolson and Joanne Trautman. Boston: Harvest Books, 1977.

———. *A Reflection of the Other Person: The Letters of Virginia Woolf*, volume 4, 1929–1931. London: Hogarth Press, 1978.

INDEX